# Responses

Practical assignments for GCSE English

**Sheila Black**

**Basil Blackwell**

© Sheila Black 1988

First published 1988

Published by Basil Blackwell Ltd
108 Cowley Road
Oxford OX4 1JF
England

ISBN 0 631 90131 0

Typeset by Opus, Oxford
in 10.5 pt Frutiger Light
Printed and bound in Great Britain by
Butler & Tanner Ltd,
Frome and London

*For Alan, who was a great help*
*and Elizabeth, who was no help at all.*

Important reminders are summed up in the 'boxes' which appear throughout the book.

# Contents

# To the pupil

Could you criticise all the examples of English on these pages for one reason or another?

If you could, then you're doing fine – you're already responding to what you read.

There's this recipe, right, and you need about eight ounces of flour. It's really nice. Well, you mix up the sugar and 3 eggs. After it's mixed you put in the cocoa and the flour. And you can put in some milk if it's a bit dry. Then just pour it in the tins and cook it. It's six ounces of sugar, did I say that? Then get them out of the tins and sandwich them together. With butter cream. I nearly forgot – if you don't grease the tins it might get stuck. Oh yeah, and before you put in the eggs you need six ounces of butter or marg.

It was dark. As Jim walked down the road someone murdered him. He hit him on the head. His wife cried when she knew he was dead.

Dear Guvnor

I wood like the job what my mate says is going down your office. I have not had a job before but dont wright to my old school as they ~~dont~~ did'nt like me much. Me mum says its time I urned some money. I spose your job will be better than nothing. I can start strait away. See ya.

love
Mr Gary Simps

As you use this book, you'll be developing your reading skills in lots of different ways. You'll also be using *reading* as a way of helping you *write*, *speak*, *listen* and *think* with greater care and greater confidence.

# U·N·I·T 1  *Skimming a book*

How can we form an idea of what's in a book without reading it all the way through? A *Contents* list (like the one on pages v–ix) can be helpful but we can also look through the book to notice drawings, photos, headings and important words or sections which are easily visible on the page. This way of looking at a book or passage to form a general impression of it is called *skimming*.

You can find out something about this book and practise the skill of skimming by answering the following questions:

## Assignments

**1**  How many pages are there in this book?

**2**  How many units are there?

**3**  About how long is each unit?

**4**  Would you estimate that the book contains: *one or two*; *a few*; *several*; *a large number* of the following:

 **a** photographs
 **b** cartoons
 **c** maps
 **d** complete short stories
 **e** poems
 **f** newspaper and magazine articles
 **g** diagrams
 **h** board games
 **i** crosswords

**5**  Does the book contain photographs of:

 **a** a Red Indian squaw
 **b** a Rolls Royce
 **c** a cinema
 **d** a bald man
 **e** bees

**6** Does the book contain drawings of

    **a** a deck chair
    **b** a football commentator
    **c** a pyramid
    **d** a fire escape
    **e** a chocolate bar

**7** Does the book contain anything about

    **a** crime
    **b** marriage
    **c** advertising
    **d** school
    **e** dieting

**8** What are the following units about:

    **a** *Weighing up the evidence*
    **b** *On the telly and in the paper*
    **c** *It all depends*
    **d** *The right candidate for the job*
    **e** *But does it make sense?*

**9** What kind(s) of material (eg story, factual passage, photo, poem, diagram etc) do each of the following units contain:

    **a** *Using comparisons*
    **b** *Solving the problem*
    **c** *Actions have consequences*
    **d** *Knowing the code*
    **e** *Clear instructions*

**10** Are pupils asked to do the following anywhere in the book:

    **a** Explain the difference between adverbs and adjectives
    **b** Put muddled fragments of a text in order
    **c** Design a flowchart
    **d** Write a diary from the point of view of a character in the story
    **e** Illustrate a poem
    **f** Write an informal letter
    **g** Tape record a play or conversation
    **h** Tell a joke
    **i** Write a persuasive magazine article

**11** On many pages of the book part of the text appears in a box. What are these boxes for?

**12** In 4–6 sentences, write a clear summary of what this book contains. Include as much information as possible in your summary. It should be intended for an English teacher who has not seen the book.

The last unit was about skimming a book; a different type of reading is called *scanning*. This is the technique to use when you want to find out specific bits of information. On the following pages there is a table of food values. It tells you how many calories or kilojoules (units of energy) certain foods contain. The answers to the questions below can all be found by looking at the table. Try to answer the questions as quickly as possible; don't read every word on the table but just run your eye over the page until you find what you need.

## Assignments

☞ **1** **a** How many calories are there in a whole grapefruit?
**b** How many kilojoules are equivalent to 5 calories?
**c** How many kilojoules are in 1oz lean bacon?
**d** How many calories are equivalent to 150 kilojoules?
**e** Are carrots less fattening than blackberries?
**f** Is it less fattening to eat an apple than a banana?
**g** Which cream would dieters prefer?
**h** Is margarine less fattening than butter?
**i** Does skimmed milk contain half the calories of whole milk?
**j** Which is the least fattening cheese listed?
**k** Which beans are most fattening?
**l** Which chocolate is less fattening? By how many calories per ounce?
**m** I want a snack of less than 100 calories. Should I have 1oz bread and 2oz cottage cheese, or 4oz canned pineapple?
**n** Is turkey less fattening than lean beef?
**o** How many types of meat are listed (excluding fish)?
**p** What is the most fattening food listed?
**q** Which foods have less than four calories an ounce?
**r** Which fruits have more than 25 calories an ounce?
**s** Which is the most fattening fish listed?

**2** Invent 20 similar questions and swap them with a friend.

# FOOD VALUE TABLE

| Food | Portion | Calories | Kilojoules |
|------|---------|----------|------------|
| Apples | 1 medium (4oz) | 40 | 150 |
| Apricots, fresh | 25g/1oz | 5 | 20 |
| canned | " | 30 | 150 |
| Asparagus | " | 5 | 20 |
| Aubergines | " | 5 | 20 |
| Avocado pear | 1 medium (10oz) | 250 | 1050 |
| Bacon, lean raw | 25g/1oz | 115 | 500 |
| Bananas | 1 medium (4oz) | 60 | 250 |
| Beans, baked | 25g/1oz | 25 | 100 |
| broad | " | 10 | 50 |
| butter | " | 75 | 300 |
| haricot | " | 75 | 300 |
| runner | " | 5 | 20 |
| Beef, very lean | " | 75 | 300 |
| Beetroot, raw | " | 10 | 50 |
| Blackberries | " | 10 | 50 |
| Blackcurrants | " | 10 | 50 |
| Bread, white or brown | " | 70 | 300 |
| Broccoli | " | 5 | 20 |
| Brussels sprouts | " | 10 | 50 |
| Butter | " | 225 | 950 |
| Cabbage, red or white | " | 5 | 20 |
| Carrots | " | 5 | 20 |
| Cauliflower | " | 5 | 20 |
| Celery | " | 3 | 10 |
| Cheese, Cheddar | " | 120 | 500 |
| cottage | " | 30 | 150 |
| cream | " | 230 | 950 |
| Edam | " | 90 | 400 |
| Cherries, fresh | " | 10 | 50 |
| Chicken, flesh only, raw | " | 10 | 50 |
| Chocolate, milk | " | 165 | 700 |
| plain | " | 155 | 650 |
| Cod, raw | " | 20 | 90 |
| Cornflakes and most cereals | " | 105 | 450 |
| Cornflour | " | 100 | 450 |
| Courgettes | " | 2 | 10 |
| Cream, double | 2 × 15ml spoons | 130 | 550 |
| single | 2 × 15ml spoons | 60 | 250 |
| Cucumber | 25g/1oz | 3 | 10 |
| Currants | " | 70 | 300 |
| Eggs, whole | 1 standard | 80 | 350 |
| Flour | 25g/1oz | 100 | 450 |
| Gooseberries, raw | " | 10 | 45 |
| Grapefruit, whole | 1 medium (4oz) | 30 | 150 |
| Grapes | 25g/1oz | 15 | 60 |
| Haddock, white, raw | " | 20 | 90 |
| smoked, raw | " | 20 | 90 |
| Hake, fillets only, raw | " | 25 | 100 |
| Ham, lean only, boiled | " | 60 | 250 |
| Herring, raw | " | 65 | 280 |
| Honey | " | 80 | 350 |
| Ice cream | " | 55 | 250 |
| Jam | " | 75 | 300 |
| Jelly, made up | 600ml/1 pint | 420 | 1800 |
| cubes | 25g/1oz | 75 | 300 |

| Food | Portion | Calories | Kilojoules |
|------|---------|----------|------------|
| Kidneys, raw | 25g/1oz | 30–35 | 150 |
| Kippers, raw | " | 30 | 150 |
| Lamb, very lean only | " | 75 | 300 |
| Lard | " | 260 | 1100 |
| Leeks, raw | " | 10 | 50 |
| Lemon, raw | " | 5 | 20 |
| Lettuce, raw | " | 3 | 10 |
| Liver, raw | " | 40–45 | 150–200 |
| Macaroni, raw | " | 100 | 400 |
|       boiled | " | 30 | 150 |
| Mackerel, raw | " | 30 | 150 |
| Margarine | " | 225 | 1000 |
| Marmalade | " | 75 | 300 |
| Marrow, boiled | " | 2 | 10 |
| Melon | " | 5 | 20 |
| Milk, whole | 600ml/1 pint | 380 | 1600 |
|    skimmed | 600ml/1 pint | 190 | 800 |
| Mushrooms, raw | 25g/1oz | 2 | 10 |
| Nuts, shelled (average) | " | 170 | 750 |
| Oil, olive or corn | 30ml/1 fl.oz | 265 | 1100 |
| Onions, raw | 25g/1oz | 5 | 20 |
| Oranges | 1 medium (4oz) | 40 | 150 |
| Parsnips, raw | 25g/1oz | 5 | 20 |
| Peaches, raw | 1 medium (4oz) | 40 | 150 |
| Pears, raw | 1 medium (4oz) | 40 | 150 |
| Peas, fresh or frozen | 25g/1oz | 20 | 90 |
| Pineapple, canned | " | 20 | 90 |
| Plums, raw | " | 10 | 50 |
| Pork, very lean | " | 35 | 150 |
| Potatoes, raw | " | 25 | 100 |
| Radishes, raw | " | 5 | 20 |
| Raspberries, raw | " | 5 | 20 |
| Rhubarb, raw | " | 2 | 10 |
| Rice, raw | " | 100 | 450 |
|     boiled | " | 35 | 150 |
| Sausage, average, raw | " | 100 | 400 |
| Soup, thin | 300ml/½ pint | 65–100 | 300–400 |
|    thick | 300ml/½ pint | 90–200 | 400–800 |
| Spaghetti, raw | 25g/1oz | 105 | 400 |
|     boiled | " | 35 | 150 |
| Spring greens | " | 3 | 10 |
| Strawberries | " | 5 | 20 |
| Sugar, white or brown | " | 110 | 500 |
| Swedes, raw | " | 5 | 20 |
| Sweetcorn, canned or frozen | " | 25 | 100 |
| Syrup | " | 85 | 350 |
| Tomatoes, raw | 1 medium (2oz) | 10 | 50 |
| Tuna, canned in oil | 25g/1oz | 75 | 300 |
| Turkey, meat only, raw | " | 35 | 150 |
| Turnips, raw | " | 5 | 20 |
| Vinegar | 30ml/1 fl.oz | 1 | 5 |
| Yoghurt, plain, low fat | 5oz carton | 75 | 300 |
|    fruit flavoured | 5oz carton | 125 | 500 |

# U·N·I·T 3 *Selling chocolate*

When a company launches a new product, a lot of thought goes into choosing the right marketing approach. Look at the description of the new chocolate bar below. Then study some of the suggestions which have been made for its name, wrapper and advertising campaign.

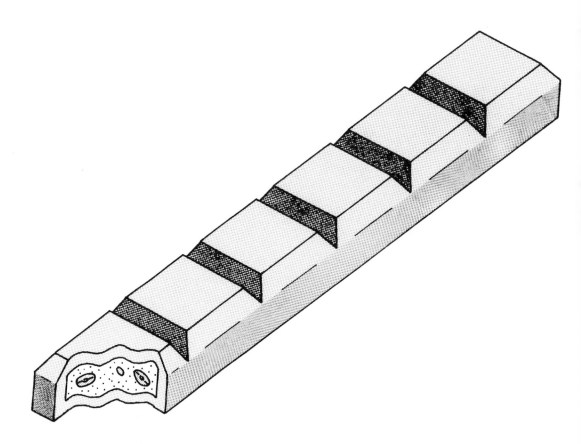

**The bar**
The new product is a milk chocolate bar measuring 15cm × 2.5cm, divided into six thick square segments. The filling is a mixture of orange creme and whole hazelnuts.

**Suggested names**

1 Scrunch    2 Tuesday    3 Zany    4 Paradise    5 Majik
6 Lustre     7 Romance            8 Nature's garden

**Suggested wrappers**

1 Plain black with name in gold
2 Dark brown with orange lettering
3 Fluorescent green, pink and yellow
4 Navy with large red stars and name in white
5 Navy with rainbow glitter effect, lettering in white
6 Black and white check, with name in bright green
7 Dark green with yellow flowers and light green lettering
8 White with green and red lettering

**Suggested slogans**

1 M'm . . . . . . so good it makes me feel zany!
2 Muncha blocka choca day
3 The day's not right without one
4 Tropical, topical, unforgettable
5 An evening for two needs . . .
6 For a fitter, sweeter you
7 Hey presto! It's gone!
8 The mean macho munch

**Suggested TV advertisements**

1 Scenes of a strong man doing very hard physical work. After work he goes into a pub. When the barman offers him a whisky he says, 'Never mind the whisky; what I need's a _____ bar.'

2 Scenes of people of all types and ages running from all corners of a town. Gradually they all pack into a small sweet shop and say, 'We'd like a _____ bar, please!'

3 A couple in swimming costumes lying on a beach on a tropical island. A waiter brings them a cocktail each and two _____ bars. The girl turns to her boyfriend and says, 'I've got all I need: sun, you *and* a _____ bar.'

4 Monsters from outer space bouncing about to weird music. Gradually we see that they are all eating chocolate bars. After eating the chocolate, they all say the name of the bar and then bounce off the screen.

5 A candlelit sitting room, soft music playing. A couple sit on the sofa and we think they're about to kiss and cuddle. Instead, he produces two chocolate bars. She winks at the camera and says the slogan in a seductive voice.

6 A sunny meadow with birds singing. Scenes of oranges and nuts being harvested and prepared. A man's voice tells us how healthy and natural _____ is.

7 A magician stands behind an empty table. He waves his wand and the bar appears. Some children come in and eat the chocolate. The magician smiles knowingly and tells us *he's* made it disappear.

8 A class of children are falling asleep as a teacher drones on. Gradually, they all pull the bar from their pockets and eat it. At once they become bright and attentive again.

---

**Writing a 'blurb'**

**Example 1**
'. . . *more exhilarating than a tropical waterfall*'
Imagine standing in the heart of a tropical waterfall. Fresh water cascading over your body, silver spray glinting in the sun. As you turn, gushes of water race over your skin – exhilarating and invigorating you. Sounds wonderful doesn't it . . . exotic, exciting? Now you can capture the very *essence* of that sensational experience in your own bathroom, any time of day you like.

**Example 2**
The easy way would be to buy in ready-made apple filling. Like most people do. The best way is to buy the finest British Bramleys and make your own apple filling. Like Sara Lee does for our Apple Danish bar. Then to add a little spice we add a little cinnamon. We get it from Sumatra, not Sri Lanka, even though it costs us twice as much. And to add a little juiciness we add plump sultanas from Greece. Then we fold the filling into delicious Danish Pastry – made from real eggs and pure butter, naturally – and finish off with a rich streusel topping. We think you'll find Sara Lee Apple Danish Bar is best served hot. And we know you'll find it irresistible.

**Some words and phrases you may like to use:**

| | | |
|---|---|---|
| new | nutritious | super |
| special | tangy | scrumptious |
| never-to-be-forgotten | zest | tasty |
| seductive | luscious | sparkle |
| crunchy | crazy | firm |
| appetising | elegant | rich |
| smooth | neat | pure |
| creamy | honest | real |
| clean | exotic | exhilarating |
| wholesome | taste of the sun | invigorating |
| chunky | today's favourite | essence |
| different | your family will love . . . | fresh |
| value for money | treat | finest |
| delicious | spoil yourself | juicy |
| natural | improved | plump |
| good for you | sensational | irresistible |

# Assignments

**1** Imagine you are the promotions team of *Eat-me Chocolate Ltd* considering the marketing suggestions for the new chocolate bar. You have to choose which suggestions to use in your advertising campaign.
**a** Decide what 'image' you would like the bar to have, and who the campaign will be aimed at.
**b** Choose one of each of the names, wrappers, slogans and TV advertisements for the new bar. Make sure that they all fit together and maintain the 'image' you decided on in **a**.

**2** Write a report (see page 19) for the company directors, informing them of what you decided in **1**, and explaining the reasons for your choices.

**3** **a** Write the 'blurb' for the new bar. This should be a short description (50–80 words) which will be used as the basis for all the publicity promotions. (To give you an idea of the kind of *register* you should use, see the box opposite. The first example comes from an advertisement for a shower, the second from an advertisement for apple streusel.)
**b** Design a one-page advertisement for a magazine, based on the approach you decided upon in your discussion. Use appropriate colours to match the wrapper you chose.

**4** Write your own promotion for the product, using *different* ideas from the ones given here. You need to think up:

**a** a name
**b** a wrapper
**c** a slogan
**d** a one-page advertisement for a magazine
**e** the 'blurb'
**f** the script for a one-minute TV advertisement
**g** the script for a 30-second radio advertisement

**5** Write the promotion for a new product (as in **4**) but this time choose a different product, which you have invented yourself.

# U·N·I·T 4 *Solving the clues*

We might not be aware of it, but when we read our brain does some very clever detective work. It continually tries to make links between all the ideas printed on the page and, usually, the ideas will make some kind of sense. When our brain meets something like the fragments on these two pages, however, it soon knows that something is wrong!

## *Assignments*

○ ☞ **1** The fragments on the following pages are taken from two different stories by 15-year-olds.
**a** Decide which sections belong to which story.
**b** List the clues in the text which helped you to decide.
**c** Note how long this activity took you.

○ ☞ **2** The different parts of the two stories still need to be put in the right order.
**a** Work out the correct order for the sections of each story (The advice in the box should help you here.)
**b** List the clues which helped you to decide on the order.
**c** Note how long this activity took you. Was it easier or harder than **1a**? Suggest reasons for this.
**d** Invent a title for each of the stories.

**3** Find or write another story. Cut it into sections and ask a friend to put them in the correct order. (A small group of you could work on several stories at once.)

---

**Deciding the right order**

● *Skim* over the paragraphs to get a general idea of what the story/passage is about.
● Think logically which sections *have* to go in a certain place.
● Look first for the sections which sound like the beginning and the end.
● Look for what seems like the first mention of a particular person, place or other detail – something which must obviously come before other mentions.
● Look for links at the beginnings and ends of paragraphs.
● When you have a suggested order, read through the whole story carefully to check that it makes sense.

**a** Once he was in the corridor, Jim sprinted, dashing in amongst the other pupils until finally he had to stop to open the door to go outside. Taking off once more, Jim nearly fell as he spun on the thin black ice that was partially covering the concrete of the playground. This warning caused him to slow down to a jog; besides, he was beginning to get a stitch now. Jim wasn't running to keep warm in spite of it being a bitter winter's day with the wind stinging as it swept across his face. No, someone was chasing him.

**b** Empowered with a strength only bestowed on the drunk and desperate, he landed a terrific right hook to the jaw of the first thug, sending him crashing into the undergrowth beside the path. Sadly, however, as he staggered from the force of the punch he himself had delivered, he did not see the second thug swinging his bottle fiercely, tearing into his left temple and cheek. He only felt a blinding pain in the left side of his face before he sank into the painless oblivion of unconsciousness.

**c** Mark Bramson was a fresh-faced wiry young man of twenty-six years. His dark hair and thin black moustache, however, belied his age and people often thought he was ten years older – an annoying fact which was, nevertheless, useful in his chosen profession – acting. Mark Bramson also knew of another annoying fact that affected him at that moment: he was broke and very depressed.

**d** Ronald Colee was also very depressed. Trust the BBC to dump their new brainchild on him from out of the blue! He had no doubt that the new soap opera, based around the lives of. a fabulously rich family of stockbrokers, would send the ratings through the roof. However, he had no desire to interview for the lead part – a rich young man in his middle thirties – especially with this week's busy schedule. Even so, the powers that be had spoken, so he might as well enjoy the job.

'Send the first candidate in, Sheila,' he spoke into his desk microphone. Then he leaned back in his padded chair, trying to picture the ideal man for the part: tall, athletic build, dark hair and moustache, looking about middle thirties. The door to his office opened and in walked the very man he had imagined. Minutes later, in a daze, he found himself saying, 'Just sign here Mr Bramson, and come in again next Monday.' A few seconds later he pressed the intercom button and spoke into his desk microphone again. 'Send the other applicants away, Sheila.'

**e** Turning into the bottom of his street, Jim quickened his step and wondered if he'd make it up the hill in front of him. Well, if he couldn't Fatty couldn't, but then ——————.

He began the trek up the hill. It seemed miles long. His legs began to tire – another look – Fatty was coping well – he had gained on him. Gritting his teeth, Jim made one last, laborious attempt. Staggering and out of breath, he reached the top and trotted forward – not far now.

**f** When he came round, Mark was aware that he was lying in a hospital bed, and that his throat felt very dry. 'Don't worry dear,' a nurse was saying to him, 'that nasty scar will have gone completely in a couple of years.'

'Oh God!' Mark croaked, feeling a furrow in his left cheek like a ploughed field, before falling again into unconsciousness.

**g** Obeying his primary instincts, Jim flew at him, flinging fists in quick succession, aiming at the taller boy's stomach, failing to acknowledge the obviously amused crowd of adults and children around him. Through the cloud of fear it suddenly dawned on him. Fatty wasn't hitting him back but, instead, was calling in a puzzled voice, 'I don't want to fight you! Stop it! I don't want to fight! Stop hitting me!'

**h** In his haste, he failed to notice the perilous patch of uneven stones by the factory wall which caught his foot and sent him flying, slapping his hands and legs against the cold, hard ground – then the pain. His gloves had protected his hands but his knees. . . . He looked down. Both were grazed, stinging and bleeding. Pain preoccupied him for precious moments and when he finally pulled himself to his feet it was to find a panting Fatty Brown, hands on hips, standing over him.

**i** The grim shadows of the giant elms flanking the path would normally have intimidated him, but not tonight. The sky above was clear; he could see the stars, and he felt like he was walking on air. Up ahead he could see two young men and a girl, each holding an empty cider bottle, silent witnesses to their intoxication. As he strode past the park bench on which they were seated along the narrow, darkened path, Mark felt a foot lash out and he stumbled. He fell heavily on his face a few yards further on. Behind him he could hear drunken cackles, the sound of two bottles breaking, and the clump of heavy boots on the path approaching him. He staggered to his feet and wheeled round to see two of the drunken youths approaching him with the jagged shards of their cider bottles grasped in their clumsy hands.

**j** At intervals, he would peer over his shoulder. Each time he would see the flushed face of Fatty Brown about fifty yards behind him. Brown had been following Jim all day – well, ever since lunch-time. What had he done? He always made sure to keep out of his way. For now, however, he would just keep running. He had no time to think of explanations.

**k** 'Dammit, if Ronald can't find the right man in time, no one can,' muttered Louis Wilson, producer of the new billion dollar blockbuster about Italian underground crime. He was looking for a man to play the leader of the Mafia, and Ronald Colee was his last chance to come up with someone slim, tall, dark and scarred before shooting began in a week's time. 'Dammit, every other detail's perfect, but not this one, the most vital part.' So lost was he in his thoughts that he strode right up the BBC steps and into a slim young man who was leaving the building. As he looked up to apologise, Louis stopped and smiled. Maybe he wouldn't need to see Ronald at all.

**l** Mark took the BBC lift down to the ground floor, crossed the impressive foyer, and entered the swing doors, his head hung low in deep depression.

**m** Jim stepped back dropping his hands, bemused by the expression on Fatty's face and for the first time he noticed what Fatty was holding in his hand.

'Here, I've been trying to catch you all day. You dropped this at dinner.' He held out a rusty war-time penknife, a treasured reminder of Jim's grandad who had died a few years back in the First World War.

**n** Having been discharged on the Sunday morning, Mark decided to go to see the director of the BBC on Monday, as arranged. The look on Ronald Colee's face was not one of surprise this time, more of horror. After thirty seconds of open-mouthed goggling, he calmly explained that Mark simply could not have the part, and that the contract must be declared void, because of the change in Mark's circumstances. Mark left the office with a sigh. Ronald Colee also sighed as he told Sheila to put the word out about 'the soap job.'

**o** There weren't many times Jim could think of when the bell for the end of school had come as a greater relief than today. He couldn't get out of the classroom quick enough and was reprimanded by the school master for his eagerness.

'Wait until you are told to leave,' the teacher had said.

'Yes sir, sorry sir,' Jim had replied.

**p** Ronald Colee sat back in his easy chair and considered how easy that job had been. 'And it gives me time for a drink before lunch,' he thought gleefully.

Later that evening Mark also celebrated with a drink at his local. He strode home across the park radiantly that night, if not a little erratically under the influence not only of a great success, but also of a little too much to drink.

*And then what happened?*

Imagine you are having a conversation with a friend who's telling you about something interesting that's happened. You're listening carefully, all the time asking questions about what happened next. Mentally you may be predicting what your friend is going to say next. Reading a story can be like this too.

This story has been divided into sections. As you read it, make a mental note of any details that strike you as significant. Then try to predict what will happen next. Write down a few notes about what you think is happening and how you think the story will continue.

**ALL BUT EMPTY**
**by Graham Greene**

*1 gas lights*

*2 corrupt*

It is not often that one finds an empty cinema, but this one I used to frequent in the early '30s because of its almost invariable, almost total emptiness. I speak only of the afternoons, the heavy grey afternoons of late winter; in the evenings, when the lights went up in the Edgware Road and the naphtha flares,[1] and the peep-shows were crowded, this cinema may have known prosperity. But I doubt it.

It had so little to offer. There was no talkie apparatus, and the silent films it showed did not appeal to the crowd by their excitement or to the connoisseur by their unconscious humour.

I suspect that the cinema kept open only because the owner could not sell or let the building and he could not afford to close it. I went to it because it was silent, because it was all but empty, and because the girl who sold the tickets had a bright, common, venal[2] prettiness.

One passed out of the Edgware Road and found it in a side street. It was built of boards like a saloon in an American western, and there were no posters. Probably no posters existed of the kind of films it showed. One paid one's money to the girl of whom I spoke, taking an unnecessarily expensive seat in the drab emptiness on the other side of the red velvet curtains, and she would smile, charming and venal, and address one by a name of her own.

I remember I went in one afternoon and found myself quite alone. There was not even a pianist; blurred metallic music was relayed from a gramophone in the pay-box. I hoped the girl would soon leave her job and come in. I sat almost at the end of a row with one seat free as an indication that I felt like company, but she never came. An elderly man got

16

entangled in the curtain and billowed his way through it and lost himself in the dark. He tried to get past me, though he had the whole cinema to choose from, and brushed my face with a damp beard. Then he sat down in the seat I had left, and there we were, close together in the darkness.

What will happen next? Will they speak? What might be said? (Turn to page 92)

# U·N·I·T 6 *Solving the problem*

On these pages you can read about the views of some pupils who regularly play truant from school.

**Aziz (13)** I go to a big comprehensive school down town. It's got about 2000 kids in it. It's too big — you don't get noticed in it so I hardly ever go now.

It's not strict enough, either. I get annoyed because when I have a lesson I like there's so many kids making a racket you can't think straight. Mind you, I suppose some days I don't want to do much either except just muck about.

Not many subjects interest me, really. I like cooking but that's about all. I hate PE, English and Maths. They're boring. Who cares what x equals or how to describe a fire?

**Alison (14)** *I don't go to school much now because I got fed up with teachers telling me what to do all the time. Like they got at me for smoking. It's my life, isn't it? It's up to me to decide if I want to smoke or not.*

*Anyway, my mates take the micky if I go to school. Most of them have left and are on the dole now. One or two have got jobs. I don't know if I'll get a job very easily. But qualifications don't help much, do they? Plenty of people with all sorts of exam passes are unemployed so what's the point of trying?*

**Norris (14)** I haven't been to school for 3 months. I never wore the uniform so they kept sending me home. Then I had my hair dyed orange and they didn't like that either. What right have they got to criticise the way I look? I don't tell the teachers what to wear, do I? It's the person inside that counts, not the clothes you wear or the colour of your hair.

I get a lot of hassle from my parents too. They think I should go to school. But they just want a quiet life. They're not really interested in what I do or what I think.

**Carrie (15)** Teachers want to get kids through exams but if the kids are not bothered then the teachers aren't. I think that if you don't want to take exams you should be allowed to leave. That's best for the kids and the teachers. I'd leave.

At the moment when I go to school I just sit and talk or read a magazine. They never tell us off. I think if they pushed me I'd work a bit harder but there's not enough discipline really. I suppose it's hard being a teacher but they choose the job, don't they?

**Claire (15)** I work in a baker's on a Saturday and I really enjoy it. It makes me feel like an adult, not a kid. I'm ready for work — school bores me. I'd like to train as a hairdresser but I don't need school qualifications for that, do I?

A lot of what you learn in school is useless. Like history and all the maths we do. As long as you've got a bit of common sense that's all you need in life. Teachers don't explain things properly anyway. They just tell you to write it down or think about it. That doesn't help you understand.

I go to school occasionally just so my mum doesn't get into trouble, but there's really nothing there for me.

**Craig (15)** *I get bored at school – mostly with the other kids. They're so immature. Most of my mates are 17 or 18 and they've all left school now. Some of the kids in my class still like grass fights and hiding the teacher's board rubber, that sort of stuff.*

*I'm thick anyway. What's the point of keeping me at school when I want to leave? I can read and write as well as I need to and I could easily do a man's job. School's all right if you're brainy but it's a waste of time for people like me who're not going to get anything out of it.*

**Earl (14)** The classes at my school are all too big. The teachers never get time to help you. They just concentrate on the bright ones – the ones who do all the talking – and if you can't do the work it's just tough luck. You need really small classes to learn anything.

Anyway, I don't go to school much. I hang about down the precinct with my mates. The only trouble is we've got no money to spend and sometimes the police hassle us. The other week I got nicked for loitering and my mum had to come down the police station to collect me.

Really, I'd like a job. Labouring or something outside would suit me. Sometimes I do a bit for my uncle and it's much better than school.

**Ellen (15)** I could be quite brainy if I worked but I never bothered. I do go to school sometimes – it depends what lessons I've got. Like computer studies – I hate that. I picked it for one of my options because the boy I was going out with did it. Now I don't like it and I don't like him either! So I never go on Tuesdays and Fridays.

When I bunk off I usually wander round the shops down town. You can be free there – no moaning teachers. I get fed up with being treated like a two-year-old in school. All the stupid rules put me off. One day I got sent home for wearing grey tights. It's so petty. Another time I got a detention for not taking a pen to a lesson. Teachers don't always remember their pens!

---

## Writing a report

- Think about who will read the report and what they will want to know.
- Decide what should be included and what left out.
- Make notes before you write your report.
- List points and number them in your notes.
- Decide which points are similar and can be grouped together.
- Put your points in what you think is the best order.
- Remember to distinguish between facts and opinions. (See page 218.)
- Keep your style concise and precise.

# Assignments

**1** Imagine that you are a Youth Officer who knows many of the truants well. The local Education Committee has become very concerned about the large number of young people truanting in your area. You have been asked to write a report explaining why they play truant. Use the views expressed here as the basis of your report.

In the first paragraph outline what you are reporting on.

In the rest of the report explain clearly the reasons the pupils give for their truancy.

---

**2** You have been asked to give the Education Committee a pupil's reaction to the statements made by the truants.

**a** Make a list of reasons the truants give for not attending school.

**b** Look again at the list and put a tick by the ones you think are reasonable.

**c** Bearing this in mind, try to answer the following questions:
- What measures could schools take to prevent truancy?
- How should persistent truants be dealt with?

**d** At the end of your discussion on **c**, draw up a straightforward list of recommendations, which could be issued to all schools.

---

**3** Write a letter to Luke Foster, chairperson of the local Education Committee telling him about your discussion and explaining that you are enclosing a list of the recommendations you decided on. (See page 102 for how to set out a formal letter.)

# U·N·I·T 7 *A visual image*

Many magazines present stories in the form of a picture strip. Read this one, for instance.

# Assignments

○ ☞ **1** How do you respond to this picture strip? Is it realistic? Does it make you think? Would you want to criticise it? If so, for what reasons?

✎ **2** This picture strip presents teenagers with some difficult moral situations. Sum up briefly and clearly what you think the situation(s) is/are.

✎ **3** Rewrite this as a story in words. Stick closely to the facts you are given but add other details of your own. For instance, try to describe Sue's personality and give a clearer idea of her feelings than a picture strip can do. You could also suggest *why* Mick behaves as he does. As the story covers a period of several months, you may like to mention other events not covered in the picture strip. Your story is likely to be longer than the picture strip.

○ **4** Exchange stories with at least one other member of your group. Read the picture strip again, then read the written version. Which version is more successful:

**a** as entertainment
**b** as a moral lesson
**c** in appealing to the emotions
**d** in making you think?

○ **5** Why do some young people prefer picture stories to those in words? Is it because the picture strips are:

**a** simpler
**b** easier to read
**c** more exciting
**d** leave less to the imagination
**e** shorter
**f** another reason (your own ideas)?

✎ **6** Shortly after the last scene in the story Sue writes to a problem page for advice. Write her letter and the reply she receives.

☞ ○ **7** Should teenage magazines try to deal with moral situations? If not, why not? If so, which of the following methods is most likely to be successful and why:

**a** picture strip
**b** story in words
**c** problem page
**d** short, sharp advice
**e** other ways (suggest some)

# U·N·I·T 8 *Sweet dreams*

The story on page 21 has a sad ending, but many romance stories present love in a rather different way. Here is a poem on the subject, written by Mädi Edwards, aged 15.

*Sweet dreams of 'Mr Right'*
Scanning the pages by a pale, dusty light,
Engrossed in a story she believes is called life.
Escaping her feelings, filling her mind,
Forgetting reality, a world left behind.
Passion and ecstasy she thinks she can feel,
A misunderstanding of what time must reveal.
Sitting and reading, alone yet at peace,
Armed with 'life's handbook' to show what love means.
Emptiness and sorrow can no longer be seen,
Searching for affection in a pitiful dream.
Always escaping, a life on the run,
Avoiding a future that one day will come.
Dreading the moment when the last page is read,
With only the memory of 'love' in her head.
Wondering and waiting, probing the night,
She's hunting, yet begging, to find 'Mr Right.'
But still she returns, truth has no effect,
Claimed by a story with a love of no depth.
Floundering in fantasy, breaking all ties,
With a life once concordant distorted by lies.

*Mädi's explanation*
It's a poem about young girls' fascination with romance novels. Some become obsessed with them, and are led to believe that such events happen in real life. Others read these books intentionally as a means of escaping reality.

Girls can be affected by these books to such an extent that they exist merely to practise the ideology of romance stories in the expectation that life always has a happy ending.

An American professor researching into women's reading habits advertised for women to write and tell her why they read and enjoy romantic fiction. This is one of the letters she received in reply to her advertisement:

Dear Ms Conway,


You ask for readers to write and tell you why they read romantic fiction. Well, I'll tell you. We live in wicked times and terrible things happen every day, but the heroines in these stories make me feel that it's a lovely world and that people are good. With this knowledge I can face life and I feel glad to be alive.

I suppose it's escapism, if you like. My reading irritates my husband sometimes because he feels I'm in a world of my own. It's not that I want to get away from him or the children, it's just that my life is full of pressures. I can't expect much romance in my life, but these books can find some for me. It would be lovely to meet a man like the ones in the romances - so strong and brave and so sensitive to the needs of a woman. I spend my life looking after others - cooking and cleaning for my husband and family. Even if I'm tired or ill I still have to go on. I have a kind of dream that I might meet a hero like those in the books, who'd look after me and love me just for being myself. I'm not saying I want an affair. It's just that if I can't be treated well myself and live a romantic life, I like to read about someone who does enjoy those things.

Besides, I learn a lot from reading. The books are set in all sorts of different places and you learn so much about geography and different general knowledge. And then there's the improvement in my vocabulary too.

A lot of people knock romance stories without ever reading them. We've all got our hopes and dreams and not many people can say they're totally happy with their life. If romance stories keep me happy, where's the harm in that?

I hope this letter has been of some use to you in your research.

Yours sincerely,

Elaine Staples

Elaine Staples (Mrs)

# ssignments

☞ **1** List the criticisms of romantic literature which the poem on page 23 makes. Add any other ideas of your own.

---

✔ ◇ **2** Write a story about the girl in the poem.

---

✔ ◇ **3** Write one of the stories she is reading. (This could be in cartoon form, if you like.)

---

◇ ☞ **4** **a** Write a list of the separate reasons Mrs Staples gives for reading romantic novels.
**b** Write a letter in reply to Mrs Staples, discussing each of the points she makes in turn. Make it clear whether or not you agree with her.

---

☞ **5** **a** List other types of reading matter and television programmes which you think might be criticised as 'escapist'.
**b** Do you think that indulging in this type of escapism is a weakness? Or can you find any good reasons for it? Give reasons for your opinions.

---

✔ ◇ **6** Using some of the ideas you have collected for **1**, **4** and **5**, write an article for a teenage magazine, entitled *either*
*The dangers of escaping into a book*
or *A little escapism never did anyone any harm.*
(Your article should be at least 400 words long)

---

**Escapism** – retreating into a fantasy world to avoid the realities of life

25

# U·N·I·T 9  *Ways of communicating*

When you want to contact someone you could choose the phone, a letter or (not often) a telegram. These days most people use the phone. Here is a transcript of a telephone conversation between two friends.

*John*: Hullo, Nick. It's John here.

*Nick*: Oh hullo. What happened to you last night then?

*John*: I was gonna come but I got diverted! D'you remember Adam, that mate of mine I worked with over at Hounslow?

*Nick*: Yeah. Went out to work in Saudi, didn't he?

*John*: Yeah, that's right. Well . . . er, he turned up last night. Right out of the blue. So I told him about your party and we was gonna come but . . .

*Nick*: What happened then?

*John*: Well, he said as he'd just got back he could have a nosh on the firm's expenses and I could go with him. So we went for this curry, right?

*Nick*: Yeah.

*John*: Well, that was about half nine. We was gonna go to the party afterwards. Anyway, he kept ordering up loads of stuff and I says to him, 'Adam, we'll never eat all this!'

*Nick*: Did ya?

*John*: Yeah! He said he was starving so we kept eating all this grub and I'd already had fish and chips at about six.

*Nick*: You pig!

*John*: Yeah, well I couldn't move when I'd finished! Adam was still keen to go to the party, like, and so was I but about eleven he suddenly felt all in. He'd been travelling a whole day all the way from Saudi! So he came back and slept on our settee.

*Nick*: So why didn't you come?

*John*: I felt so full. I couldn't move! I fell asleep watching the late night horror movie.

*Nick*: You glutton!

*John*: Anyway, what was the party like? All right, was it?

*Nick*: Yeah – excellent. You missed a really good do!

## Assignments

☞ **1** Conversation is obviously different from written English.
**a** List all the examples of *slang* you find in this conversation (see page 113).
**b** List any other expressions you notice which are common in speech but not in written English.

✎ ☞ **2** Imagine that Nick lives some distance from John and is not on the phone. Write a letter from John which serves the same purpose as the telephone conversation (see page 99 for an example of an informal letter).

26

# U·N·I·T 10 *A choice of endings*

This short radio play has two possible endings. As you read it, try to decide whether you think its ending should be humorous or horrific. (Ignore the letters and stars in the margin for now – they'll be used later.)

**MANIACS**
**by Peter Whalley**

**The Cast**

George    *the boilerman, early sixties, aggressive, self-confident*
Fred      *the groundsman, late forties, slow, gentle*
Mr Fish   *the headmaster, young, well-educated, polite*

**A school boiler-house**
*The boiler is heard faintly throughout.*

| | |
|---|---|
| George | Can I offer you some tea this morning, Fred? Or have you got your flask? |
| Fred | Oh, I've got me flask. |
| George | I thought you would have. |
| Fred | It's useful if I'm over by t'cricket square. Saves trekking back here. |
| George | Hang on a minute. |

*He moves away. We hear him fill a kettle and switch it on.*

| | |
|---|---|
| | (*distant*) And why do we need a cricket square in November? Or is that a state secret? |
| Fred | You need one in November so that you can have one July following. |
| George | (*returning*) Then why have one at all, eh? I mean the time that you, as groundsman, have to put into that. Why have one at all? |
| Fred | I suppose it's to play cricket on. |
| George | Well, there's no denying that. Would you like an Eccles cake? |
| Fred | No thanks, George. I've got me pipe. |
| George | No, what I mean is, what does a school that caters exclusively for the ungrateful, the unwashed and the downright bloody unspeakable want with a cricket square? Now a barracks square – I could understand that. |
| Fred | They won't have any sort of square left by the next year if I don't get on top of that moss. |
| George | They don't even wear proper flannels. What I've seen of 'em. Denims they wear. Denims. Next year I daresay it'll be swimming trunks. |
| Fred | It were swimming trunks last year. |
| George | My God. |
| Fred | And pads. They're not allowed to play without pads. |
| George | Not allowed! They're allowed to do owt they want. (*Pause*) Used to be a game for gentlemen did cricket. Mind you so did a lot of things. And what happened, eh? |
| Fred | To cricket? |
| George | To everything. At what point did the scum rise to cover the surface? |
| Fred | Oh aye. |
| George | And why did we allow it, eh? Why did we allow 'em to take over everything? Streets, football grounds, shopping precincts. |

27

| | |
|---|---|
| Fred | Cricket squares. |
| George | The worst thing this country ever did was to end national service.[1] |
| Fred | There were a gang of 'em out there again this morning. I don't know what lesson they were supposed to be doing. |
| George | Rural studies. |
| Fred | I don't know. |
| George | It'd be rural studies. He sends 'em out. Look into the distance, he says, and see what you can see. And that's the lesson. |
| Fred | Well, they just look to be hanging about to me. Till they saw that I were sweeping leaves up off tennis courts. |
| George | Hang on. Me kettle's boiling. |

*He moves away.*

| | |
|---|---|
| Fred | Then they came and started kicking all t'leaves about. The piles I'd made. Just kicking 'em about. Great lads of fifteen or sixteen. |

*George returns with the kettle and makes his tea.*

| | |
|---|---|
| George | What, the leaves that you'd collected? |
| Fred | They kept shouting, 'Who loves you,[2] Fred! Who loves you, Fred!' |
| George | Mental. |
| Fred | Great, gangling yobs. Fifteen or sixteen. Who loves you, Fred! You wouldn't credit it. |
| George | Mental they are. Want locking up, most of 'em. |
| Fred | When I'd go to sweep em up again, they'd go, 'Leave the leaves, Fred! Leave the leaves!' |
| George | Barbarians! The new barbarians of the Welfare State. Pouring out of comprehensive schools everywhere. |
| Fred | Aye. Though I suppose . . . |
| George | What? |
| Fred | Well, I sometimes think they can't be *all* that bad. Not every last one. |
| George | You'd think not, wouldn't you , but . . . (*he sighs*) |
| Fred | Some of the girls aren't unpleasant. |
| George | And some of 'em are worse than the flaming lads. Some of 'em. Dirty little devils some of 'em. |
| Fred | Oh aye. |
| George | You ought to listen to the wife after she's cleaned the girls' toilets of a night. |
| Fred | Aye, it can't be a picnic cleaning them. |
| George | It's an indictment[3] of what modern education's all about, Fred. It is. The combination of literacy and sex education has wreaked havoc over them walls. And what's astonishing is the way that their spelling picks up when they come to t'dirty words. I don't know how to account for that, do you? |
| Fred | No. |
| George | No. You're sure you won't have this Eccles cake? She always puts me two in. |

1 *At one time, all boys had to do two years' military training*
2 *Phrase spoken by the American TV detective* Kojak
3 *Accusation against*

| | |
|---|---|
| Fred | No, ta, George. I'll stick to me pipe. |
| George | You know we can sometimes spend two hours of a night talking about us experiences. Her with her cleaning and me with my caretaking. Sometimes I think they should change that board outside so that it says Sodom and Gomorrah[4] High School. |
| Fred | The sights I see over by the long jump pit. |
| George | I'll bet. |
| Fred | The sights I've seen there. |
| George | They should be gelded.[5] Most of 'em. Gelded when they come into t' first year. At that age they wouldn't know what they were missing. |
| Fred | Well, I've stopped bothering about it. I mean, they don't bother. So why should I? |
| George | Oh, they don't. If I ever stop a couple of 'em at it behind this boiler-house, I get a right mouthful in return. |
| Fred | If I'm out with tractor I just carry straight on till they move. |
| George | How did we ever get to this stage, eh? |

*He lights a cigarette.*

| | |
|---|---|
| Fred | I reckon I've stopped a few babies that way. |
| George | A tide of filth is what we face, Fred. A tide of filth and ignorance. Ever since Mr Fletcher went. |
| Fred | Fletcher. |
| George | The finest headmaster this school has ever had. |
| Fred | Before my time he was. |
| George | Wonderful man. The kids walked in fear of him. Terrified they were. And the staff for that matter. |
| Fred | Aye? |
| George | I'll tell you what. He'd have put paid to one or two of these young thugs that we have swaggering about here. |

(*Pause*)

| | |
|---|---|
| Fred | Knackenhead. |

*George gives a small cry and we hear the crash of his cup to the floor.* **A**

| | |
|---|---|
| George | Oh, look at that now! |
| Fred | Sorry, George. |
| George | Damn. And I've had that cup for, what, must be five year. |
| Fred | Sorry, George. |
| George | Nay. You took me by surprise, that's all. I wasn't prepared for it. For the name. Knackenhead. |
| Fred | It just put me in mind of him when you said . . . |
| George | Oh yes, yes. |
| Fred | Would you like a drop from me flask? There's a spare beaker on it. **B** |
| George | Aye. Go on then. |

*And we hear Fred pour it.*

---

4 *According to the Book of Genesis, in the Old Testament, God destroyed these two cities because they were so evil*
5 *castrated*

|          | (*joking*) Steady me nerves. I mean the thought of him's worse than any **C** horror film. |
|----------|-------------|
| Fred     | (*giving him the tea*) There. |
| George   | Ta. |
| Fred     | He should have had an X-certificate hung round his neck. |
| George   | Aye. The ultimate in horror. Frankenstein, Dracula and King Kong meet **D** Knackenhead! |

*They both have a quiet laugh.*

|          | (*turning serious*) Still, it's no joke though, is it? A great lout like that loose **E** around t'corridors. And with most of teachers scared of him. |
|----------|-------------|
| Fred     | Oh aye. |
| George   | That's why they send him out so often. Out of classes. Mind you, he looked a sight in 'em. |
| Fred     | I'll bet he did. |
| George   | I once went into, oh, Mrs Quincey's class it were. You know, little twitchy woman, teaches art. |
| Fred     | Drives a Mini. |
| George   | Yes. |
| Fred     | Keeps a Yorkshire terrier. |
| George   | That's her. Well, I went into her class to fetch a step-ladder. She'd borrowed it for a still life. And it were still an' all. Two weeks later it were still there. So I went to retrieve it. Well, minute I opened door they all started yelling out. |
| Fred     | Oh aye. |
| George   | You know the sort of thing. |
| Fred     | I do. |
| George   | All right, George! Going up in the world, George! All that kind of crap. Anyway, in't middle, there sat Knackenhead leering at me and mouthing obscenities. |
| Fred     | I can imagine. |
| George   | But I had to smile to meself, you know. Seeing him there, this great six foot two article, dressed like a circus parade . . . |
| Fred     | A punk. |
| George   | Aye. Though I would imagine even other punks found him offensive. Anyway, there he was, all squeezed in behind this little desk. And holding a pen – My God, I thought, I've seen everything now – holding a pen in his great fist. I'm not kidding, it were like seeing, you know, an elephant at a circus doing tricks. Unnatural. |
| Fred     | He should have been down a coal-mine. |
| George   | He should have been down a coal-mine from the age of five. But no, he ✳ has to go to school. |
| Fred     | Aye. |
| George   | Only teachers won't have him in their classes. So they send him out. |
| Fred     | Aye. |
| George   | And where does he end up? Where does Knackenhead go when he's sent out of classes because his teachers are all scared rigid of him? |
| Fred     | Down here. |
| George   | Right. Down here in this boiler-room. *My* boiler-room if you please. |
| Fred     | They always do, don't they? |
| George   | Like a magnet this place is to 'em. All the thugs and the louts and the ✳ yobbos. I could run a borstal down here with the visitors I get. |

30

| | |
|---|---|
| Fred | You could. |
| George | Dirty, filthy yobbos hanging about, smoking their fags and telling their dirty, crude stories to one another. |
| Fred | Well, it's somewhere warm, isn't it? In winter. When it's summer they ✳ come digging up my cricket square. |
| George | They come barging their way in. Let's have a warm, George. Got any dirty books for us, George? Getting it regular, are you, George? |
| Fred | Aye, and it's funny how . . . |
| George | Effing and blinding as though I weren't here! As though I were deaf! |
| Fred | Aye. |
| George | Maniacs. |
| Fred | And it's funny how you get one that stands out every year, isn't it? |
| George | Like Knackenhead. |
| Fred | This year yes. The pick of this year's crop, Knackenhead. |
| George | Spitting on my floor. Spitting like old feller chewing tobacco. |
| Fred | Aye. |
| George | Spit, spit, spit! It's a wonder they're not dehydrated, some of 'em. |
| Fred | There's always one though. Do you remember Slack? |
| George | Slack! Do I remember Slack! |
| Fred | Pick of last year's crop were Slack. |
| George | Slack with his aerosol cans. |
| Fred | He made a grand mess of my cricket pavilion. |
| George | He made a grand mess of anything he got twenty yards of did that ugly little runt. D'you see that up there? |
| Fred | What? |
| George | On that wall. Still there. I couldn't get it off. |
| Fred | Oh aye. |
| George | That were Slack. I once said to him, 'Do you spray your walls at home? Do you go round doing that at home?' |
| Fred | What did he say? |
| George | I'll not repeat what he said, Fred. I won't. Though the gist of it was that he would aerosol whatever took his fancy and that my questions were not welcome. That was the gist of it. |

(*Pause*)

| | |
|---|---|
| Fred | Well, I've a hockey pitch to mark out before dinner time. |
| George | Course you know who I blame. You know why we have to put up with these maniacs spitting and smoking and foulmouthing in my boiler-house? |
| Fred | Teachers. |
| George | Well, don't you think so? |
| Fred | Oh aye. |
| George | They can't cope, can they? I mean, can you see little twitchy Mrs Quincey handling Knackenhead? |
| Fred | Or Slack. |
| George | Or Slack. She wouldn't have a cat-in-hell's chance. Slack'd cover her in rude words from head to foot with his aerosol while Knackenhead 'd stand there chewing on her Yorkshire terrier. |

*A door opens and closes as Mr Fish enters.*

(*whispering*) Eh up. Here's the man at the top.

| | |
|---|---|
| Mr Fish | (*approaching*) Morning George. Fred. |

31

| | |
|---|---|
| George | Mr Fish. |
| Fred | Morning. |
| Mr Fish | Don't let me disturb you if you're having your break. Only when you've a minute, George, I wonder if you can do something about the chairs in the hall. I think I've mentioned it to you before . . . |
| George | I've been meaning to get round to it. |
| Mr Fish | Oh yes. Yes. I'm not suggesting . . . |
| George | It's on me list. Only do you know, Mr Fish, that I spent two hours last night clearing mud from the ceilings of the teaching block. |
| Mr Fish | Really, yes. |
| George | From the ceilings! I mean I know we've got some very clever individuals in this school but I didn't know any of 'em could walk on the ceilings. |
| Mr Fish | No. (*Intrigued*) What, er, what exactly is it that they're doing? |
| George | Flicking. |
| Mr Fish | Flicking? |
| George | Flicking mud balls. |
| Mr Fish | Ah, I see. |
| George | Which then stick and dry out. Two hours it took me going round with a step-ladder and a paint-scraper. |
| Mr Fish | Yes. Yes, I can see that it must be a problem. And I'm not sure just what the answer is. |
| George | Dirty little devils. |
| Fred | And that mud'll be taken from off my cricket square. |
| Mr Fish | Well, er, leave that one with me, George. I'll alert the staff to what's going on. |
| George | I would be grateful. |
| Mr Fish | Hmm. Anyway, these chairs. As I say, one or two are a bit worse for wear and I wondered if you could . . . have a go at them. |
| George | Whoever designed them chairs wants his head examining. |
| Mr Fish | Really? Are they not, er, all they might be? |
| George | There are two screws just underneath your . . . just underneath the seat. And if you take them out the whole thing falls to bits. |
| Mr Fish | Oh yes. Yes, I'm aware of that. |
| George | Well, all they need is a nail-file or a penknife and . . . |
| Mr Fish | Oh yes, yes. But I've spelled it out. In assembly to the whole school. I explained about the screws and what happens if they are removed. |
| George | Oh well, at least they'll know how to do it properly then, won't they? |

(*Pause*)

| | |
|---|---|
| Mr Fish | Hmm. Well, if you could get some screws from the craft block and have a go. Otherwise I fear that assembly will continue to be punctuated by the sound of falling bodies. And how are you, Fred? Everything all right, is it? |
| Fred | Not too bad, thank you. |
| Mr Fish | Did we get those rugby posts back, could you just remind me? I think we got to the bottom of that one, didn't we? |
| Fred | Yes, in a manner of speaking. |
| Mr Fish | Good, good. I wouldn't want you to feel that you didn't have our full support in these matters. |
| Fred | Chopped up. |
| Mr Fish | What? |
| Fred | Posts. They came back chopped up. I've got 'em piled up now behind the |

32

|          | pavilion. Longest piece isn't above two foot. |
| Mr Fish  | Ah. And there's no chance of sticking . . .? No, I suppose not. Well, we'll have to see if the PTA[6] can help us out. |
| George   | I know it's not my place to say it, Mr Fish, but the louts that we have here ✳ don't deserve the facilities they're given. |
| Mr Fish  | Oh . . . |
| George   | Maniacs most of 'em. Destroy anything they can get their hands on. I'm not saying the teaching staff's to blame, don't get me wrong . . . |
| Mr Fish  | Oh, I think you're being a bit hard on the children there, George. I think I'd have to quarrel with you on that one. |
| George   | With all due respect, Headmaster, you don't see 'em like we do. |
| Mr Fish  | Well, I do spend a lot of time walking around this school and I must say I get immense satisfaction from seeing all the good work that goes on. I can ✳ walk down a corridor and there's a French class here, a History class there, they're dissecting something in Biology, baking something over here, studying the Russian Revolution over there . . . |
| George   | And flicking mud balls at the ceiling. |

*Mr Fish manages an unconvincing laugh.*

| Mr Fish  | Oh, we do have . . . we do have our recalcitrants.[7] One or two wayward ✳ souls who haven't yet seen the light. |
| George   | Well, that's as may be, but some of the language and behaviour that we have to put up with . . . eh, Fred? |
| Fred     | Has to be seen to be believed. |
| George   | And perhaps you don't see it, Mr Fish. |
| Mr Fish  | Well, I, er, I do try and spread myself as far as possible. . . |
| George   | Real rogues' gallery we have sometimes in here. Isn't that right, Fred? |
| Fred     | Aye. |
| Mr Fish  | Well, I can't deny that some of our lost souls may fetch up on your shores. ✳ I suppose this is something of a sanctuary for some of them. |
| George   | You can say that again. |
| Mr Fish  | But you mustn't let that prejudice you against our worthy citizens, George. And they are in the majority. I can assure you of that. ✳ |
| George   | Well, I'll take your word for that. But it's the rotten apples – isn't it – it's the rotten apples that turn all the rest. Unless you get 'em out in time. |
| Mr Fish  | Except that we are not, after all, we are not dealing with apples, are we? Oh, I'll tell you something that might cheer you up a bit. Relevant to what we've been talking about. You know . . . Knackenhead? |
| George   | Oh yes. |
| Fred     | Unfortunately. |
| Mr Fish  | Yes, I think he might rate as one of your rotten apples, mightn't he? ✳ |
| George   | To the bloody core that one. |
| Mr Fish  | Well, I think with a bit of luck you might not be bothered with him for a while. |
| George   | Oh? |
| Mr Fish  | Seems he's run away from home. Mother rang this morning. She hasn't seen him since the day before yesterday. |
| George   | Well, that's the best news I've heard for a long while. |

6 *Parent Teacher Association*
7 *Pupils who refuse to obey instructions*

| Mr Fish | Yes, I think there'll be a few fingers crossed that he doesn't hurry back to the maternal bosom. Anyway, I'll leave you to it. (*Then coyly as he departs*) You won't forget the chairs, will you? |
|---|---|

*We hear the door close as he exits.*
*A moment's silence, then George laughs softly.* **F**

| George | Well, that's one rotten apple that won't spoil the barrel. |
|---|---|
| Fred | Aye. |
| George | You've cleaned that spade up, haven't you? |
| Fred | Yes, yes. Clean as a new pin. **G** |

*George laughs again.*

| George | You know I didn't tell you, did I? Mrs Quincey stopped me yesterday. **H** Said, 'Oh, thank you, George, I don't know what you did to the boiler but it's the first day I've been properly warm since we've been back this term.' And you know what she's usually like, all twitchy and starved to death. |
|---|---|
| Fred | Aye |
| George | First day I've been properly warm, she said. I nearly told her, 'Well, you've got Knackenhead to thank for that, love. He's providing the fuel!' |

*Fred laughs.*

| Fred | First useful thing he's done. **I** |
|---|---|
| George | And the last. |
| | (*Pause*) |
| Fred | Well, I'll get on with that hockey pitch. |
| George | And I'd better look at his damn silly chairs. Before he bursts into tears over 'em. |
| Fred | I'll tell you what though, George. |
| George | What's that, Fred? |
| Fred | There's never been one as good as Slack, eh? **J** |
| George | What, you mean for giving off heat like. |
| Fred | Well, it weren't that so much as throwing all his aerosol cans in after him. Hearing 'em explode inside boiler. |

*George laughs.*

| | Little squirt. |
|---|---|
| George | And what was that one before him? Pilkington? |
| Fred | Summat like that. You forget their names after a time. They're that much alike. |
| George | Aye. All wanting to be t'boiler. Wanting a warm. **K** |

*They both laugh.*

---

> **Plot** – a traditional plot for a story or play consists of a sequence of events in a logical order. Generally the events should arouse interest and lead to a conclusion which the reader or audience finds satisfying.
> **Character** – characters are one major aspect of the plot. Events are bound to affect the characters but, equally, characters may also affect events.

# Assignments

☞ **1**  **a** In a few sentences summarise clearly the 'plot' of the play.
     **b** Do you find this ending believable? Give reasons.
     **c** Do you find this ending satisfying? Give reasons.

Now read the alternative ending which follows on from the last stage direction: *'They both laugh'*.

*The door opens.*

| | |
|---|---|
| Mr Fish | (*from the door*) Er, sorry . . . |
| George | Eh up. |
| Mr Fish | Sorry to pop back like this, chaps, but I thought I should warn you. Knackenhead has returned to us. |
| George | (*quietly*) Oh God! |
| Mr Fish | Yes, I'm afraid so. |
| Fred | Couldn't we have a whip-round? Send him off somewhere again? |
| Mr Fish | Walked up to me as bold as brass. All right boss, he said, I just couldn't keep away from your nice little prison. |

*He gives an uncertain laugh.*

| | |
|---|---|
| | Quite a sense of humour, really. |
| Fred | For a gorilla. |
| George | I thought he'd left home? |
| Mr Fish | Perhaps he got homesick . . . |

*George and Fred give way to gloomy laughter.*

(*not pleased*) Well, I'll . . . I'll leave you to get on with your work.

*He exits. Their laughter dies.*

| | |
|---|---|
| George | Knackenhead! |
| Fred | Returned. |

(*Pause*)

| | |
|---|---|
| George | If only we could, eh? |
| Fred | Aye. |
| George | Fight back. Take up arms against Knackenhead and his tribe! |
| Fred | We'd lose our pensions. |
| George | Oh, it wouldn't be understood. Wouldn't be well-received in the local press. |
| Fred | They can't stop us dreaming though. |
| George | No. |
| Fred | No. |
| George | Sweet dreams, eh? Sweet bloody dreams! |

☞ **2**  The BBC used the second ending when this play was broadcast on radio. Why do you think they chose it?

☞ **3**  The letters **A–K** alongside the text trace the thread of horror running through the play.
**a** Explain clearly how this thread is developed.
**b** Why do you think there is such a long gap after **E**, before the thread is taken up again at **F**?

☞ **4**  **a** Most of our insight into the three characters is gained from hearing their opinions. The chart below lists some of the things they give opinions on. Find a short quotation from the play to go in each box. (The passages marked * should help you here).

*One entry has been done as an example.*

| George's opinions | Fred's opinions | Mr Fish's opinions | About |
|---|---|---|---|
| | | | pupils in general |
| | | | louts at the school |
| | 'I don't know what lesson they were supposed to be doing.' | | modern teaching |
| | | | the boiler-room |
| | | | Knackenhead |

**b** Sum up briefly what you learn about each of the three characters from these opinions and from any other relevant parts of the play.
**c** How seriously do you think the playwright means us to take these characters?

☞ **5**  Looking back at your conclusions in **3** and **4**, think again about the sort of ending that the play should have.
**a** What do we have to believe in order to accept the first ending?
**b** What do we have to believe in order to accept the second ending?
**c** How important is it that the ending should be believable?
**d** Bearing in mind your answers to **a–c**, do you prefer the first or the second ending? Give your reasons.

✔ ✐ **6**  Write a *third* ending for the play which is completely different from the other two.

✔ ✐ **7**  The chart opposite shows a plan for a short play or story which could be developed in several different ways. Begin at START and follow the arrows in any direction you choose until you come to a box marked END. This will give you one possible plot for the story. Now follow the arrows in a different direction and you have a second plot.

Write two versions of a play or story using the two plots you have selected. (Remember: character, suspense, dialogue etc are also important 'ingredients' of a successful play or story.) Now make up your own story chart and write two or more versions of your story or play.

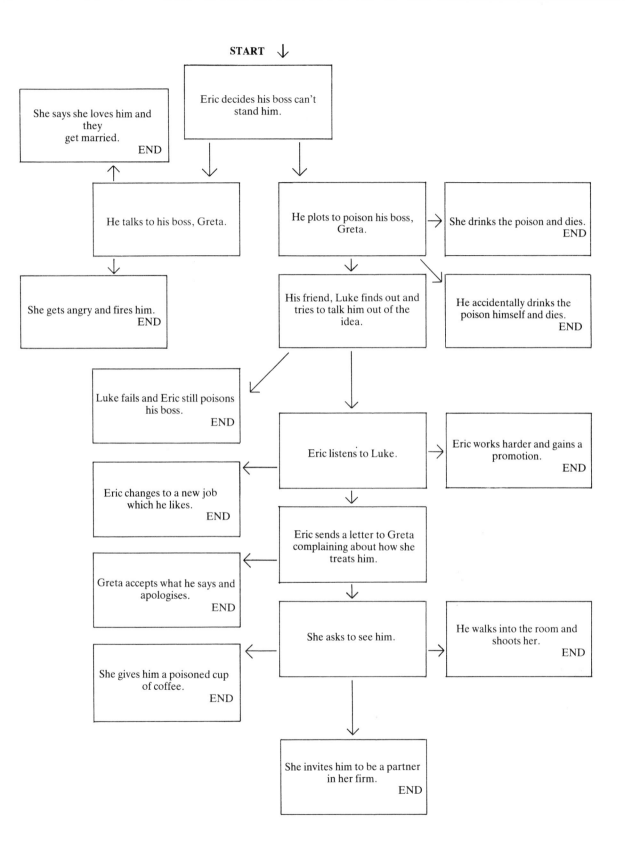

START ↓

Eric decides his boss can't stand him.

She says she loves him and they get married.
END

He talks to his boss, Greta.

He plots to poison his boss, Greta.

She drinks the poison and dies.
END

She gets angry and fires him.
END

His friend, Luke finds out and tries to talk him out of the idea.

He accidentally drinks the poison himself and dies.
END

Luke fails and Eric still poisons his boss.
END

Eric listens to Luke.

Eric works harder and gains a promotion.
END

Eric changes to a new job which he likes.
END

Eric sends a letter to Greta complaining about how she treats him.

Greta accepts what he says and apologises.
END

She asks to see him.

He walks into the room and shoots her.
END

She gives him a poisoned cup of coffee.
END

She invites him to be a partner in her firm.
END

# U·N·I·T 11 *Using comparisons*

When a writer uses a comparison it often gives the reader a mental picture which helps to make the meaning clearer or more interesting.

**Trout**
Hangs, a fat gun-barrel,
deep under arched bridges
or slips like butter down
the throat of the river.

From depths smooth-skinned as plums
his muzzle gets bull's eye;
picks off grass-seed and moths
that vanish, torpedoed.

Where water unravels
over gravel-beds he
is fired from the shallows
white belly reporting

flat; darts like a tracer-
bullet back between stones
and is never burnt out.
A volley of cold blood

ramrodding the current.
                              *Seamus Heaney*

> **Similes, metaphors, personification**
>
> A **simile** is a comparison in which something is said to be *like* something else eg His wit is *as sharp as a razor* or His wit is sharp, *like a razor*.
>
> A **metaphor** is also a comparison, but in a metaphor the comparison is only implied, not directly stated eg *His sharp wit cut through our conversation* or *He's so sharp he'll cut himself*!
>
> **Personification** is a particular kind of metaphor in which an object or animal is described as though it were human eg *The sun smiled down on them*.

# Assignments

☞ **1**  **a**  Identify all the comparisons used in this poem. For each one say whether it is a simile or a metaphor.

**b**  When a comparison is made, it should be possible to say which two things are being compared and to suggest a reason for the comparison (ie what the two things have in common). Using your answers to **a**, copy and complete this chart. (An example of the sort of thing you could write has been done for you.)

|  | What two things are compared | Reason | Comment |
|---|---|---|---|
| 1) | Trout and fat gun-barrel. | Both deadly and precise. Shape? | I like this. It's an unusual way to think of a fish. Usually fish seem slower and gentler. |
| 2) |  |  |  |

**c**  Paying particular attention to the comparisons, write about the poem *Trout* and your reactions to it.

**2**  Represent this poem visually – as a picture, a series of pictures, a collage, or in any other way you like.

Here is another poem which uses comparisons in a different way.

## Our Love Now

I said,
    observe how the wound heals in time,
    how the skin slowly knits
    and once more becomes whole.
    The cut will mend, and such
    is our relationship.

She said,
    Although the wound heals
    and appears cured, it is not the same.
    There is always a scar,
    a permanent reminder.
    Such is our love now.

I said,
    observe the scab of the scald,
    the red burnt flesh is ugly,
    but it can be hidden.
    In time it will disappear,
    Such is our love, such is our love.

She said,
    Although the burn will no longer sting
    and we'll almost forget that it's there
    the skin remains bleached
    and a numbness prevails.
    Such is our love now.

I said,
    remember how when you cut your hair,
    you feel different, and somehow incomplete.
    But the hair grows – before long
    it is always the same.
    Our beauty together is such.

She said,
    After you've cut your hair,
    it grows again slowly. During that time
    changes must occur,
    the style will be different.
    Such is our love now.

I said,
    listen to how the raging storm
    damages the trees outside.
    The storm is frightening
    but it will soon be gone.
    People will forget it ever existed.
    The breach in us can be mended.

She said,
    Although the storm is temporary
    and soon passes,
    it leaves damage in its wake
    which can never be repaired.
    The tree is forever dead.
    Such is our love.

*Martyn Lowery*

○ ☞ **3** Look at the comparisons in *Our Love Now*.

**a** In what way is this rift in a relationship like a wound? a scald or burn? hair being cut? a storm?
**b** Give each of these four comparisons marks out of 10 according to how well you think it works in the poem.
**c** Each of the four comparisons can work in two different ways. Is this a strength or a weakness?

✔ ○ **4** **a** In a pair or small group, practise reading this poem aloud. Experiment with reading it in different ways. Is it best read across or down?
**b** Tape record your reading or perform it to an audience.

✔ ◇ **5** Write two conversations based on this poem, in which:
**a** the boy talks to a friend about the girl
**b** the girl talks to a friend about the boy

◇ **6** Write a poem of your own using the same framework. Choose any subject you like; think of four things it can be compared with (even if they seem quite unlikely comparisons), and use each comparison in two different ways. If you can, set your poem out like the verses in *Our Love Now*.

# U·N·I·T 12 *Poem or prose*

This poem, written by a fifth former, explores the feelings of a young mother.

**Starting school**
Don't go into the nursery today.
You can cut the atmosphere with a knife.
Teddy's got the sulks and
With Jonathan jack-in-the-box
Exchanges emotions little dreamt of
Five years ago.
Like two old men remembering the good times.
Has it come to this?
Play clothes strewn on the floor are
Shrinking ghosts of former pleasures
When bricks and dollies were treated
With deserved respect.
Now who's this high and mighty personage,
This jumped-up besmartened businesswoman
Who packs her satchel, sings school songs
And does her sums with all the willingness
Of the clock to tick?
Teddy's eternal summer shall not fade
Nor Jonathan's either,
But one child's spring
Already turns to summer.

## Assignments

☞ ○ **1** In the chart opposite, the poet has broken the poem into sections and placed alongside each section a literal explanation of its content. Compare the two versions. In each case decide what qualities the poem has which the prose explanation doesn't. For instance, you may think that the poem:

**a** sounds more effective
**b** creates a clearer mental picture
**c** evokes more emotion
**d** is more confusing
**e** is more concise
**f** is more startling

**g** creates a better mood
**h** gives us more to think about
**i** is more boring
**j** is less clearly expressed
**k** is more lively and interesting

Add other reasons of your own.

| Poem | Prose |
|------|-------|
| Don't go into the nursery today<br>You can cut the atmosphere with a knife | There is a tense atmosphere in the nursery today. |
| Teddy's got the sulks and<br>With Jonathan jack-in-the box<br>Exchanges emotions little dreamt of<br>Five years ago | The teddy bear has an emotional quality – silent and resentful. Five years ago the emotions suggested by it and the jack-in-the box were very different from those they suggest now. |
| Like two old men remembering the good times.<br><br>Has it come to this? | They remind me of two old men talking about the past.<br><br>Have things really changed so much? |
| Playclothes strewn on the floor are<br>Shrinking ghosts of former pleasures. | On the floor are the clothes she wore for play before starting school. They are reminders of all the fun she has had, but soon they will be too small. |
| When bricks and dollies were treated<br>With deserved respect. | That was in the days when she was interested in her bricks and dolls. |
| Now who's this high and mighty personage. | It's hard to recognise her now. She seems to have such a high opinion of herself. |
| This jumped-up besmartened business-woman | She's suddenly an important person. She looks so grown-up, smart and efficient now. |
| Who packs her satchel, sings school songs<br>And does her sums with all the willingness<br>Of the clock to tick? | She packs her satchel, sings school songs and does her sums with no effort – you would think she has done this willingly since the beginning of time. |
| Teddy's eternal summer shall not fade<br>Nor Jonathan's either. | The teddy bear and jack-in-the-box will never grow old. |
| But one child's spring<br>Already turns to summer. | But this child is already starting to grow up. |

☞ **2**  **a** Would you want to alter the prose explanation at all? Are there any places where you feel it does not adequately convey all that the poem conveys? (Think about: *metaphors, similes* and *personification* – see page 39 in particular.)
**b** What does this assignment suggest to you about the nature of poetry?
**c** Do you prefer the poem or the prose version? Give your reasons.

**3**  Write a third column for the chart, headed *Mother's thoughts*, and enter what you think the writer might be feeling at each stage. For example, your first entry might read:

> I don't want to go into the nursery today.
> I find the atmosphere in there oppressive.

**4**  **a** Write a poem of your own about childhood or growing older. Include as many comparisons as you can.
**b** Now write a prose explanation of what the poem is saying. How do the two versions differ?

# U·N·I·T 13 *On the telly and in the paper*

Passages **A** and **B** describe a football match between United and City. For both teams it is only their second match of the new season. **A** is a report given on a television sports programme only 15 minutes after the match. It is written here exactly as it was spoken by the commentator. **B** appeared in a newspaper on the following day. (The names of teams and players have been altered.)

(If these questions are being answered under timed conditions allow one hour.)

**A** ❛ Well, one of the hallmarks of a great side is patience. It's a quality bred from confidence, knowing that class will eventually tell. Well, United have been patient and now with their two new signings they seem to have ended the drought and could well be on the road to success at last.

It was Stone, the plucky little Scot who scored the first goal in the ninth minute after a brilliant pass from Mayhew. What a way to waken up City! And what a start to a tingling game! Well, United went on to dominate the game despite some brave efforts from City. But for all City's competitiveness and astute chances, they were woefully short of confidence in front of the goal. Several times they sprayed the ball around and seemed on the verge of scoring, notably in the 30th minute when a Duncan header hit the bar. But it was triumphant United who scored the second goal in the 37th minute. This time it was young Fair who headed to perfection after Archer took a free kick.

United increased the pace after half time but, although the City defence was stretched and tested to the very limit, they failed to score a third goal. United can take heart, too, that Patel still looks a quality player.

And what about City? Well, we'll see what happens when they field their two new signings, but on this showing, you know, manager Gordon Loot can't be a happy man. Especially since, almost inevitably, Tommy Clogger was booked. **,**

**B**

## United 2   City 0

Strenuous pre-season preparation and legs tanned from friendlies in Spain paid off handsomely for born-again United at Goodluck Park where David Fair netted two goals in a match in which City were always panting behind.

The two sides had splashed out two million pounds between them during the summer in the hope of offering better competition to the northern teams and bringing back some of their lost supporters. But, whereas United fielded both Paul Baines and Steven Stone fit and well and raring to go, City had to keep two of their new jewels, Lockhart and O'Ryan locked up in the back safe, and rely on a defence which conceded 74 goals last season.

Baines made the most significant entrance, dominating the United penalty area to such an extent that Perkins in goal could just as well have brought his knitting. Baines is what you might call your actual old-fashioned centre-half.

After this, manager Alan Drake praised Baines' maturity and what he called qualities of leadership. This kind of disciplined performance is obviously just what the new manager is looking for in the construction of the new United.

Undoubtedly Steven Stone will help them too, although with City not putting a winger against him, the questions asked were in the infants' class.

In the first thirty minutes when United tormented City from all angles, Patel fully answered speculation that his place in the United side would hinge not only on fitness. City had no answer to his positioning and passing, and it was more than coincidence that United never matched their early brilliance after he was injured in a first half tackle by Clogger which eventually brought Patel's departure. Odd, then, that the only man booked was Naylor.

Alkirk playing in midfield made the first goal as he beat Nash in the 11th minute, splitting the City defence with a crossfield pass to Mayhew before Fair slotted in. The second came when Archer headed a free kick down to Fair in the 37th minute.

City kept running as usual and would have had a better chance had a header from Duncan gone in instead of hitting a post before United scored their second. Haylo shot against the crossbar before the match was quite out of reach.

Those yearning to stimulate their soccer appetites with a morsel of something exquisite could do worse than travel to Old Trafford next week-end to see Drake's young heroes take on the mighty Manchester United.

# Assignments

1. How does each account rate the general performance of

   **a** United
   **b** City? (*10 marks*)

2. In your own words, explain what passage **B** tells us about:

   **a** Baines
   **b** Patel. (*6 marks*)

3. What other information does each of the reports give us, apart from the account of the match? (*8 marks*)

4. What factual differences do you notice between the two reports? (*8 marks*)

5. Which report would you expect to be more accurate? Give reasons for your choice. (*4 marks*)

6. Both match reports have been prepared for an audience that already knows certain facts. Find two examples which show that this is the case. (Your examples may be from **A** or **B**.) (*6 marks*)

7. What evidence is there that report **A** is in spoken rather than written English? (*8 marks*)

8. Write down two descriptive comparisons used by the writer of report **B**. For each, explain what is being compared to what and suggest why the comparison has been made. (*6 marks*)

9. Why, do you think, does passage **B** contain more of these descriptive details than passage **A**? (*4 marks*)

10. Which of the two reports do you think gives a better sense of the atmosphere at the game? Quote from the reports to support your view. (*6 marks*)

11. Reports **A** and **B** were composed for similar, but slightly different, purposes. Explain carefully what you think these different purposes are. (*8 marks*)

12. Which of the two accounts do you prefer and why? (*6 marks*)

# U·N·I·T 14 *What do you expect?*

This is the first part of a story set in the USA in the nineteenth century. It is being told by a man looking back on his childhood.

**LOST SISTER**
**by Dorothy**
**M Johnson**

Our household was full of women, who overwhelmed my Uncle Charlie and sometimes confused me with their bustle and chatter. We were the only men on the place. I was nine years old when still another woman came – Aunt Bessie, who had been living with the Indians.

When my mother told me about her, I couldn't believe it. The savages had killed my father, a cavalry lieutenant, two years before. I hated Indians and looked forward to wiping them out when I got older. (But when I was grown, they were no menace any more.)

'What did she live with the hostiles for?' I demanded.

'They captured her when she was a little girl,' Ma said. 'She was three years younger than you are. Now she's coming home.'

High time she came home, I thought. I said so, promising, 'If they was ever to get me, I wouldn't stay with 'em long.'

Ma put her arms around me. 'Don't talk like that. They won't get you. They'll never get you.'

None of the three sisters, my aunts, had ever seen Aunt Bessie. She had been taken by the Indians before they were born. Aunt Mary had known her – Aunt Mary was two years older – but she lived a thousand miles away now and was not well.

Even after Army officers had come to our house several times and there had been many letters about Aunt Bessie's delivery from the savages, it was a long time before she came. Major Harris, who made the final arrangements, warned my aunts that they would have problems, that Aunt Bessie might not be able to settle down easily into family life.

This was only a challenge to Aunt Margaret, who welcomed challenges. 'She's our own flesh and blood,' Aunt Margaret trumpeted. 'Of course she must come to us. My poor, dear sister Bessie, torn from her home forty years ago!'

The major was earnest but not tactful. 'She's been with the savages all those years,' he insisted. 'And she was only a little girl when she was taken. I haven't seen her myself, but it's reasonable to assume that she'll be like an Indian woman.'

My stately Aunt Margaret arose to show that the audience was ended. 'Major Harris,' she intoned, 'I cannot permit anyone to criticize my own dear sister. She will live in my home, and if I do not receive official word that she is coming within a month, I shall take steps.'

Aunt Bessie came before the month was up.

The aunts in residence made valiant preparation. They bustled and

48

swept and mopped and polished. They moved me from my own room to my mother's – as she had been begging them to do because I was troubled with nightmares. They prepared my old room for Aunt Bessie with many small comforts – fresh doilies everywhere, hairpins, a matching pitcher and bowl, the best towels and two new nightgowns in case hers might be old. (The fact was that she didn't have any.)

Margaret warned her anxious sisters, 'Now, girls, we mustn't ask her too many questions at first. She must rest for a while. She's been through a terrible experience.' Margaret's voice dropped way down with those last two words, as if only she could be expected to understand.

Indeed Bessie had been through a terrible experience, but it wasn't what the sisters thought. The experience from which she was suffering, when she arrived, was that she had been wrenched from her people, the Indians, and turned over to strangers. She had not been freed. She had been made a captive.

Aunt Bessie came with Major Harris and an interpreter, a half-blood with greasy black hair hanging down to his shoulders. His costume was half Army and half primitive. Aunt Margaret swung the door open wide when she saw them coming. She ran out with her sisters following, while my mother and I watched from a window. Margaret's arms were outstretched, but when she saw the woman closer, her arms dropped and her glad cry died.

She did not cringe, my Aunt Bessie who had been an Indian for forty years, but she stopped walking and stood staring helpless among her captors.

The sisters had described her often as a little girl. Not that they had ever seen her, but she was a legend, the captive child. Beautiful blonde curls, they said she had, and big blue eyes – she was a fairy child, a pale-haired little angel who ran on dancing feet.

The Bessie who came back was an aging woman who plodded in moccasins, whose dark dress did not belong on her bulging body. Her brown hair hung just below her ears. It was growing out; when she was first taken from the Indians, her hair had been cut short to clean out the vermin.

Aunt Margaret recovered herself and instead of embracing this silent stolid woman, satisfied herself by patting an arm and crying, 'Poor dear Bessie, I am your sister Margaret. And here are our sisters Hannah and Sabina. We do hope you're not all tired out from your journey!'

Aunt Margaret was all graciousness, because she had been assured beyond doubt that this was truly a member of the family. She must have believed – Aunt Margaret could believe anything – that all Bessie needed was to have a nice nap and wash her face. Then she would be as talkative as any of them.

The other aunts were quick-moving and sharp of tongue. But this one moved as if her sorrows were a burden on her bowed shoulders, and when she spoke briefly in answer to the interpreter, you could not understand a word of it.

Aunt Margaret ignored these peculiarities. She took the party into the front parlor – even the interpreter, when she understood there was no avoiding it. She might have gone on battling with the major about him,

but she was in a hurry to talk to her lost sister.

'You won't be able to converse with her unless the interpreter is present,' Major Harris said. 'Not,' he explained hastily, 'because of any regulation, but because she has forgotten English.'

Aunt Margaret gave the half-blood interpreter a look of frowning doubt and let him enter. She coaxed Bessie. 'Come, dear, sit down.'

The interpreter mumbled, and my Indian aunt sat cautiously on a needlepoint chair. For most of her life she had been living with people who sat comfortably on the ground.

The visit in the parlor was brief. Bessie had her instructions before she came. But Major Harris had a few warnings for the family. 'Technically, your sister is still a prisoner,' he explained, ignoring Margaret's start of horror. 'She will be in your custody. She may walk in your fenced yard, but she must not leave it without official permission.

'Mrs. Raleigh, this may be a heavy burden for you all. But she has been told all this and has expressed willingness to conform to these restrictions. I don't think you will have any trouble keeping her here.' Major Harris hesitated, remembered that he was a soldier and a brave man, added, 'If I did, I wouldn't have brought her.'

There was the making of a sharp little battle, but Aunt Margaret chose to overlook the challenge. She could not overlook the fact that Bessie was not what she had expected.

Bessie certainly knew that this was her lost white family, but she didn't seem to care. She was infinitely sad, infinitely removed. She asked one question: 'Ma-ry?' and Aunt Margaret almost wept with joy.

'Sister Mary lives a long way from here,' she explained, 'and she isn't well, but she will come as soon as she's able. Dear Sister Mary!'

The interpreter translated this, and Bessie had no more to say. That was the only understandable word she ever did say in our house, the remembered name of her older sister.

When the aunts, all chattering, took Bessie to her room, one of them asked, 'But where are her things?'

Bessie had no things, no baggage. She had nothing at all but the clothes she stood in. While the sisters scurried to bring a comb and other oddments, she stood like a stooped monument, silent and watchful. This was her prison. Very well, she would endure it.

My Indian aunt accustomed herself, finally, to sitting on the chair in her room. She seldom came out, which was a relief to her sisters. She preferred to stand, hour after hour, looking out the window – which was open only about a foot, in spite of all Uncle Charlie's efforts to budge it higher. And she always wore moccasins. She never was able to wear shoes from the store, but seemed to treasure the shoes brought to her.

After I found that she was usually at the window, looking across the flat land to the blue mountains, I played in the yard so I could stare at her. She never smiled, as an aunt should, but she looked at me sometimes, thoughtfully, as if measuring my worth. By performing athletic feats, such as walking on my hands, I could get her attention. For some reason, I valued it.

The sisters and my mother took turns, as was their Christian duty, in visiting her for half an hour each day. Bessie didn't eat at the table with us – not after the first meal.

The first time my mother took her turn, it was under protest. 'I'm afraid I'd start crying in front of her,' she argued, but Aunt Margaret insisted.

I was lurking in the hall when Ma went in. Bessie said something, then said it again, peremptorily, until my mother guessed what she wanted. She called me and put her arm around me as I stood beside her chair. Aunt Bessie nodded, and that was all there was to it.

Afterward, my mother said, 'She likes you. And so do I.' She kissed me.

'I don't like her,' I complained. 'She's queer.'

'She's a sad old lady,' my mother explained. 'She had a little boy once, you know.'

'What happened to him?'

'He grew up and became a warrior. I suppose she was proud of him. Now the army has him in prison somewhere. He's half Indian. He was a dangerous man.'

He was indeed a dangerous man, and a proud man, a chief, a bird of prey whose wings the Army had clipped after bitter years of trying.

However, my mother and my Indian aunt had that one thing in common: they both had sons. The other aunts were childless.

There was a great to-do about having Aunt Bessie's photograph taken. The aunts who were stubbornly and valiantly trying to make her one of the family wanted a picture of her for the family album. The government wanted one too, for some reason – perhaps because someone realized that a thing of historic importance had been accomplished by recovering the captive child.

Major Harris sent a young lieutenant with the greasy-haired interpreter to discuss the matter in the parlor. (Margaret, with great foresight, put a clean towel on a chair and saw to it the interpreter sat there.) Bessie spoke very little during that meeting, and of course we understood only what the half-blood *said* she was saying.

No, she did not want her picture made. No.

But your son had his picture made. Do you want to see it? They teased her with that offer, and she nodded.

If we let you see his picture, then will you have yours made?

She nodded doubtfully. Then she demanded more than had been offered: if you let me keep his picture, then you can make mine.

No, you can only look at it. We have to keep his picture. It belongs to us.

My Indian aunt gambled for high stakes. She shrugged and spoke, and the interpreter said, 'She not want to look. She will keep or nothing.'

My mother shivered, understanding as the aunts could not understand what Bessie was gambling – all or nothing.

Bessie won. Perhaps they had intended that she should. She was allowed to keep the photograph that had been made of her son. It has been in history books many times – the half-white chief, the valiant leader who was not quite great enough to keep his Indian people free.

His photograph was taken after he was captured, but you would never guess it. His head is high, his eyes stare with boldness but not with scorn, his long hair is arranged with care – dark hair braided on one side and with a tendency to curl where the other side hangs loose – and his hands hold the pipe like a royal scepter.

Bessie kept his picture on her dresser when she was not holding it in her hands. And she went like a docile, silent child to the photograph studio, in a carriage with Aunt Margaret early one morning, when there would be few people on the street to stare.

Bessie's photograph is not proud but pitiful. She looks out with no expression. There is no emotion there, no challenge, only the face of an aging woman with short hair, only endurance and patience. The aunts put a copy in the family album.

But they were nearing the end of their tether. The Indian aunt was a solid ghost in the house. She did nothing because there was nothing for her to do. Her gnarled hands must have been skilled at squaws' work, at butchering meat and scraping and tanning hides, at making tepees and beading ceremonial clothes. But her skills were useless and unwanted in a civilized home. She did not even sew when my mother gave her cloth and needles and thread. She kept the sewing things beside her son's picture.

She ate (in her room) and slept (on the floor) and stood looking out the window. That was all, and it could not go on. But it had to go on, at least until my sick Aunt Mary was well enough to travel – Aunt Mary who was her older sister, the only one who had known her when they were children.

After several weeks Aunty Mary came, white and trembling and exhausted from her illness and the long, hard journey.

Margaret went to the Indian woman's door and explained volubly who had come, a useless but brave attempt. Then she stood aside, and Aunt Mary was there, her lined white face aglow, her arms outstretched. 'Bessie! Sister Bessie!' she cried.

And after one brief moment's hesitation, Bessie went into her arms and Mary kissed her sun-dark, weathered cheek. Bessie spoke. 'Mar-y,' she said. 'Ma-ry.' She stood with tears running down her face and her mouth working. So much to tell, so much suffering and fear – and joy and triumph, too – and the sister there at last who might legitimately hear it all and understand.

But the only English word that Bessie remembered was 'Mary', and she had not cared to learn any others. She turned to the dresser, took her son's picture in her work-hardened hands, reverently, and held it so her sister could see. Her eyes pleaded.

Mary looked on the calm, noble, savage face of her half-blood nephew and said the right thing: 'My, isn't he handsome!' She put her head on one side and then the other. 'A fine boy, sister,' she approved. 'You must' – she stopped, but she finished – 'be awfully proud of him, dear!'

Bessie understood the tone if not the words. The tone was admiration. Her son was accepted by the sister who mattered. Bessie looked at the picture and nodded, murmuring. Then she put it back on the dresser.

Aunt Mary did not try to make Bessie talk. She sat with her every day for hours, and Bessie did talk – but not in English. They sat holding hands for mutual comfort while the captive child, grown old and a grandmother, told what had happened in forty years. Aunt Mary said that was what Bessie was talking about. But she didn't understand a word of it and didn't need to.

'There is time enough for her to learn English again,' Aunt Mary said, 'I think she understands more than she lets on. I asked her if she'd like to come and live with me, and she nodded. We'll have the rest of our lives for her to learn English. But what she has been telling me – she can't wait to tell that. About her life, and her son.'

'Are you sure, Mary dear, that you should take the responsibility of having her?' Margaret asked dutifully, no doubt shaking in her shoes for fear Mary would change her mind now that deliverance was in sight. 'I do believe she'd be happier with you, though we've done all we could.'

Margaret and the other sisters would certainly be happier with Bessie somewhere else. And so, it developed, would the United States government.

Major Harris came with the interpreter to discuss details, and they told Bessie she could go, if she wished, to live with Mary a thousand miles away. Bessie was patient and willing, stolidly agreeable. She talked a great deal more to the interpreter than she had ever done before. He answered at length and then explained to the others that she had wanted to know how she and Mary would travel to this far country. It was hard, he said, for her to understand just how far they were going.

Later we knew that the interpreter and Bessie had talked about much more than that.

Next morning, when Sabina took breakfast to Bessie's room, we heard a cry of dismay. Sabina stood holding the tray, repeating 'She's gone out the window! She's gone out the window!'

And so she had. The window that had always stuck so that it would not raise more than a foot was open wider now. And the photograph of Bessie's son was gone from the dresser. Nothing else was missing except Bessie and the decent dark dress she had worn the day before.

# Assignments

☞ **1** Imagine the comments below are made by people who have read this first half of the story. Gather as many details as you can from the story in order to prove these opinions right, wrong, or somewhere between the two.

Margaret is an interfering old woman. All she cares about is running other people's lives.

Bessie is so different from what they expected. She takes them all by surprise.

Bessie never complains about her new home so she can't mind it that much.

It's obvious there's something fishy about that interpreter!

There's a kind of under-standing between Bessie and the boy's mother.

The aunts are good women really. They're just a bit stupid.

You can't tell where Bessie's gone. There's no clue. She's probably just run away.

By the time Mary arrives, they're all fed up with Bessie.

Bessie's cold. She doesn't care about anything.

Mary's visit comes as a great relief to the other aunts.

The main attraction of the interpreter's visits for Bessie is just speaking her own language again.

✔ 📖 **2** From what you have read so far:

**a** Where do you think Bessie has gone?
**b** What could her reasons be?
**c** How do you think the story will end?
**d** Using all the evidence from what you have read, write your own ending to the story.

Now turn to page 237 for the rest of the story.

# U·N·I·T 15 *Life or death*

Sometimes the way information is written can be a matter of life or death. For example, instructions on safety must be concise and easy to understand. This passage deals with safety in the garden.

**Clothes**

Usually the clothes one wears for gardening are dictated by the prevailing weather conditions, but there are a few important guidelines to bear in mind. When using an electrical appliance in the garden, particularly a lawn-mower, it is important to wear strong flat-heeled shoes. The same applies to those using sharp implements such as spades and forks. A person mowing the lawn should never work barefoot or in open sandals. If the ground is wet the safest footwear is rubber boots which offer the best protection if an electrical fault should occur. It is also important to avoid belts or flapping clothing which could get trapped in appliances or trip someone up.

**Children and pets**

Children and pets need to be kept firmly under control when electrical equipment or sharp tools are being used outside. Young children should never be allowed to operate equipment or to distract the attention of an adult who is using it.

When chemicals such as weed-killers are used in gardens, care should be taken that bottles and packets are read and that manufacturer's instructions are followed to the letter. Many garden chemicals are highly poisonous to pets, and owners must take precautions accordingly. Similarly, children should be warned never to eat berries or plants found growing in the garden.

When the lay-out of a garden is planned, hidden or awkward steps and sudden changes of height should be avoided. These could be a danger to children and to elderly or disabled people; gentle slopes are preferable.

If the garden is adjacent to a road, children and pets need to be protected by secure fences and gates. Greenhouses and cold frames should be checked regularly to ensure that no fragments of broken glass are left lying around. It is imperative, too, that all garden tools should be safely locked away when not in use.

**Electrical equip-
ment – general
guidelines**

New electrical equipment should only be purchased if it carries a label stating that it complies with British safety standards. Plugs should be fitted securely and correctly fused and wired. (Most appliances now have a blue wire for neutral, green/yellow for earth and brown for live, but note that most gardening equipment has no earth wire.) It is important to ensure that all equipment has no worn or loose parts and that the flex is not damaged in any way. Ideally, all electrical equipment should be serviced by a qualified electrician at least every three years. When appliances are used, it is important for the flex to be positioned correctly so as to avoid the risk of cutting through it. Appliances should have brightly coloured flex which shows up clearly against most backgrounds. If the flex does become caught in the appliance, it must not be touched until the current has been turned off and the plug removed from the mains socket. No-one should ever examine, clean or adjust equipment before removing the plug, even if it does not appear to be working. All garden appliances should be cleaned with a dry cloth – never washed with water. Electrical garden equipment must not, of course, be used when it is raining.

Additional protection against electric shock can be gained by fitting a residual current circuit breaker to the socket where garden appliances are usually plugged in. This device quickly cuts off power to the equipment if the machinery develops a fault or if the flex is accidentally cut.

**Lawn-mowers and hedge trimmers**

Before using a lawn-mower, it is important to ensure that there are no stones or other small loose articles on the lawn. These could damage the equipment or fly out and injure someone. When the lawn is being mown the flex should be kept behind the person using the mower. It could be trailed over a shoulder or a short loop of flex can be held in one hand. The lawn should always be cut away from and not towards the flex. There is also a danger that hover type mowers can drift back over a foot or over the flex.

Anyone using a hedge trimmer should make sure that there is enough flex to allow mobility and that the trimmer is kept well clear of the flex. A hedge trimmer should always be operated with both hands on its handles.

**Extension leads**

Extension leads which are used outside should have rubber connectors to keep out the damp. It is important not to fit a plug to both ends of an extension lead as live prongs are extremely dangerous. When an extension lead with a connector is used, the pronged half should be fitted to the equipment, and the socket end connected to the mains. The connectors should be fitted together before the appliance is plugged in to the mains. To avoid overheating, extension leads should be fully unwound and of a current rating appropriate for the tool used. (Follow the manufacturer's guidelines on this.) Under no circumstances should extension leads be used outside permanently – for instance, to heat or light a greenhouse.

# Assignments

☐ ☞ **1** Draw a diagram, or a number of diagrams, to illustrate as many as possible of the safety guidelines mentioned in the text. Label the diagram(s) to show clearly where the dangers lie. (The picture on page 57 may give you some ideas.)

☐ ☞ **2** **a** Rewrite these guidelines as a set of brief, clear instructions.
**b** Look at your instructions critically, to see whether you can make them any shorter or easier to understand. Remember that the language you use must be clearly understood by a child or by an old person.
**c** Reorganise your instructions into two lists, headed 'Do' and 'Don't'.

✔ ☐ **3** Write a story, poem or cartoon strip to teach children about a particular aspect of garden safety. (You could choose more than one of these options, to illustrate different dangers – which do you think is the most effective way of communicating the information?)

✔ ☐ **4** Your local council wishes to distribute a leaflet on *Safety in the Garden* to every home in your area next summer. Using the information on these pages, and any other suitable material you can find, prepare a four-page leaflet for this purpose. You may include written text, illustrations, diagrams, lists . . . in any way you think appropriate. Before you begin, look at some other information leaflets to see how they are set out, and plan your work carefully.

✔ ○ **5** **a** Plan a ten-minute radio programme on safety in the garden. Think about how to make your presentation as varied as possible: you could include interviews and/or dramatic dialogue as well as straightforward advice, or you could make it a phone-in programme, where listeners ring in for advice. If you like, you could aim the programme at a specific audience, such as old people or parents with young children.
**b** Perform the programme for the rest of the class, or tape-record it. (Perhaps there is a local organisation who would benefit from hearing your tape?)

**6** Look back at the different forms of presentation you have used in these assignments. Bearing in mind that the aim of this type of information is to save lives and prevent accidents, what do you think is the best way of conveying it? What might influence your choice of presentation? Explain your views fully.

# U·N·I·T 16 *Reading the minutes*

Have you ever been to an official meeting? Perhaps you serve on a committee of some kind, or perhaps your school has a School Council and you have attended a meeting. At most meetings of this type a secretary takes *minutes* (see box). These help people remember what was said, and by whom. In addition, they are recognised as a truthful record of what was said – an important point if disputes occur later. Finally, they provide information for people who did not attend the meeting but who wish to know what was discussed.

---

**Official meetings**

**Chairperson** – the person responsible for organising and introducing the meeting, and ensuring that all topics are discussed fairly. The chairperson should not state his/her own views.

**Minutes** – an official record of what was said, by whom, at a meeting. The record must be accurate and clear. It must mention all the topics discussed, but omit irrelevant comments – summarising the most important points of lengthy discussions.

**Apologies for absence** – the meeting is informed of anyone unable to attend.

**Agenda** – a list of what is to be discussed at the meeting. Usually topics are placed in order of importance. The agenda should be made public or circulated shortly before the meeting.

**Agree previous minutes** – everyone attending has a duty to read the minutes of the previous meeting. At the beginning of the meeting they are expected to confirm that this was an accurate record of what took place last time.

**Matters arising** – at this point people have a chance to comment on anything relating to the previous meeting.

**Any other business** – any matter not on the agenda but which someone at the meeting would like to discuss.

---

Here are the agenda and minutes of the April Council meeting at St Colin's School, Stanwick. The council meets once a month and consists of four teachers and 14 pupils – two from each school year.

# St Colin's School
## STANWICK

ST COLIN'S SCHOOL COUNCIL

Agenda for meeting 28th April

1 Members present
2 Apologies for absence
3 Agree previous minutes
4 Matters arising
5 School dinners
6 Charity work
7 Jewellery
8 Paintings
9 School trips
10 Any other business

---

ST COLIN'S SCHOOL COUNCIL

### Minutes of the School Council meeting  28th April

MEMBERS PRESENT

| | |
|---|---|
| Mr Spratt | Mr Meaner |
| Mrs Waterhouse | Miss Cooper |
| John Cussons (Head Prefect) U6B | George Perry U6F |
| Jim Kenyon L6S | Dorothy Eden L6L |
| Peter Tidd  5T | |
| Gail Riminton 4M | Tony Rutherford 4D |
| Kate Tudor 3B | Carol Bennett 3R |
| Malcolm Griffiths 2K | Kate Dorsett 2K |
| Amos Brown 1H | Geraldine Daw 1N |

Apologies for absence were received from Mr Lucas, who was out at a conference. He nominated Mr Spratt to take his place. No apologies were received from Nicola Florey (5T).

AGREE PREVIOUS MINUTES

The last minutes were agreed.

MATTERS ARISING FROM PREVIOUS MINUTES

1  John Cussons passed on a message from the Parents' Association to the effect that the fifth form's request for a coffee machine has been duly noted and will be discussed at the next PA meeting.

2  Gail Riminton said that following the Council's discussion on recycling, the Headmaster had agreed to see her to discuss the topic.

60

ITEMS ON AGENDA

1 <u>School dinners</u>

The first and second year representatives felt strongly that it is
unfair that they should be the last ones in to dinner every day. The
choice of food was often very limited and many items were cold. Fifth
and sixth formers pointed out that everyone had been through this when
they first joined the school. Miss Cooper said that at the last school
she taught at, a rota system had been operated very successfully. Mr
Spratt felt this might be complicated and would make it hard for staff
to arrange meetings of rehearsals at a convenient time.
   Amos Brown wondered whether anyone had spoken to kitchen staff about
the poor food at the end of the lunch hour. After all, everyone had
to pay the same amount and they should all get good, hot food. It was
suggested that a rota system could be used next term on a trial basis.
John Cussons agreed to put this proposal to the Headmaster.


2  <u>Charity work</u>

Kate Tudor and Carol Bennett, both third year representatives, felt
that the school's record on raising money for charity was very poor.
Last year only £56.00 had been raised. They proposed that the school
have a charity week at the end of term and that each form should
organise an event to raise money. The Council approved this idea
unanimously. All representatives were asked to discuss with their forms
which charities they would like to support.

3 <u>Jewellery</u>

The fourth form representatives proposed that girls should be allowed
a free choice of jewellery. Mrs Waterhouse said that this issue had
been discussed almost every year at the council and each time it was
agreed that jewellery should be restricted to watches and plain gold
ear-studs. A vote was taken on whether the Council wanted to discuss
this issue further:

              For:  5          Against:  19

4  <u>Paintings</u>

Jim Kenyon raised the question of artwork in the school corridors. His
form (L6S) felt that the paintings were dull and outdated. George Perry
argued that the paintings were all very famous ones and were an
important part of our heritage. Jim Kenyon said that he was not
proposing to get rid of the old paintings but to buy some more modern
ones to be put up in addition. Peter Tidd remarked that paintings were
expensive and that the request for a coffee machine should take
priority. Jim Kenyon said that things like pictures add an important
dimension to school life: a more cultural and harmonious environment.
Tony Rutherford found this idea unlikely. A vote was taken on raising
this matter with the Headmaster.

              For:  18         Against:  6

5 School trips

The first form representatives stated that there are not enough holidays abroad arranged for first and second year classes. Mr Spratt pointed out that teachers are not obliged to arrange any school trips for anyone. Miss Cooper said that there had been none in her day. There was general discussion at this point but no further comments made openly. John Cussons asked whether the meeting wanted to vote on the issue of more holidays for first years. Mr Spratt felt this would be most impertinent and that there would be no further trips at all if pupils tried to lay the law down. At this point the bell rang. John Cussons asked for all items for next month's agenda to reach him by 18th May.

6 Any other business

1 Mr Meaner reminded the Council that they should all be present at Friday's Open Evening at 6.30 sharp.

2 The next meeting was fixed for 24th May at 12.45 in Room 121.

# Assignments

**1** Imagine you are one of the pupils named in these minutes. Write at least 400 words justifying your strong views on one of the following issues:

**a** school dinners
**b** art in school
**c** raising money for charity
**d** school trips
**e** school uniform

**2** Write a playscript for part of the meeting.

**3** On the opposite page are some rough notes taken by the School Council secretary at the next meeting, which took place on 24th May. Write an agenda for this meeting based on these notes. (Use the agenda for the previous meeting to guide you.)

Council 24th

Present? Peter Tidd in detention (Mr Sahat won't let him off)
Dorothy Eden at interview

Everyone else here.

## Minutes    — OK

## Matters arising
1. PA meeting on coffee machine next Wed. (30th)
2. GR said HM thinking about recycling exercise books.
   He thinks bottle bank cd. be dangerous.
3. JC says HM against dinner rota. No reason!
4. HM pleased about paintings idea. Will ask PA for money.

## TODAY'S ITEMS
School trips for 1st & 2nd year
Vote taken on whether to discuss this further:
          for : 5    against : 18

Charities  — loads of suggestions
Vote needed perhaps?
JC says ask all forms suggest 2 only, then take vote.
KT said committee was needed to arrange charity week.
Miss C — all shd be involved. TR - nothing done if too many involved.
committee set up : AB, NF, CB, MG
1st meeting next Wed after school (Rm 118)

Uniform  — 1st form want to abolish it
Various silly comments — no sensible discussion.
JC took vote on further discussion :
          for : 3    against : 21

Pets  — 1st form want school pets
Mr M — Who'd look after them? — suggested rota.
Mrs W — What about holidays?
CB said there would always be volunteers.
Much discussion — general feeling it was impractical
(time, money, space...) Many pupils have pets at home anyway.

Revising  5th & 6th form joint statement on revising.
Not enough peace & quiet in library. Hard for exam people
to study properly ∴ great stress. All v. concerned
about this. JC told to put this to HM as urgent matter.
Miss C — perhaps library shd always be supervised by
staff? — staff short of time & reluctant to give
Mr M — general agreement. Perhaps another room cd be
up more in this way.
made available? staff meeting shd discuss this. Teachers' all
GR said they'd pass this on.

AOB

Mr M thanked us for helping at Open Evening

JC wants items for next agenda by June 19th

Next meeting — June 23rd. Room 121

4 Write up the minutes of this meeting, following closely the method used for the previous meeting. Note in particular that all abbreviations must be written in full.

5 Hold a meeting on similar lines to the ones described, in a group of about 12–20 people.
a Draw up an agenda of topics to discuss. These can be suggested by members of the group.
b Elect a chairperson and then conduct the meeting.
c Everyone present at the meeting should take notes on what is said.

6 a Write up the minutes of the meeting held for 5 above. Follow the method used on pages 60–62.
b Exchange minutes, and read what as many other people as possible have written. Is there any general agreement as to whose account of the meeting is most accurate and clear? Can you suggest any reasons why this might be the case?

# U·N·I·T 17 *Revising a poem*

Great writing does not always 'flow from the pen'; it has to be worked at. Here are two versions of a poem by Wilfred Owen, a soldier who fought in and wrote poems about the First World War.

**Anthem for Doomed Youth**
What passing-bells for these who die as cattle?
  Only the monstrous anger of the guns.
  Only the stuttering rifles' rapid rattle
Can patter out their hasty orisons.[1]
No mockeries now for them; no prayers nor bells,
  Nor any voice of mourning save the choirs,—
The shrill, demented choirs of wailing shells;
  And bugles calling for them from sad shires.

What candles may be held to speed them all?
  Not in the hands of boys, but in their eyes
Shall shine the holy glimmers of good-byes.
  The pallor of girls' brows shall be their pall;[2]
*1 prayers*        Their flowers the tenderness of patient minds,
*2 funeral shroud* And each slow dusk a drawing-down of blinds.

**Anthem for Dead Youth**
What passing-bells for you who die in herds?
  —Only the monstrous anger of the guns!
  —Only the stuttering rifles rattled words
Can patter out your hasty orisons
No chants for you, nor balms, nor wreaths, nor bells,
  Nor any voice of mourning, save the choirs,
And long-drawn sighs of wailing shells;
  And bugles calling for you from sad shires.

What candles may we hold to speed you all?
  Not in the hands of boys, but in their eyes
Shall shine (the) holy lights of our goodbyes.
  The pallor of girls' brows must be your pall.
Your flowers, the tenderness of comrades' minds,
And each slow dusk, a drawing-down of blinds.

**Some notes on poetry**

**Alliteration** – the repetition of consonants, especially in a line of poetry eg *Fluttering, floating flakes are flying*.

**Onomatopoeia** – the use of words whose sound echoes their meaning eg *Murmuring of innumerable bees*. Words like 'crash', 'gurgle' and 'whisper' are all onomatopoeic.

**Assonance** – the repetition of vowel sounds, especially in a line of poetry eg 'i' sounds in *The light was white and fine and shining*.

**Sonnet** – a poem of 14 lines, usually expressing personal thoughts or emotions. The two most common rhyme schemes are the Italian (abba abba cde cde) and the Shakespearian (abab cdcd efef gg) but variations occur.

**Rhyme scheme** – the pattern in which the rhyme sounds occur in verse eg an aabccb pattern!

| | |
|---|---|
| I know you're n*ear* | a |
| For I can h*ear* | a |
| The echo of your str*ide* | b |
| I miss you *so* | c |
| Though you don't kn*ow* | c |
| I need you by my s*ide* | b |

# Assignments

☞ ✔ ○ **1**  **a** What is the one main difference between the two versions? How does this alter the effect the poem has on you?

**b** List all the other differences between the two versions.

**c** Now consider possible reasons for the variations. Below are some extracts from a conversation one group of pupils had about the poems. They may give you some ideas.

**d** Which version of the poem is the final one, do you think?

❛ *The alliteration and onomatopoeia are more effective, more noisy.*
*The comparison makes them sound more degraded somehow.*
*The shells sound insane in that one, don't they?*
*I think it's less definite than 'lights'.*
*Well, it's not just their comrades who have tender thoughts.*
*'Mockeries' could refer to more than one thing, couldn't it?*
*The rhythm sounds better.*
*It fits in better with the other bits about the church service.*
*That way it makes the shells sound too sympathetic.*
*The commas slow the lines down.*
*The full stop seems sad but the exclamation mark doesn't.*
*'Doomed' is sadder than 'dead'* ❜ .

✔ ◇ **2**  Using your answers to question **1**, write an essay about the two versions making it clear which version you prefer and why.

✔ ◇ **3**  Revise a poem that you have written yourself. Write a second version of it taking a different approach to your subject or improving on the words you used before. Then write an account of what you have changed and why you changed it.

# U·N·I·T 18 *Actions have consequences*

When something out of the ordinary occurs, it can result in a lot of writing: newspaper articles, reports, letters. Take this incident on the school bus, for example:

# School Buses threatened as pupils go berserk

Police were called last night to Sloan Street High school when a public service bus supposed to be taking over a hundred pupils home turned back. Driver Chris Atkins, 32, took this highly unusual step after describing the pupils as behaving 'like animals'.

According to Mr Atkins, pupils were pelting each other with flour bombs and eggs and some were squirting fizzy drinks at each other. In another incident a boy's shirt was ripped from his back and a fight broke out. Said Mr Atkins, 'I warned them twice about their behaviour but they were uncontrollable. So I carried out my threat to return them to school. I just couldn't concentrate on my driving and I am not prepared to work under these conditions.'

Two elderly members of the public who were aboard the bus were said to be shocked and frightened.

The pupils were apparently celebrating the end of term but things got out of hand. Many had obviously planned the pelting attacks in advance and had brought flour and eggs from home.

When the bus returned to Sloan Street, Mr Atkins demanded to see the Headteacher, Mrs Wills and insisted that the police be called. He also made the pupils clean the bus. His trade union is now discussing what measures can be taken to safeguard drivers against future incidents of this kind. If bus services are cut, many pupils living in outlying villages will find it very difficult to get to school.

Mrs Wills has promised a full investigation into the incident and has said that the pupils involved will be severely punished.

# Assignments

☞ **1**  Mrs Wills asked some people travelling on the bus to give their version of what happened. Write the accounts given by:

    **a**  Giles Toogood (Head Prefect)
    **b**  Jason Smart (5th former, currently suspended)
    **c**  Mrs May Whiting, aged 82

☞ **2**  Write a letter from Mrs Wills to the parents of all pupils who travel on buses explaining what has happened and making it clear that the situation is a very serious one. Outline what measures will be taken to prevent recurrences of this kind of incident.

**3**  **a**  Write a letter from Mrs Gertrude Smyth-Carp to the newspaper. She has read about this incident and wishes to register her disgust at the way young people today behave. The *tone* of the letter should be bossy and self-righteous.
    **b**  Write Giles Toogood's reply to her letter. He wishes to point out that many young people today are hard-working, considerate and well-behaved. The *tone* of his letter should be reasonable yet rather hurt. (For *tone*, see pages 127–131.)

---

**Formal letters**

- Put your address on the right, the recipient's address on the left
- Put the date under your address
- Begin *Dear Sir or Madam*, if you don't know the recipient's name
- End *Yours faithfully*, if you began *Dear Sir or Madam*
- End *Yours sincerely*, if you began *Dear Mr/Ms ——,*
- Sign your name on the line below
- See page 100 for an example.

# U·N·I·T 19 *Doing it again*

A modern poet, Simon Rae, has this to say about how he drafts and redrafts his poems:

> ❛ The first drafts of my poems tend to be *inclusive*, especially if they are descriptive. Later drafts become increasingly *exclusive* (ie more gets left out), until the final draft, which is stripped of everything that can be left out. In the early, experimental stages, I give lines and images the benefit of the doubt. The process is a little like trying on clothes in a clothes shop. Does this go with that? Is that really *me*? It's rare to get it right first time. Often you cling to things against your better judgment, jettisoning them only at the last minute. ❜

> **Image** — words used by a writer to convey a mental picture. Images are often similes or metaphors (see page 39).

Here are the first and final drafts of Simon Rae's poem *Night driving: autumn.*

**First draft**

**Night driving: autumn**
The headlights probe the back of the fog's throat
like a doctor's pencil torch
as the incline tilts us. The engine
says 'Aargh'. Then a sergeant
with luminous stripes directs us
round a corner as a five-barred gate
just misses us and the moon hangs herself
from the gibbet of an elm. The ghost train
hits the straight and the road's
ill-repaired punctures jolt the tyres.
Leaves click against the windscreen
like inaccurate moths, and the blurred pelts
pass easily over the carpet of the bright room
we push before us. When we finally
flood it with darkness and swing the doors open
the cold stings the throat like ammonia,
and the stars have crystallized
to powdered glass underfoot.

**Final version**
The headlights probe the back
of the fog's throat like a doctor's
pencil torch, and the engine
says 'Aargh' as we climb. Then
a sergeant with three luminous
stripes leaps out to direct us
round a corner. A barn looms
like a ghost-train facade, slams
silently past, while from
an arthritic gibbet of elm
the moon hangs herself tragically.
Blurred pelts pass easily
over the carpet of the bright
room we push before us. When we
flood it with darkness and swing
the doors open, the cold stings
like ammonia and the stars
have crystallized to a confetti
of ground glass underfoot.

# Assignments

☞ **1**   **a** List all the differences you notice between the two versions of the poem.
**b** Suggest reasons why the poet made these changes. (See page 65 for some ideas here and note Simon Rae's comments above, too.)
**c** If you were the poet, would you want to make any other changes?

☞ **2**   **a** Which of the two versions do you prefer and why?
**b** Now read Simon's own account of why the changes were made, on page 119.

# U·N·I·T  20  *Begging your pardon*

This is the beginning of a passage about Victorian beggars. As well as giving an insight into some of the tricks of the beggars' trade, the passage contains a number of slang words and phrases that the beggars used.

i)    In the morning, when the residents were getting themselves ready for the day's work, the kitchen of a beggars' lodging house must have presented a grotesque scene. Many 'gegors', or professional beggars, made their way by exhibiting wounds and sores, and faking them realistically was a traditional art always open to fresh variations. It was known as the 'scaldrum dodge'.

ii)    One simple trick was to cover a patch of skin with a layer of soap and apply strong vinegar, so that what appeared to be large, yellow, matter-filled blisters formed; another was to hide a lump of raw meat under an elaborate clotted dressing. Even beggars with genuine mutilations found that a bit of artifice helped, and before starting work they would touch up the stumps of healed amputations so that they looked inflamed and purulent. Other poor wretches went to the lengths of searing and discolouring parts of themselves with gunpowder, or used vitriol to raise fresh sores and aggravate old ones. In the end they must often have produced a real injury by the means they used to fake one.

iii)    A common site for an artificial sore was the shin, where it justified a limp and could easily be shown without offending even a lady's modesty; but sometimes an eye or ear was inflamed and made to produce the effect of a discharge. The standard procedure was to cover the focus of interest with a coil of filthy bandage. When the gegor had waylaid someone suitable, he slowly unravelled the bandage as he talked, all the while urging closer inspection – which the revolting appearance of the dressing effectively discouraged.

iv)    'Working the shallow' was another common way of playing on physical
*1 Chap*    distress. The typical 'shallow cove'[1] was a man who called at houses in
*2 System*    a half-naked state asking for money and clothes. Some who followed the lay[2] became expert wheezers and shakers, with graveyard coughs and an ability to fall into ghastly shivering fits that greatly increased their appeal. (A too-persistent shaker was in danger of acquiring an involuntary palsy so that he started vibrating at any time, in season and out.) The shallow was best worked in bad weather, and many of those who followed it had little need of pretence: they were already ill-clad and if they took off any of their few clothes in the hope of filling their bellies they must have suffered greatly for meagre gains.

v)    The advantage of the system was that old clothes were easier to get than other forms of charity, while the importance Victorians attached to ample body covering (on grounds of health as well as propriety[3]) no doubt made them all the readier to respond. If sixpences were rare, old shirts and waistcoats (known professionally as 'mittings' and 'bends') were fairly common and, according to the wear left in them, they are said to have fetched from three-halfpence to fourpence apiece from the barrow man or dollyshop.[4] Barefoot 'limpers' specialized in collecting boots and shoes which, even when badly worn, still realized a copper or two: second-hand boot vampers[5] could work temporary miracles with glue, heelball and varnish.

Since cast-offs were only to be got at people's homes, each begging expedition had to cover a fresh house-to-house round. This did not mean that shallow coves were continually on the pad:[6] that would have been an inconvenient way of life for anyone who needed all the time to be within reach of a market for old clothes. Probably, like other house-to-house beggars, they often gave the impression of being tramps when in fact they were working from a fixed centre, usually a big town, and covering different sectors of the surrounding area in turn. An important advantage of this plan was that, except in London, there were likely to be different police authorities for the middle of the town, where the beggar lodged, and the residential areas outside it, where house-begging was most profitable. Experienced cadgers would make their way out to the edge of a great city and then, towards evening, come limping dustily back through the better-class suburbs, ready to explain that they were tramping artisans[7] without means of a night's shelter. A favourite 'blob'[8] was to say one had trekked through England because there was work near-by for men trained in such-and-such a speciality, but it was useless applying in rags or without some particular item of craftsman's kit.

vii)    Some beggars practised a form of the shallow by hanging about the streets in scanty tatters asking for alms; but the beggar who exposed too much of himself in a busy, respectable street risked attracting altogether too much notice and landing up in the House of Correction. On the whole, static begging was best practised by decorous-looking women[9] and children, and of course by those (genuine or bogus) who were obviously cripples. Many beggars carried a card, slung round their necks or fixed to a tray of 'snells' (hawkers' trifles) on which the way they had been crippled and their claims to charity were set out, sometimes at astonishing length. This procedure was known as 'standing pad on a fakement'[10] and, compared with accosting, it was less likely to get one taken up or moved on as a nuisance.

*9 Respectable-looking*

*10 Pretence*

# Assignments

**1**  **a** Make notes on the passage. For example: *scaldrum dodge* = fake wounds
   1) soap + vinegar → yellow blisters
   2) raw meat under dressing
   3) vitriol → sores
   4) gunpowder → discoloured skin
   *Real wounds* eg stumps – made to look worse
   **b** Look through your notes and compare them with the passage. Check that you have not omitted anything important.
   **c** Give your notes on each paragraph a suitable heading.

**2**  You have to write an entry about Victorian beggars for a children's encyclopaedia. Using your notes, summarise clearly what paragraphs i–vii have to say. (Remember to use appropriate language for your audience.)

**3**  Imagine you are one of the beggars in the passage. Write an extract from your autobiography, describing either
   **a** a typical day's work; or
   **b** a particular incident.

**4**  In pairs, act out a discussion between two beggars about the tricks of their trade *or* act out an interview with one of the beggars for television or radio.

---

**Making notes**

- Leave out all the unnecessary words
- Use signs where this helps, eg
   = instead of *means*;
   ∴ instead of *therefore*;
   → instead of *results in*.
- Use side headings to make main points clearer
- Underline important words and phrases
- Number points
- Never repeat information.

74

Derek has just left home to study history at college. A couple of days after his departure, his Mum writes him this letter.

14 Longleaf Lane
Guildford
Surrey
GU2 3AF

October 8th

Dear Derek,

Well, you've finally left home! It seems very quiet here without you. (It must be your loud music we miss.) After we all saw you off on the train, I must admit I wiped a few tears away. Dad and Karen said I was an old softie but I think they're missing you too. Karen sends her love and says she misses your help with her maths homework. Dad said to ask you if you'll be back for City's game against United on October 29th? He thinks it will be an all-ticket affair and says he'll treat you to a ticket if you want to go.

Gran came round yesterday and brought some strawberry jam which she says I'm to give you next time you come home. She's worried that they won't feed you properly and wonders who will do your washing (not me, I hope!) She says to tell you that if you get a cold you should buy some lemons and squeeze the juice in hot water. Put some honey in and then drink it! Anyway, I expect she will write to you herself, so no doubt you'll get more medical advice then!

Well, how are things with you? What's your room like at the college? And is the food O.K.? You eat anything so you should be all right. I just hope they're giving you enough of it! No doubt you've made lots of friends already. Tell us about them — you know we like to hear about all the characters you meet.

cont.

I suppose it's too much to hope that you've done any work yet. What with your hectic social life I suppose history lectures have been the last thing on your mind. Seriously though, Derek, do work hard. It's no good leaving all the studying till the last minute like you always did at school. You've got to begin as you mean to go on or when you get to the exams next summer you just won't be able to catch up. Your father and I are having to support you financially while you're studying (The grant doesn't go far, does it?) and we don't want our money wasted.

By the way, I saw your old flame Kathy Knight yesterday. She asked me when you'd be home! I told her you'd only just gone. I think she is still sweet on you but Karen says she has another boyfriend now.

Well, I'd better sign off now. Dad is nodding off in the armchair — I told him that film would be boring. Karen is trying out _another_ hairstyle. As you see, everything's much the same here.

Take care of yourself, love, and do remember to write to us. (soon)

Lots of love,
Mum, Dad and Karen.

P.S. Fred sends licks and woofs.
P.P.S. Send your letter 1st class.

# Assignments

☞ **1**　**a** If you were Derek, would you enjoy reading this letter? Give reasons for your answer.
**b** What do you think might be the *tone* of Derek's reply to this letter? (See page 127.)
**c** Write Derek's reply, remembering to answer all his mother's questions and comments. (You can invent an address for his college.)

☞ **2**　**a** How would you describe the tone and content of Derek's Mum's letter?
**b** Imagine that Derek received other letters from:
his father; Karen; Kathy Knight; his old history teacher.
In each case, suggest what you expect the tone and content of the letter to be.
**c** Write one of these letters.

**3**　**a** Imagine that Derek phones his family after receiving the letter from his Mum. Act out the conversation.
**b** List the good and bad things about letters and phonecalls as ways of sharing news with family and friends.

✔ ▱ **4**　**a** Write a long letter to a friend or relation who lives some way from you. Tell him/her all your latest news and ask about what s/he has been doing.
**b** Post your letter and wait for the reply.

# U·N·I·T  22  *Knowing the code*

All advertising is covered by the British Code of Advertising Practice, a strict set of rules to make sure that it is fair. Here are some extracts from the code.

**Section B**

**Truthful presentation: use of 'free'**

8.1 When a product is advertised as being 'free', incidental costs which will necessarily be incurred in acquiring it, and which are known to (or can be accurately assessed by) the advertiser, should be clearly indicated; and when such incidental costs exceed those that would typically arise if a comparable product was *bought* from a comparable source, the product advertised should not be described as free.

**Section C.I**

5.1 **Cure**

No advertisement should employ words, phrases or illustrations which claim or imply the cure of any ailment, illness or disease, as distinct from the relief of its symptoms.

5.4 **Appeals to fear, and exploitation of credulity**

No advertisement should cause those who see it unwarranted anxiety lest they are suffering (or may, without responding to the advertiser's offer, suffer) from any disease or condition if ill health; or suggest that consumption or use of the advertised product is necessary for the maintenance of physical or mental capacities, whether by people in general or by any particular group.

**Section C.II**

**Hair and scalp products**

1.1 No advertisement should contain any of the claims set out below in sub-paragraph 1.2 unless that claim is backed by substantiation which includes data derived from practical trials, on human subjects of sufficient rigour in both design and execution as to warrant general acceptance of the conclusions upon which the claim is based.

1.2 The claims referred to above are:
– that baldness can be prevented or its progress retarded:
– that hair loss or thinning of the hair can be arrested or reversed;
– that hair growth can be stimulated or improved:
– that hair roots can be fed or nourished; and
– that the hair itself can be strengthened or its health, as distinct from its appearance, improved.

**Section C.X**

**Children – General**

1.1 Direct appeals or exhortations to buy should not be made to children unless the product advertised is one likely to be of interest to them and one which they could reasonably be expected to afford for themselves.

1.2 Advertisements should not encourage children to make themselves a nuisance to their parents, or anyone else, with the aim of persuading them to buy an advertised product.

1.3 No advertisement should cause children to believe that they will be inferior to other children, or unpopular with them, if they do not buy a particular product, or have it bought for them.

1.4 No advertisement for a commercial product should suggest to children that, if they do not buy it and encourage others to do so, they will be failing in their duty or lacking in loyalty.

# Assignments

**1**  **a**  The two advertisements on the opposite page obviously infringe the British Code of Advertising Practice. For each, write the numbers of the sub-sections of the code which you think are being infringed.
**b**  Write two letters of complaint, one about the *Planet-trekker* robotobile car advertisement, the other about the *Hirsute* advert. Each letter should mention clearly your personal reaction to the advert, and should refer to the parts of the Code you think are being infringed. Write one letter to the Advertising Standards Authority and one to the product's manufacturers. (These are formal letters and should begin *Dear Sir or Madam* and end *Yours faithfully* – see page 102.)

**2**  Design two alternative advertisements for the *Planet-trekker* robotobile car and *Hirsute* lotion, which do not infringe the Code.

**3**  Invent a product of your own and design an advertisement for it which infringes the code. Ask a friend to tell you which subsections of the code it infringes. (You could display a collection of these adverts in the classroom.)

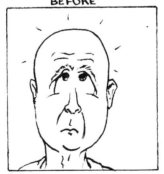

**4** Conman Cosmetics Ltd are being prosecuted because not only is their advertising dishonest, the product itself is also a complete fake. A reporter in court makes these notes on the case.

> **Case against Conman**
>
> Prosecuting lawyer - Ms Madeleine Swan
> Proved their ad. infringes ad. code (check details)
> Main witness - Dr Jonathan Walser, hair expert
> His scientific analysis on Hirsute lotion shows it contains mainly olive oil, colouring, salt + shampoo!!
>
> Defence lawyer - Mr Peter Furness
> Witnesses - Rachel Knowles, scientist, 32, claims to have 'discovered' H's secret formula
> Won't say exactly what it is
> 3 hairy men who swear they were bald before using H. lotion
>
> Case continues tomorrow
>
> Must get some photos + interviews!

**a** Write the reporter's article on the court case. It should be about 400 words long.

---

### Writing newspaper articles

- Give the article a suitable headline
- Sum up all the main facts of the case (Who? What? Where? When? How? Why?) in the first paragraph of the article
- Put less important information towards the end of the article

---

**b** The editor suddenly says that space in the newspaper is very limited. The article must be reduced to 150 words. Rewrite your article, keeping only the most important facts.

**5** **a** Look through magazines and newspapers and make a collection of advertisements for hair products and adverts aimed at children. Write a paragraph about each, explaining whether or not you think it is likely to infringe the Advertising Code.
**b** Explain which of these adverts you think is the best, giving your reasons in full.

# U·N·I·T 23 How predictable can you get!

Certain types of writing, particularly in newspapers and magazines, use the same key words and phrases over and over again. It could be argued that as long as you have these, you can fill in the rest — it's all so predictable.

## Assignments

📖 ☞ 1   Copy out at least four of these horoscopes and add words which will make sense of them. (You may check some horoscopes from a newspaper first, if you like.)

***Aries*** *(22nd March–20th April)*

_____ high spirits _____

_____ moon in Leo _____ goals and

ambitions _____ peak.

***Taurus*** *(21st April–21st May)*

_____ interesting developments _____

_____ home front _____ finance.

Beware _____ matters _____ hurry.

***Gemini*** *(22nd May–23rd June)*

_____ family activity _____ busy.

_____ good news _____ old friend, _____

_____ partner _____ jealous.

***Cancer*** *(22nd June–23rd July)*

_____ thinking _____ money _____ week, _____

_____ rush _____ major purchase, _____

_____ advice _____ regret _____.

**Leo** (24th July–23rd August)

_____ lazy mood _____ but _____

_____ letters. Mercury _____ birth sign

_____ romantic.

**Virgo** (24th August–23rd September)

_____ lots of enjoyment _____ children or

young people _____ _____ creative _____

_____ new hobby.

**Libra** (24th September–23rd October)

Friendship _____ important _____ forget

relatives _____. Money troubles _____ mind,

but _____ eventually.

**Scorpio** (24th October–22nd November)

Now _____ holiday _____ friends _____

_____ close to you. _____ forget _____

plan _____ future.

**Sagittarius** (23 November–22nd December)

_____ keen _____ new plans _____

too hasty _____ disappointed _____

_____ trust _____ newcomers.

**Capricorn** (23rd December–20th January)

_____ solutions _____ problems _____

_____ worrying _____ long time _____

energy and enthusiasm _____ help _____.

**Aquarius** (21st January–19th February)

_____ spectacular week _____ fun, parties _____

_____ careful _____ overdo _____

_____ tired.

82

*Pisces* (20th February–21st March)

_____ emotionally happy and fulfilled, _____

going wrong recently _____ effort _____

_____ fears _____ seem.

○ ☞ **2**    **a**   Compare your versions with those of a friend. How similar are they?
       **b**   Make a list of the words and phrases you think are most predictable.

☞ **3**    Collect other types of writing you could do this with, for example, 'Scandal' stories from newspapers; reports of football matches or sports events; lyrics of pop songs; letters to problem pages.
      Write out a version of one of these which only contains the key words and phrases and ask a friend to complete it.

✐ **4**    Using at least four different samples like those suggested in **3**, try to analyse some of the predictable words and phrases and suggest a reason(s) for their use. For instance,

     **a**   The writer hasn't thought hard enough
     **b**   There's no other way of saying this
     **c**   It's supposed to shock readers
     **d**   It's supposed to amuse readers
     **e**   It's familiar so we immediately know what the writer is talking about
     **f**   It arouses our emotions
     **g**   It's an accurate expression
     **h**   It's an attractive expression
     **i**   It's what we expect in this type of writing
     **j**   It sounds right.

Add other reasons of your own.
     Draw up a table like the one below to show the results of your analysis.

| Sample | Word/phrase | Reason? | My comment on word/phrase |
|---|---|---|---|
| 1 Newspaper article on football violence | mindless thugs | a, f, i, j | A bit common. Are they mindless? It says some have good jobs so they must be clever. |
| | scum | f, i | Over-emotional? But they *are* very violent and stupid. |

✐ **5**    Try rewriting one of your samples without using any of the key words and phrases. Make your style as clear and original as possible.

# U·N·I·T 24 *Making plans*

The information on the next six pages all relates to Ilfracombe, in North Devon, and the surrounding area.

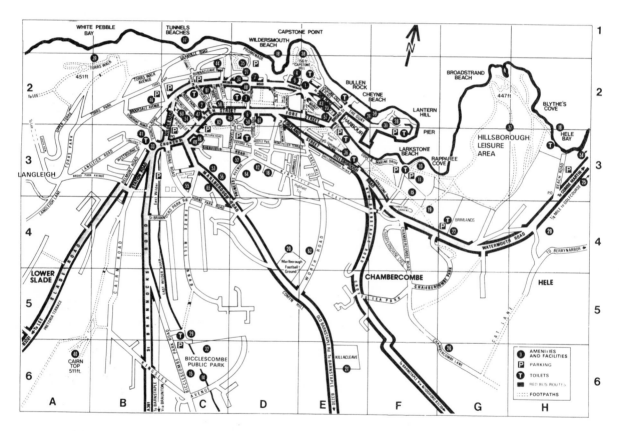

| 1. | **Tourist Information Centre** | E2 | 16. | Bowling Green | D3 | 28. | St Nicholas Chapel | F2 |
|---|---|---|---|---|---|---|---|---|
| 2. | Council Offices | C2 | 17. | Tunnels Bathing Beaches and | | 29. | Corn Mills (Restored) | C5 and H4 |
| | | | | Sports Canoes | C1 | 31. | Lifeboat Station | F2 |
| | **ENTERTAINMENTS** | | 18. | Children's Paddling | | | | |
| 4. | Pavilion Theatre | D2 | | Pools | D2 and H3 | | **PARKS, GARDENS AND OPEN** | |
| 6. | Cinema | D2 | 19. | Indoor Swimming Pool | F4 | | **SPACES** | |
| | | | 20. | Football Club | D4 | 32. | Bicclescombe Park | C6 |
| | **AMUSEMENTS & RECREATION** | | 21. | Cricket Club | E6 | 33. | Garden of Remembrance | B3 |
| 3. | Indoor Skating Centre | D2 | 22. | Rugby Club | G4 | 34. | Runnymede Gardens | D2 |
| 7. | Crazy Golf | D2 | 23. | Sub Aqua Club | E2 | 35. | Southern Slope & Jubilee | |
| 7. | Children's 'Karts' | D2 | 24. | Yacht Club | E2 | | Gardens | D2 |
| 9. | Putting | D2 | 25. | Golf Club | H3 | 36. | St James' Park | E3 |
| 10. | 'Karting' | F3 | | | | 37. | Hillsborough | GH2–3 |
| 11. | Pitch & Putt | F3 | | **PLACES OF INTEREST** | | 38. | Capstone Hill | DE2 |
| 14. | Children's Boating Pool | | 4. | Art Exhibition | D2 | 39. | Torrs Walk & Lee Down (NT) | AB2 |
| | and Park | C6 | 26. | Chambercombe Manor | G6 | 40. | Cairn Hill-top (CA) | A6 |
| 15. | Tennis Courts | C6 and F3 | 27. | Museum | D2 | | | |

**CHURCHES**
Church of England
| 41. | Holy Trinity | B3 |
|---|---|---|
| 42. | St Peter's | D3 |
| 43. | St Philip & St James | E2 |

**Roman Catholic**
| 44. | Our Lady, Star of the Sea | C2 |
|---|---|---|

**Other Denominations**
| 45. | Baptist | C2 |
|---|---|---|
| 46. | Evangelical | B2 |
| 47. | United Reformed | C2 |
| 48. | Methodist | D2 |
| 49. | Christian Fellowship | C3 |
| 50. | Salvation Army | D2 |
| 51. | Christian Spiritualist | C2 |
| 66. | Jehovah's Witnesses | C3 |

84

## Assignments

(If you answer the assignments as a timed exercise, allow one and a half hours.)

**1** Your cousin who lives in the USA is coming to England next Easter. S/he plans to spend a week with you visiting Ilfracombe and has written asking you to find out what the town and surrounding area have to offer. You have collected up the tourist information in this unit. Write a reply to the letter, giving details about what can be seen and done. (*20 marks*)

**2** You will be meeting your cousin in London and travelling from Paddington to Barnstaple by train (changing at Exeter) on Saturday April 7th and returning on April 14th. On both occasions you intend to set out fairly early in the morning. Consult the timetables and set out clearly the trains you will catch on your outward and return journeys. (*8 marks*)

**3** Write a letter to the manager of the Cozynight Hotel, Ilfracombe, reserving two single rooms for the week. Ask for a hotel car to meet you from Barnstaple railway station at the appropriate time. (*12 marks*)

**4** On Sunday April 8th you will be able to collect a hired car for the week. Assuming that the weather will not be warm enough for sunbathing, write a plan for what you will do every day from Sunday–Friday inclusive. Your cousin enjoys being outdoors, is interested in English history and will want to do something different every day. (*20 marks*)

# Ilfracombe

Ilfracombe, set snugly in the middle of Devon's majestic Atlantic coast-line, is the jewel in the County crown.

Whether you take your leisure on one of the many coves or beaches, ambling along the flower-decked Prom, discovering the Quay and the High Street shops – or taking the car to explore the Moor, the nearby sandy beeches, a stately home or castle, there's something for everyone to enjoy.

In the balmy sunny evenings stroll among the coloured lights enjoying the atmosphere of charm and character that is Ilfracombe. Or if the mood takes you there are the theatre, bars, cinema, discos, skating and dancing. Whilst on Lantern Hill the tiny Chapel keeps its age-old vigil over the ancient harbour. By day or by night here truly is a resort of delight.

Ilfracombe, the leading holiday resort in North Devon, has all the advantages of sheer natural beauty. Built round its ancient harbour and quay, nestling snugly into a breath taking coastline, here are the natural focal points of the town – but you're never far from the sounds and the smell of the sea. Above the harbour, like a sentinel, stands Hillsborough looking down over the ever popular pier and quay, and beyond to the promenade. Capstone Hill with its fluttering vantage point, and the famous Torrs Walks. The hills and cliffs give Ilfracombe its essential character yet plenty of the shops are on level ground near to the centre of the town. So too are many of the holiday amenities. The famous Tunnels beaches with their safe tidal pools and fascinating history, are just along the Promenade – as are the Pavilion Theatre, the colourful Jubilee Gardens and Southern Slopes – enchantingly floodlit at night. Further afield, but still within walking distance, enjoy the beauty of Bicclescombe Park or the charm of Chambercombe Manor.

But Ilfracome is intriguing from the water too – whether you are sailing your own boat, taking a coastal cruise or one of the rare trips to the mystic Island of Lundy. Ilfracombe was just made for holidays whether you seek tranquility or the excitement of activity, exploration or adventure. Travel just a short distance and you'll find a whole lot more to see and do.

# The Coastal Path

## Hele Bay-Ilfracombe-Shag Point (3¾ miles 6km)

**Going**: this section contains two easy stretches of cliff-walking each side of Ilfracombe.

From Hele Bay the Coast Path zig-zags up Hillsborough Hill (447ft) bringing you over the top and down the other side where it runs close to the edge of the cliff.

*In the spring and early summ you have a very close view of nesting herring gulls, fulmars, and kittiwakes.*

As you come over the top of Hillsborough a fine panormama of Ilfracombe with its harbour and prominent Lantern Hill. The Path brings you out through pleasure gardens to the Harbour, usually full of sailing craft and a small coaster or two, passing above two beaches: Larkstone Beach and Rapparee Cove, with rocks and grey sand.

*Ilfracombe (pop 8900) has been a fishing port of some importance since the Middle Ages. Granted a charter by Edward I in 1278 it was regularly called upon to provide ships and men in times of war. Holy Trinity church is 15th century with earlier parts, and the Chapel of St Nicholas on Lantern Hill, probably 14th century, recently restored. Of the number of pubs the oldest is undoubedly the George and Dragon, dating from 1360. It was renovated in 1641!*

*Ilfracombe started to become a popular resort early in the last century and is now the largest on the North Devon coast. From its harbour a steamer runs trips in the summer to the Welsh coast and the island of Lundy, both of which can be seen on a clear day.*

The Coast Path west of Ilfracombe starts on Torr's Walk, reached by Osborne Road which runs east of Holy Trinity church. Keep climbing until you come out on the cliff high above the town. The very good Path the continues along the side of the 400ft cliff with more close views of breeding gulls, also stonechats, whitethroats, and other birds fond of gorse and bramble. You eventually come out on an open stretch of turf where a stile and a sign indicates the start of the National Trust Flat Point, a fine open cliff-top area. From Shag Point, along the route, there is a good view ahead of Bull Point, of characteristic shape.

# BRITISH RAIL TIME-TABLES

## Exeter Central – Barnstaple – Exeter Central (Saturdays)

|  | | | | | | | | |
|---|---|---|---|---|---|---|---|---|
| Exeter Central | d | 08 49 | 10 19 | 12 44 | 14 28 | 15 52 | 17 12 | 19 19 |
| Exeter St David's | a | — | — | 12 47 | — | 15 55 | — | 19 22 |
| Exeter St David's | d | 09 06 | 10 38 | 12 50 | 14 42 | 16 00 | 17 30 | 19 25 |
| Newton St Cyres | d | — | — | — | — | — | 17 38 | 19 32x |
| Crediton | d | 09 16 | 10 49 | 13 03 | 14 55 | 16 10 | 17 43 | 19 39 |
| Yeoford | d | 09 24x | — | 13 10x | — | — | 17 49 | 19 46x |
| Copplestone | d | 09 30x | — | — | — | — | 17 55 | — |
| Morchard Road | d | 09 33x | — | — | — | — | 17 58 | — |
| Lapford | d | 09 38x | — | 13 22x | — | — | 18 03 | 19 55x |
| Eggesford | d | 09 45 | 11 10 | 13 27 | 15 15 | 16 32 | 18 10 | 20 00 |
| Kings Nympton | d | 09 51x | — | 13 33x | — | 16 38x | 18 15 | 20 05x |
| Portsmouth Arms | d | 09 56x | — | — | — | — | 18 20 | — |
| Umberleigh | d | 10 03x | — | 13 44x | — | 16 49x | 18 26 | 20 14x |
| Chapelton | d | 10 08x | — | — | — | — | 18 30 | — |
| Barnstaple | a | 10 19 | 11 37 | 13 57 | 15 41 | 17 00 | 18 40 | 20 27 |
| Barnstaple | d | 05 45 | 07 45 | 09 20 | 10 42 | 12 15 | 14 03 | 16 00 |
| Chapelton | d | — | 07 51x | — | — | — | — | 16 08 |
| Umberleigh | d | 05 56 | 07 55x | — | 10 52x | — | 14 13x | 16 13 |
| Portsmouth Arms | d | — | 08 02x | — | — | — | — | 16 19 |
| Kings Nympton | d | 06 06 | 08 06x | — | 11 03x | — | 14 24x | 16 24 |
| Eggesford | d | 06 13 | 08 13 | 09 47 | 11 10 | 12 42 | 14 29 | 16 33 |
| Lapford | d | 06 19 | 08 17x | — | 11 14x | — | 14 35x | 16 39 |
| Morchard Road | d | — | 08 22x | — | — | — | — | 16 44 |
| Copplestone | d | — | 08 25x | — | — | — | — | 16 48 |
| Yeoford | d | 06 30 | 08 30x | — | 11 24x | — | 14 45x | 16 54 |
| Crediton | d | 06 38 | 08 36 | 10 06 | 11 31 | 13 04 | 14 54 | 17 01 |
| Newton St Cyres | d | — | 08 40x | — | — | — | — | — |
| Exeter St David's | a | 06 50 | 08 50 | 10 17 | 11 45 | 13 16 | 15 06 | 17 12 |
| Exeter St David's | d | — | 08 53 | — | 11 50 | — | — | — |
| Exeter Central | a | — | 08 56 | 10 31 | 11 53 | 13 38 | 15 41 | 17 36 |

## London Paddington – Penzance – London Paddington

| | ■ 125 ⊕ | ■ 125 ⊕ | ■ | ■ ☕ | ■ 125 ⊕ | ■ 125 ☕ | ■ | ■ ☕ | ■ 125 ⊕ |
|---|---|---|---|---|---|---|---|---|---|
| London Paddington | 07 45 | 08 45 | 08 50 | 09 35 | 10 12 | 10 50 | 11 23 | 11 35 | 12 25 |
| Reading (depart) | 08 10 | 09 10 | 09 34 | 10 08 | 10 37 | — | 11 54 | 12 06 | 12 51 |
| Taunton | — | 10 31 | 11 07 | — | 11 55 | — | 13 21 | 13 40 | — |
| Tiverton Parkway | — | 10 45 | — | — | 12 09 | — | — | — | — |
| Exeter St Davids | 10 12 | 11 02 | 11 40 | 12 18 | 12 26 | 12 50 | 13 54 | 14 13 | 14 35 |
| Newton Abbot | 10 34 | — | 12 14 | — | 12 56 | 13 32 | 14 18 | 14 44 | 15 43 |
| Paignton | 11 17 | — | 12 37 | — | 13 19 | 13 55 | — | 15 07 | 16 06 |
| Plymouth | 11 18 | 12 01 | — | 13 33 | — | 13 50 | 15 05 | — | 15 34 |
| St Austell | 12 15 | 13 00 | — | 14 34 | — | 14 49 | — | — | 16 30 |
| Truro | 12 33 | 13 18 | — | 14 53 | — | 15 09 | — | — | 16 47 |
| Penzance | 13 11 | 14 02 | — | 15 36 | — | 15 49 | — | — | 17 25 |

| | 125 ⊕ | 125 ⊕ | 125 ⊕ | ■ 125 ⊕ | ■ 125 | ■ 125 ⊕ | ■ | ■ 125 | ■ ☕ |
|---|---|---|---|---|---|---|---|---|---|
| Penzance | — | — | 05 35 | 06 18 | — | 07 20 | — | 08 45 | — |
| Truro | — | — | 06 05 | 06 56 | — | 08 00 | — | 09 22 | — |
| St Austell | — | — | 06 22 | 07 14 | — | 08 18 | — | 09 40 | — |
| Plymouth | — | 06 00 | 07 30 | 08 25 | — | 09 25 | — | 10 38 | — |
| Paignton | — | 06 03 | 07 15 | 08 20 | 09 00 | 09 15 | 10 30 | — | 11 20 |
| Newton Abbot | — | 06 38 | 08 09 | 09 01 | 09 21 | 10 04 | 10 51 | — | 11 41 |
| Exeter St Davids | — | 07 00 | 08 31 | 09 23 | 09 54 | 10 27 | 11 21 | 11 36 | 12 11 |
| Tiverton Parkway | — | 07 17 | 08 48 | 09 16 | 10 11 | — | 11 38 | — | 12 28 |
| Taunton | 06 25 | 07 31 | 09 02 | 09 51 | 10 25 | 10 55 | 12 00 | — | 12 44 |
| Reading (arrive) | — | 09 03 | 10 36 | 11 11 | 11 52 | 12 15 | 13 40 | — | 14 22 |
| London Paddington | 09 05 | 09 33 | 11 06 | 11 41 | 12 22 | 12 45 | 14 15 | 13 36 | 14 57 |

■   Compulsory seat reservations required for journeys to Taunton, Reading and Paddington.
125   InterCity 125 High Speed Train.

Catering available for all or most of journey

✗   Restaurant (Mondays to Fridays) serving meals
⊕   Buffet serving hot dishes, drinks and light refreshments
☕   Buffet serving drinks and light refreshments.

89

# U·N·I·T 25  *But does it make sense?*

Don't just assume that because you've read something in a book it must be right! As you read, you should be continually asking yourself questions about the words in front of you. For instance, suppose your Geography textbook contained the map and chart below together with the words which follow?

1 Ireland
2 United Kingdom
3 Portugal
4 Spain
5 France
6 Belgium
7 Netherlands
8 Switzerland
9 West Germany
10 Austria
11 Italy
12 Greece
13 Norway
14 Sweden
15 Finland

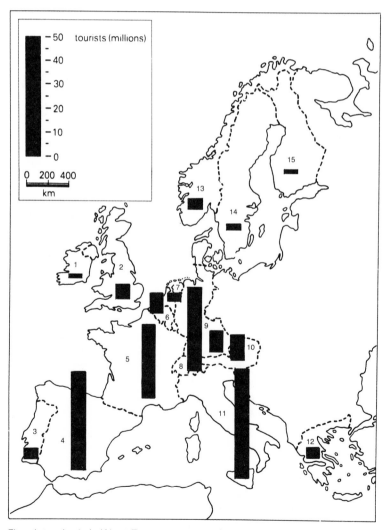

Tourist arrivals in West European countries

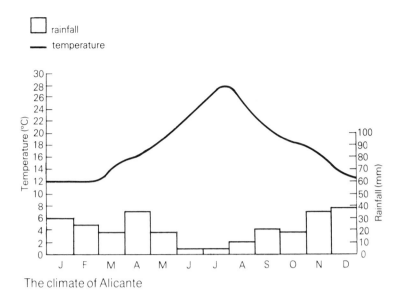

rainfall
temperature

The climate of Alicante

The map gives information about the numbers of tourists visiting countries in Western Europe. More than five thousand visit the United Kingdom each year, making it one of the most popular tourist destinations in Europe. Italy is the most popular since it receives about forty thousand tourists a year, but France is a close second. All the countries in the southern part of Europe receive large numbers of visitors and all the countries in the northern part have far fewer visitors. Holland and Sweden are the least popular countries, perhaps because they do not have much coastline.

Alicante has an ideal holiday climate with very low rainfall all year round, except for the summer when it increases sharply. The temperature is fairly warm all year round, and even in December it is still above 60 degrees. The wettest month is April when there are nearly eight inches of rain, but by then the temperature has gone up to about 80 degrees, so summer is well on the way. The warmest, driest time for your holiday is probably July. (August is also dry but is a bit cooler.)

# Assignments

☞ 1   **a** The map and chart are both correct but the person who wrote the text has not interpreted them carefully enough. What mistakes can you find?
**b** Write a revised version of the text in which the map and chart are correctly interpreted.

✐ 2   **a** Find a chart, map, diagram, graph or table of figures (perhaps in one of your school textbooks) or make one up. Write 200–300 words about it, deliberately making mistakes in what you say.
**b** Swap with a friend. Ask him/her to spot your mistakes and write a correct version.
**c** Check the rewritten versions against the map, diagram, graph or table you selected for **a**. Is your friend's version accurate enough? Do you want to suggest further improvements?

**ALL BUT EMPTY**
Part 2

*1 Playacting*

The flat figures passed and repassed, their six-year-old gestures as antique as designs on a Greek coin. They were emotional in great white flickering letters, but their emotions were not comic nor to me moving. I was surprised when I heard the old man next to me crying to himself – so much to himself and not to me, not a trace of histrionics[1] in those slow, carefully stifled sobs that I felt sorry for him. I said:

'Can I do anything?'

He may not have heard me, but he spoke: 'I can't hear what they are saying.'

The loneliness of the old man was extreme; no one had warned him that he would find only silent pictures here. I tried to explain, but he did not listen, whispering gently, 'I can't see them.'

I thought that he was blind and asked him where he lived, and when he gave an address in Seymour Terrace, I felt such pity for him that I offered to show him the way to another cinema and then to take him home. It was because we shared a desolation, sitting in the dark and stale air, when all around us people were lighting lamps and making tea and gas fires glowed. But no! He wouldn't move. He said that he always came to this cinema of an evening, and when I said that it was only afternoon, he remarked that afternoon and evening were now to him 'much of a muchness.' I still didn't realize what he was enduring.

Only a hint of it came to me a moment after, when he turned suddenly towards me, and whispered:

'No one could expect me to see, not after I've seen what I've seen,' and then in a lower voice, talking to himself, 'From ear to ear.'

What has happened? What might 'from ear to ear' refer to? (Turn to page 98.)

The Office of Fair Trading is an independent organisation which offers us advice about our rights when we buy things. Read the Office's advice about buying a motor bike and then see how general advice like this can be used in specific situations.

First-time buyer or experienced rider, whether you go for a new bike or a used one, you want value for money. There is now a code of practice promoted by the motorcycle industry and backed by the Office of Fair Trading, to help you get a fair deal. Begin your search by going to a reputable dealer, who supports the code. Look for one of the code symbols shown on the back page.

## A word about the law

When you buy a new or second-hand bike from a **dealer** you are backed by three shopping laws. First, the bike must be *of merchantable quality*. This means it must be reasonably fit for the job it's meant to do. You don't expect the frame to break as you ride home. Obviously, a second-hand bike won't be as good as a new one, but it must still do the job. Second, it must be *as described*—whether in a sales brochure, on a showroom display card, in an advert, or by the dealer personally. Does the bike have all the features claimed for it? Your new bike should be the same as the one on display, unless it is made clear that some of the equipment costs extra. Third, it must be *fit for any particular purpose* made known to the dealer. For example, if you say you want a bike for travelling long distances, it's not much use if the dealer sells you a moped.

If you think your bike fails any of the three laws, see the dealer. You might be able to get the bike put right or some or all of your money back or, if you agree, have the bike replaced. It depends on the kind of fault and how long you've had the bike. If you were shown the faults or they were obvious when you examined the bike, you have no right to compensation. If you buy from someone who isn't in business, take great care. See **Buying privately**.

## Buying from a code dealer

### New bikes

1 Check that the law lets you ride the bike you want. (Get leaflet D100 from the Post Office.)

2 Work out the full cost of putting the bike on the road. Helmet, tax and insurance? Clothing and other equipment?

3 Code dealers must carry out the manufacturer's standard **pre-delivery inspection**. Make sure you get a copy of the completed checklist when you buy the bike.

4 Ask about the manufacturer's **warranty**. This is a kind of guarantee, a simple way of having certain faults put right at little or no cost to you if they appear during the warranty period. A warranty is a bonus over and above your legal rights. Read it carefully. There may be conditions which you should know about. For example, it may not cover faults resulting from servicing or repair by anyone other than the manufacturer's dealer.

## Second-hand bikes

1 All code dealers must carry out a **pre-sale inspection** of the bike. Ask to see the completed checklist before you buy and examine it carefully. You should get your own copy when you buy. *Any faults shown will be your responsibility unless the dealer agrees to put them right.*

2 If the bike's history is available—service records, repair bills, inspection reports, handbooks, and copies of warranties—the code dealer should give you whatever documents he has.

3 Code dealers must check the bike's mileage. The mileometer reading may be unreliable.

4 If the dealer makes any special claims about the bike—for example, that any new parts, such as a reconditioned engine, have been fitted—ask him to put them in writing.

5 If the dealer offers a warranty, check what parts are covered and for how long.

6 Work out the full cost of putting the bike on the road. You'll need an MoT test certificate if the bike is over three years old.

# Buying from non-code dealers

If you buy a bike from a dealer who doesn't support the code, you have your full rights under the law, but you will not be able to seek the help of the *trade associations*. See **If things go wrong**.

# Buying privately

You have fewer rights when you buy privately—from a friend or someone who is not in business to sell bikes. It is vital to take extra care. The law says only that bikes sold privately must be *as described* (see **A word about the law**). For example, you might be able to sue the seller for *misrepresentation* if he said something about the quality of the bike that wasn't true. So your rights will largely depend upon what is said between you and the seller. Take someone along to hear what's said. Ask the seller to put any important facts in writing.

Don't rely on an MoT test certificate—it doesn't necessarily mean the bike is in good condition.

### Make sure that you:

1 Examine the bike carefully. If necessary, take along someone who really knows about bikes. Don't buy unless you're absolutely sure the bike's o.k.

2 Get a vehicle registration document.

3 Get a receipt.

4 Don't ride a bike until you're insured, and have a driving licence and a Road Fund tax disc. (Get leaflet D100 from the Post Office.)

**BEWARE.** Some traders operate from their homes using small ads in newspapers. It's fine as long as they make it clear that they are traders. But some pretend to be private sellers to cheat you of your legal rights. If you suspect this, go to your local Trading Standards Department.

# Watch out at auctions

You don't always have the same legal rights when buying at auctions as when you buy from a dealer. Follow three golden rules:

1 Before you make a bid, visit some auctions to see how they work.

2 Read any notice and the auctioneer's terms and conditions carefully.

3 It is up to you to decide on the condition of the bike, and whether you're getting value for money. Good looks aren't necessarily a guide to a bike's condition!

# More about the law

The *Trade Descriptions Act* 1968 says that new and used bikes must be described truthfully, either in writing or in speech, or by illustration. Any statement the dealer makes must be true. If you think a dealer has misled you, tell a Trading Standards Officer, who can prosecute if necessary. In England, Wales and Scotland, the courts can award you compensation, if you have suffered as a result of the offence. This Act does *not* apply to private sales.

Under the *Road Traffic Act* 1972 it is illegal for anyone to sell an unroadworthy bike—unless he makes it quite clear that it is only fit for scrap unless repaired before use on the road. If you have been sold an unroadworthy bike, tell your Trading Standards Department. The seller could be prosecuted.

If you are buying a bike and see a *'disclaimer'*, like 'We take no responsibility for...', this does not always mean the seller can legally avoid responsibility. The notice may only be effective if the dealer can prove in court that the clause w: reasonable. For example, if your bike is damaged while it is in for repairs or a service, ignore any disclaimers and get advice from a consumer adviser.

# Assignments

☐ ☞ **1** A magazine called *The Teenager* is running an advice page for readers who want to buy a motor bike. Below are some of the letters readers have sent to the page. Use the facts you are given in the extract and write answers to these letters. (In each case the section you need to read is given in brackets.)

**a**
Dear *Teenager*,
I have heard that it is best to buy a bike from a code dealer. Please can you tell me what the code is and why it is important. (A)

**b**
Dear *Teenager*,
I bought a bike from a code dealer two months ago. I frequently travel five hundred miles to see my girlfriend. The dealer sold me a 50cc moped and said it would be 'just the job' for long journeys. It obviously isn't. Do I have any rights under the code? (A)

**c**
Dear *Teenager*,
I would like to buy a second-hand bike from a code dealer. Please could you tell me what I should get in writing from him before handing over my money. (C)

**d**
Dear *Teenager*,
My mum's friend's cousin's neighbour is selling a bike which looks all right. It has got an MoT certificate valid for six months. Do you think it would be a good buy? (D)

**e**
Dear *Teenager*,
Do you think it is a good idea to buy a motor bike at an auction? (E)

**f**
Dear *Teenager*,
Two weeks after I bought my second-hand bike it fell to pieces. I thought I could get my money back, but I have now found the dealer's disclaimer which says, 'We take no responsibility for what happens to this bike once it is sold.' Do I have any legal rights? (F)

**g**
Dear *Teenager*,
I bought a motor bike for £10. The dealer said it was only good for scrap. I patched it up, though, and have ridden it for three years with no mishaps until yesterday, when it suddenly exploded. I was furious. Am I entitled to my money back? (A)

**2** Now here are some replies which appear on the same letter page. Write suitable letters for these answers.

**a**
Well, motorbiking can be an expensive undertaking. Work out first what you need to spend on a bike, helmet, tax and insurance. Then put a little aside for any repairs that might crop up. If you have enough money for all this, you can probably afford to run a new bike. (B)

**b**
He sounds like a dealer to me. He is not allowed to pose as a private seller so contact your local Trading Standards Department. (D)

**c**
No, under no circumstances should you buy this bike! It is obviously only fit for the scrapheap! (?)

**d**
As long as you have this in writing, it should all be fine. (D)

**e**
You should not have to pay extra for this. Ask for some of your money back. (A)

**f**
It seems that the dealer deliberately deceived you. Go back to him and either ask for a free repair or for some of your money back. (A)

**g**
If the warranty made this clear, then the dealer is within his rights, I'm afraid. (B)

**3** Choose a subject you know something about and write a similar letters page on it for a teenage magazine. You should, of course, supply both the letters and the answers. Suitable subjects might include: a sport; a hobby; a place you have visited; dress sense; organising a party or social event; buying presents; problems with school. Before you begin, obtain some leaflets or books about your chosen subject and check that all your information is correct.

**ALL BUT EMPTY**
Part 3

That startled me because there were only two things he could mean, and I did not believe that he referred to a smile.

'Leave them to it,' he said, 'at the bottom of the stairs. The black-beetles always come out of that crack.'

It was extraordinary how he seemed to read my thoughts, because I had already begun to comfort myself with the fact of his age and that he must be recalling something very far away, when he spoke again: 'Not a minute later than this morning. The clock had just struck two and I came down the stairs, and there he was. Oh, I was angry. He was smiling.'

'From ear to ear,' I said lightly.

'That was later,' he corrected me, and then he startled me by reading out suddenly from the screen the words, 'I love you. I will not let you go.' He laughed and said, 'I can see a little now. But it fades, it fades.'

I was quite sure then that the man was mad, but I did not go. For one thing, I thought that at any moment the girl might come and two people could deal with him more easily than one; for another, stillness seemed safest. So I sat very quietly.

After a while he spoke again so low that his words were lost in the tin blare of the relayed record, but I caught the words 'serpent's tooth' and guessed that he must have been quoting scripture. He did not leave me much longer in doubt, however, of what had happened at the bottom of the stairs, for he said quite casually, his tears forgotten in curiosity:

'I never thought the knife was so sharp. I had forgotten I had it reground.'

What is the old man talking about? What might the storyteller do now?
(Turn to page 141.)

The local youth club leader, Pat Clark, receives this letter from the Head of Amenities at the Town Hall.

---

**LONDON BOROUGH OF ROMFORD**

Amenities Department,
Town Hall,
Romford,
Essex

Mrs P Clark,
RM9 7AZ
Mill Youth Club
Romford
19th May 19

Dear Pat,

I enclose a copy of a letter I have received from a resident living opposite the youth club. I do not know whether her allegations are true or false and I am unwilling to take any further action until I know the facts. Will you and your committee please investigate and let me have your observations in writing during the next few days.

Yours sincerely,

*Frank Waters*

---

This is a copy of the resident's letter:

148 Mill Street
Romford
Essex RM13 4PR
24th May 19__

Amenities Department
Town Hall
Romford
Essex

Dear Sir or Madam,

I live opposite the youth club and wish to complain about the noise, disturbance and damage caused by the members of the club.

On Mondays, Wednesdays and Fridays they keep their record player going at full volume from 7 o'clock until 10. As the doors and windows are always open the noise can be heard all along the street. In addition to this the young people run around our street shouting, singing and generally misbehaving.

On Saturdays when they have a disco the music is really deafening and the boys always get rowdy around 9 o'clock. After the disco a lot of the young people hang around the premises and along the street till as late as midnight laughing, talking and shouting. They also smoke and I have seen some aged only about fourteen with cans of beer which they leave empty in people's front gardens. I am frightened to tell them off as you never knew how they will react these days. I have also heard that some of the neighbours have had chalk scrawled on their fences and flowers and shrubs have been uprooted.

I think that this club is out of control and should be closed down before the hooliganism gets any worse. My husband and I are pensioners and he suffers with his nerves. We cannot take much more of this.

Yours faithfully,
Irene Smithers (Mrs)

The youth club leader holds a full investigation into Mrs Smithers' complaints and finds that some of what she says is true while some is exaggerated. Here are the notes she makes before replying to the two letters:

MON, WED, FRI — record player has been getting louder & louder recently. Windows are usually open, especially in summer.

Younger members of the club do keep running in & out of club during evening.

SAT DISCOS — music no louder than Mon-Fri, but does go on till 11.

Some boys from town (not this club) had a big fight outside club 4 weeks ago. We called police. Otherwise behaviour not too bad. Members say there are rarely fights. Other youth leaders & I send kids home from street around 11.30. Sometimes they're noisy but high-spirited. - nothing unpleasant.

GENERAL POINTS — some members do smoke. We stop those under 16 & try to advise those over 16! Beer (& drugs!) absolutely banned. Members all hotly deny having any drink at all near club.

They're annoyed about comments about gardens — say no-one ever goes near neighbours' gardens. Some members visit elderly residents nearby & we have annual party for over-60s. Club has a members' committee who try hard to keep behaviour sensible.

We need at least 2 more adult helpers. All our youth leaders work v. hard but we've had fewer organised activities lately because not enough staff - maybe kids are a bit bored?

# Assignments

**1**  Write Pat Clark's letter to Mr Waters stating clearly what was found out during the investigation. Say what precautions you are going to take to prevent the possibility of further complaints.

**2**  Pat Clark then decides that she should write to Mrs Smithers herself. Write her letter, in which she tries to reassure Mrs Smithers. Be honest about the facts, and keep the *tone* (see page 127) of the letter polite and respectful. Remember to apologise where appropriate.

**3**  How can youth clubs avoid this situation? Draw up a list of 'dos' and 'don'ts' about acceptable behaviour, attitudes etc, to be issued to all youth club members.

---

## Formal and informal letters

Mrs Smithers writes a *formal* letter to the Town Hall because she does not know the name of the person she is writing to.
Note: Dear Sir or Madam,
        Yours faithfully,

Frank Waters' letter to Pat Clark is *informal* (even though it is on council notepaper) because he knows Pat.
Note: Dear Pat,
        Yours sincerely,

---

**4**  **a**  The youth club goes on to hold a meeting with elderly local residents, aimed at improving understanding.
   Choose one person to be Pat Clark and chair the meeting; half the class to be youth club members; the other half to be elderly neighbours (including Irene Smithers).
   Act out what happens at the meeting.
**b**  Write up the minutes of this meeting (see pages 60–62).

In the early chapters of a novel, the author may include incidents which appear to have little relevance to the plot. By looking at the details carefully, however, we can often pick up clues about how characters will behave later. Read this passage, which comes from a book set in Africa.

The hills and the ridges now lay behind. This was a plain, the only such level stretch of land in this country. If you strained your eyes and peered into the misty distance you could see the land of Ukabi. It was all peaceful on this plain, which was said to have been a field of battle, once long ago. A few cattle pulled and mauled the grass while others lay down looking vacantly into space, chewing.

Suddenly, two boys emerged from the bush. They began to fight. One was tall and his unusually long neck and limbs made him appear older than he really was. He was Kamau, son of Kabonyi from Makuyu. The other, Kinuthia, was shorter with surprisingly strong muscles. His slow wide eyes well matched his smooth forehead. He lived with his uncle at a village beyond the two ridges away from Makuyu. His father had died early.

At first the boys fought with the sticks they had gone to fetch from the bush. The green sticks caught each other in mid-air several times and were soon in pieces. The boys threw them away and one piece touched a cow, which stood up quickly, frightened. It moved a few paces from the struggling pair, waking two others on the way. Then it looked in the opposite direction, unconcerned with the fight.

Kamau and Kinuthia were now wrestling. Their arms were inter-locked and the two boys went round and round without either getting the better of the other. Kinuthia tried to lift Kamau off the ground and then trap him with his right leg. The attempt always failed. Kamau had his struggles too. Though not usually voluble, today he was eloquent with threats.

'You will know who I am,' he warned, at the same time using his right knee to hit Kinuthia's stomach.

'Cow,' cried Kinuthia with pain.

'Hyena.'

'Even you,' Kinuthia hissed back.

Kinuthia appeared much more collected, and an observer would have thought that he would win. But he tripped over a sharp stone and soon was lying prostrate on his stomach. Kamau bent over him and pinned Kinuthia's hands behind his head. His face was grim and con-torted as he used his head to dig into Kinuthia's face, making his nose bleed. The boy underneath Kamau's knees felt pain. He thrust his legs in the air hoping to catch Kamau by the neck between the legs. Blows fell on him and he was bewildered, not knowing when and where the next blow would follow.

Two cows that had moved away together turned their heads and watched the struggle for a while. Then they bent their heads, thrusting out their tongues to pull and maul the grass like the others.

Just then, another boy came running from a group of cows a distance away.

'Stop fighting!' he shouted breathlessly as he stood near the pair. Kamau stopped, but he still sat on Kinuthia.

'Why are you fighting?'

'He called me names,' answered Kamau.

'He is a liar. He laughed at me because my father died poor and . . .'

'He called my father a convert to the white man.'

'He is!'

'You beggar.'

'White man's slave.'

'You . . . you . . .'

Kamau became furious. He began to pinch Kinuthia. Kinuthia looked appealingly to the other boy.

'Please stop this, Kamau. Didn't we swear that we of the hills were comrades?' He felt helpless. It was three days earlier that they had sworn to be brothers.

'What do I care about comrades who insult my father?' asked Kamau.

'I will do it again,' retorted Kinuthia between tears.

'Do now.'

'I will.'

'Try!'

Kamau and Kinuthia began to struggle. The boy felt an irresistible urge to fall on Kamau; he pulled a blade of grass and began to chew it quickly, his eyes dilating with rage and fear.

'Kamau,' he burst out.

The tremor in the boy's voice sent a quiver of fear up Kamau. He quickly looked up and met the burning eyes, gazing at him. Meekly he obeyed the unspoken command. But his face went a shade darker than it normally was. He slunk away, feeling humiliated and hating himself for submitting. Kinuthia stood up unsteadily and looked gratefully at the boy. The boy kept on lowering his face, gazing at the same spot. The feeling of pride and triumph he had suddenly felt at seeing Kamau obey him had as suddenly subsided to one of regret at having done that to him. Perhaps it might have felt better if Kamau had stuck it out and he had had to use force to remove him.

The boy's name was Waiyaki, the only son of Chege. He was quite young; not of Kamau or Kinuthia's age. He had not even gone through his second birth. Waiyaki was, however, already tall for his age. He had a well-built, athletic body. His hair was tough and dry with kinks that finished in a clear outline on the forehead. Just above the left eye was a slightly curved scar. He had got it from a wild goat. The goat had run after one of the herdboys. Seeing this, Waiyaki had taken a stick and run after the goat shouting. The goat turned on him and jabbed him with his horns, tearing the flesh to the bone. His father arrived in time to save him. That was a long while ago. The wound had healed, leaving him a hero among the boys although he had run after the goat for sheer fun and enjoyment of the scene. That, however, was not the sole reason why the other boys, young and old, promptly followed him.

104

**Writing about characters**

**1** Make close observations from the text:
- What characters *say* may reveal their attitudes and the way(s) they relate to other people.
- What they *do* (their actions) can reveal abilities and feelings.
- What we're *told* about them (what other characters say or think about them; what the author tells us about their personalities and thoughts) can give us additional insights.

**2** Draw conclusions from your observations – ask questions about what you have noticed. For instance
- Does the observation help us to deduce more about this character? Or about another character?
- Does it help us understand a relationship between two characters?
- Does it tell us more about what is happening? About what has happened? Or about what will or might happen?
- How does this observation further our understanding of the story?

## *Assignments*

☞ **1** Study the passage carefully, then copy and complete this chart on Kinuthia.

| ***What he says*** | ***What we conclude from this*** |
|---|---|
| 1 He calls Kamau animal names. | 1 Perhaps he is a typical small boy fighting. |
| 2 He calls Kamau a liar and says he laughed at him because Kinuthia's father died poor. | 2 |
| 3 | 3 He scorns tribesmen who are converted to the white man's religion. |
| ***What he does*** | |
| 1 He wrestles with Kamau. | 1 |
| 2 | 2 He looks likely to win the fight. |
| 3 He looks at Waiyaki for help. | 3 |
| 4 He looks gratefully at Waiyaki for stopping the fight. | 4 |
| 5 He is older than Waiyaki but still obeys him. | 5 |
| ***What we're told about him*** | |
| 1 He is small but strong. | 1 He looks weaker than he is. |
| 2 His father died early. | 2 |
| 3 He had sworn to be a brother to Kamau. | 3 |

☞ **2**  Now do the same for this chart on Kamau.

| What he says | What we conclude from this |
|---|---|
| 1 | 1 He seems to want to assert himself. |
| 2 He says Kinuthia began the fight. | 2 |
| 3 | 3 He mocks poor people. |
| 4 | 4 He seems to bear a grudge. |
| **What he does** | |
| 1 He fights fiercely with Kinuthia. | 1 |
| 2 He stops fighting as soon as he hears Waiyaki's voice. | 2 |
| 3 He lets the fight break out again. | 3 |
| 4 He obeys Waiyaki. | 4 |
| **What we're told about him** | |
| 1 He is tall and looks old for his age. | 1 |
| 2 He is not usually talkative. | 2 |
| 3 | 3 He seems to take the fight very seriously. |
| 4 | 4 He seems strangely afraid of Waiyaki. |
| 5 | 5 He didn't want to stop the fight. |
| 6 He feels humiliated. | 6 |

☞ **3**  Using the same headings, make out a similar chart of your own for Waiyaki.

○ **4**  Judging by this incident in their early life, which of the three do you think will turn out to be:

    **a** A respected and loved (although not always wise) leader of men?
    **b** A weaker man yet a good friend to the leader?
    **c** Someone who wanted to be leader but who did not have the strength of character?

Give reasons based on this passage to support your answer.

○ **5**  Look back at the passage and say whether each of the following statements is true, partly true or false. Give a reason for each answer.

    **a** Kamau is sensitive about his father's memory.
    **b** Waiyaki has a charismatic personality.
    **c** Kamau and Kinuthia have been rivals for a long time.

**d** The white man's religion is held in low regard.
**e** Waiyaki shows a realisation that some of his decisions are not made wisely.
**f** Kamau is afraid of Waiyaki.

**6** **a** In about 200 words write an outline for a novel featuring three main adult characters.
**b** Describe the personalities of each of the three main characters. (Use 50–100 words for each.)

**7** Write a chapter from the beginning of the novel in which all three main characters are seen as children. Make sure that the personalities they are to have as adults are already apparent.

Are different newspapers written for certain types of readers?

It is often interesting to see how different newspapers treat the same subject. Here are three accounts of boxer Frank Bruno's world title fight against Tim Witherspoon.

# BRAVE BRUNO FAILS

**A** The haunting theme tune from The Greatest Story Ever Told, the movie of Muhammad Ali's life, floated through Frank Bruno's dressing room, adding its own touch of pathos.

Terry Lawless, sat sadly alongside his beaten fighter, clutched Bruno as the words drifted across: 'They can't take your dignity away . . .'

'Just listen, Frank – because those words apply to you. Nobody can say you didn't give it everything,' said Lawless.

The big man sprawled next to him listening, an ice-bag held to the side of his face to ease the throbbing pain in his bruised and swollen right jaw, dark glasses shielding the bumps and swellings around his eyes.

Frank Bruno's dream of conquering the world had ended some two hours earlier.

Across the narrow corridor that separates the different worlds of winners and losers dressing rooms at Wembley Stadium, Tim Witherspoon was beginning his celebrations.

### Disappointed

His 11th-round victory kept the WBA heavyweight title in American hands, frustrating once again a nation's longing to see a Briton crowned king for the first time this century.

And Bruno, as if feeling personal responsibility for the whole lot of 'em, said: 'I'm just disappointed for all those fans. I feel I have let them down.

'It was a very tough fight. I had him going a few times but in the end I lost to a better fighter.

'He just knew a bit too much for me. And he done me, good and proper.'

The words came out in little more than a whisper. Bruno was finding it difficult to speak through the pain of that jaw.

They say that four o'clock in the morning is the lowest time of the day. Nobody in Bruno's vicinity would argue with that.

*But don't feel guilty, Frank, we told him.*

There's no shame in a performance full of strength and courage that at least showed the world one Briton with the heart of a lion.

(*Star*)

## BRUNO LEFT IN A WASTELAND

**B** Frank Bruno was like an intrepid explorer trekking the icy waste: the wind began to bite and suddenly he slipped into a crevasse, dragging down with him the paraphernalia of the operation which had launched him and raised the hopes of thousands.

The way in which Tim Witherspoon, the World Boxing Association champion, had suddenly turned their heavyweight fight at Wembley Stadium in the early hours of yesterday – reducing Bruno to a crumpled heap, his face distorted and swollen – had magnified all the doubts about the British hope's fighting skills.

Round by round the rigidity and stiffness of Bruno's boxing contrasted with the swinging street-corner style of the man from Philadelphia.

And for moments during the first seven rounds it looked as though the open-mouthed, heavy-breathing Witherspoon, lumbering clumsily as he threw his swinging rights which often merely cut through the air, would be exhausted by his own efforts. But then the neatness which Bruno had remembered to bring with him from Canning Town, proved to be no more than drawing board material.

He did not have the flexibility or the speed to profit from the loopholes in Witherspoon's approach. From the outer darkness beyond the Wembley touchlines it probably looked as though Bruno was doing rather well in those early rounds. His jabs and hooks sometimes connected, but they were often no more than taps to remind the American that the Englishman held all the aces when it came to reach.

Bruno ought to have produced more sweeping moves across the ring, danced a little in rhythm with his left jab. In retrospect, bouncing in and out would have been a way to pluck something from the untidy and ungainly Witherspoon.

A left to the head drove Bruno back into a neutral corner, lifting his hands to paw away the danger. He slid across the ropes into Witherspoon's corner, and slowly went down under a flailing barrage of punches which continued long after he was unable to defend himself.

A first cursory examination which indicated that Bruno's jaw was broken proved to be unconfirmed, but the pain of the injury to his pride from which Bruno was suffering kept him locked in his dressing room away from the media.

Witherspoon was magnanimous to a courageous opponent, 'I thought he was ahead, then I was ahead. It was a close, hard fight and he should not think about retiring. I said those rippling muscles of his were no good, but I'm sure he can come back again.'

(*Guardian*)

# FANS HAIL BRUNO AS TITLE BID FAILS

C    The only thing Frank Bruno lost at Wembley in the early hours of yesterday was a fight. In the 11 rounds he battled with world heavyweight champion Tim Witherspoon he grew in status as a fighting man and earned an undying place in the affection of the fans.

The reaction of the 42,000 crowd after Bruno had crumpled in a corner was wonderfully uplifting.

They paid more than £2 million hoping to cheer Britain's first heavyweight champion of the world this century. They stayed on to try to console him.

They cheered and they chanted his name. They sang 'Frankie, we love you' in a demonstration which came from the heart.

What they had seen was the best attempt by any British fighter since the war to win the greatest prize in sport.

They took to Bruno because he gave the last ounces of his heart and guts – and showed ability enough to suggest a long way into the fight that he had a real winning chance.

It was a classic clash of Street Fighter and Gym Fighter and the unfortunate thing was that the manufacturing of Bruno was incomplete.

For five rounds the British optimism continued. Witherspoon tried for an early knock-out but Bruno frustrated him and landed punches enough not only to take a points lead but to hurt him.

More significant was the draining effect on Bruno of those perilous, flattering early rounds.

The snap began to go out of his punches and gradually Witherspoon forced him into the battle of attrition he knew he would win.

In that time Bruno took punches which answered the question about the strength of his chin. So many quick wins in his career meant he lacked experience of pacing a fight and of developing stamina.

Yet he was still trying to win the fight when he lost it. Knowing the fight was slipping away from him he shook Witherspoon with good punches and dropped his guard to put extra weight into another right. A split second after it landed Witherspoon connected with a countering right.

As Bruno backed off. Witherspoon landed two more rights. There was a left hook then four more rights – only one was less than perfect.

**Mindless**

Bruno was slumping as he took the last two and there was no question he would be allowed to take more. The bell went as the count reached three but referee Isidro Rodriguez had already decided to stop it and the towel thrown by Terry Lawless made the decision unanimous.

(*Daily Mail*)

# Assignments

☞ **1**　**a** Which of the three articles gives the most detailed account of the fight?
**b** Which of the three concentrates almost entirely on Bruno himself?
**c** Which one has most to say about the fans' admiration for Bruno?

☞ **2**　**a** What attitude towards Bruno does each article adopt?
**b** What impression of Witherspoon does each article convey?

☞ **3**　**a** Describe in your own words why you think Bruno is compared to an 'intrepid explorer' (*Guardian*).
**b** Why do you think the *Star* mentions the theme tune from *The Greatest Story Ever Told*?
**c** Explain the meaning of the first sentence in the *Daily Mail* article.
**d** The *Guardian* writer offers Bruno advice on his fighting technique. What does he suggest?
**e** The *Star* includes Bruno's own words. What do you think this adds to the article?
**f** The *Daily Mail* questions the strength of Bruno's chin. What does it give as the answer?

**4**　**a** Can you find any *clichés* (see p 120) in any of the three articles? If so, write them down. Explain your reactions to each of the expressions you have picked out.
**b** Can you find any *metaphors* or *similes* (see p 39)? If so, write them down and suggest why you think the writer(s) use(s) them.
**c** How would you describe the *tone* of each of the articles (see p 127)?

**5**　**a** Explain the approach of the three opening paragraphs.
**b** Sum up the mood of the final paragraph of each article.

**6**　**a** List all the daily papers you know that are printed in this country.
**b** If possible, obtain a copy of each of them. Suggest what kind of reader each paper is aimed at.
**c** How does consideration of a particular type of reader affect the sports pages? Note down the differences in: how many sports pages there are; what sports are covered; which sports seem most popular; how they are covered.
**d** Look back at the three articles in this section, and your answers to assignments **1–5**. Do your findings there agree with your answers to **6a**, **b** and **c**?

✔ ✎ **7**　Compare and contrast the three articles, explaining carefully what you like and dislike about them. You might like to consider the following:

- the organisation of the article
- the way the two fighters are presented
- details included about the fight
- mood or emotion created
- language.

Remember to quote or refer closely to particular words and paragraphs from each article to support what you say.

**8** Copy out this crossword and complete it. Each answer can be found in one of the articles about Bruno's fight. *Scan* the three articles until you find words similar to those in the clue. The answer will then be close by.

**Clues**

*Across*
2 They hoped he'd be _____ ____ the world (8,2)
3 Not the street-corner style (8)
4 (Explorer's) bits and pieces (13)
5 The corner Frank visited after a left to the head (7)
6 Frank's good punches did this to Tim (5)
7 Celebrations starting for Tim (9)
8 Between the worlds of winners and losers (8)
9 All agreed when Lawless threw in the towel (9)
10 Frank's undying place is in the fans' _____ (9)
11 Witherspoon was magnanimous to a courageous one. (8)

*Down*
1 Did he really trek the icy waste? (5,5)

# U·N·I·T  30  *What form of English?*

The form of English used in a piece of writing is very important. Just as you need to think about this carefully before you begin writing, so you also need to be aware of it as you are reading. In the box are definitions of some of the technical terms associated with forms of English. You will need to refer to this as you do the work which follows.

**Register** – a form of language, especially vocabulary, appropriate for a particular situation eg local dialect and slang when talking to a friend; legal terms when writing a legal document; Standard English when writing something to be understood by all English speakers.

**Dialect** – special words, word order, grammar and accent used in a certain form of English. A dialect is usually spoken in a particular area, but it may also belong to a particular social class or occupational group. For example, *Moi friend whass the nurse say hiz now comin* (Norwich dialect – My friend, who's the nurse, says he's on his way); *The wee'er laddies fight with other yins a round the scheme* (Edinburgh – The smaller boys fight with the other ones all round the estate).

**Accent** – the way words are pronounced, usually in a certain area, but also often associated with a particular social class, eg *Me Fahver's very fin* (London – My father's very thin); *I've gorra gerra job dere* (Liverpool – I've got to get a job there); *He nahz that short's too lang* (Newcastle – he knows that shirt's too long).

**Standard English** – a form of English known and understood by most English speakers, eg the English used on television and radio news bulletins; formal English appropriate for most writing tasks.

**Colloquial language** – chatty language used only in speech and not usually considered appropriate in written English, eg *nosy*; *trendy sort of chap*; *use your loaf – you're supposed to be brainy!*

**Slang** – a more extreme form of colloquial language, used when the writer/speaker is very sure of his reader/listener. It is often more vulgar, humorous, unusual and obscure than colloquial English, eg *I get a kick out of winding him up*; *that bird you fancy is starkers*; *the gaffer gave that geezer the bullet*.

Writers may choose to use different registers for a number of different reasons. For instance, read this extract from *Sons and Lovers* by D H Lawrence, a novel set in Nottingham.

At half-past eleven her husband came. His cheeks were very red and very shiny above his black moustache. His head nodded slightly. He was pleased with himself.

'Oh! Oh! waitin' for me, lass? I've bin 'elpin' Anthony; an' what's think he's gen me? Nowt b'r a lousy hae'f-crown, an' that's ivry penny ——'

'He thinks you've made the rest up in beer,' she said shortly.

'An' I 'aven't – that I 'aven't. You b'lieve me. I've 'ad very little this day, I have an' all.' His voice went tender. 'Here, an' I browt thee a bit o' brandysnap, an' a coconut for th' children.' He laid the gingerbread and the coconut, a hairy object, on the table. 'Nay, tha niver said thankyer for nowt i' thy life, did ter?'

As a compromise, she picked up the coconut and shook it, to see if it had any milk.

'It's a good 'un, you may back yer life o' that. I got it fra' Bill Hodgkisson. "Bill," I says, "tha non wants them three nuts, does ter? Arena ter for gi'ein' me one for my bit of a lad an' wench?" "I ham, Walter, my lad'" 'e says; "ta'e which on 'em ter's a mind." An' so I took one, an' thanked 'im. I didn't like ter shake it afore 'is eyes, but 'e says, "Tha'd better ma'e sure it's a good un, Walt." An' so, yer see, I knowed it was. He's a nice chap is Bill Hodgkisson, 'e's a nice chap!'

'A man will part with anything so long as he's drunk, and you're drunk along with him,' said Mrs Morel.

'Eh, tha mucky little 'ussy, who's drunk, I sh'd like ter know?' said Morel. He was extraordinarily pleased with himself, because of his day's helping to wait in the Moon and Stars. He chattered on.

Mrs Morel, very tired, and sick of his babble, went to bed as quickly as possible, while he raked the fire.

## *Assignments*

☞ **1** First, work out what happens in the passage by answering these questions:

  **a** Where has Walter been?
  **b** Why does his voice go tender, do you think? (line 8)
  **c** What does he accuse his wife of? (lines 10–11)
  **d** Why does it say 'as a compromise', do you think? (line 12)
  **e** Where did Walter get the coconut from?
  **f** Give a line from the passage which shows how Mrs Morel feels about her husband.

**2** **a** Mr Morel speaks in the Nottingham dialect. Copy out the chart below and use the passage to complete this glossary.

| Standard English | Nottingham dialect |
| --- | --- |
| from | |
| every | |
| | afore |
| Aren't you | |
| | ha'ef |
| | tha |
| knew | |
| | nowt |
| | lass |
| | 'ussy |

**b** Find some other examples of your own from the passage, to add to the glossary.

**3** **a** What do you notice about the way Mrs Morel speaks?
**b** Do the registers chosen for the two characters suggest anything about social class? How might this affect their relationship?

**4** Using *ALL* the evidence from the passage, write about the relationship between Mr and Mrs Morel, as you see it.

This extract is from a story about a girl called Lorraine, written by Farrukh Dhondy.

She was a coloured kid, or at least she was a half-caste or something like that. We always called them 'coloured' when I first went to school because we didn't think there was nothing wrong with it; but after, some of them would thump you if you called them 'coloured'. They didn't like that, they wanted to be called 'black'. I'm not really sure to this day what she was, on account of never seeing her mum or dad. All the other kids would talk about their mums and dads and the gear they had indoors, but Lorraine always kept herself to herself. She wasn't much to look at and she didn't get on with any of the other girls, because some of the white girls were right snobbish. The other coloured kids would talk black when the teachers weren't there, and they left Lorraine out because she never.

She was good at sports and she was good at drama. I wouldn't have noticed her, I tell you, because at that age I wasn't interested in girls. The other lads would talk about what they done with girls and that, but I couldn't be bothered, and because I was skint till the fourth year, I never took no girls out or even let the kids in the class know who I fancied. It was a girl in our class called Wendy. She had a nasty tongue, but I liked her. I remembered the first time Lorraine and I stood in the free dinner queue, Wendy said, 'She looks like she needs them and all.' The other kids laughed, and I must have blushed all over my fat cheeks. Old Cobblers didn't tell Wendy off or have a go at her, and Lorraine just pretended she didn't hear.

☞ 5 Here are a number of words and phrases from the passage which may be considered *dialect*, *colloquial* or *slang*. (Sometimes it is difficult to distinguish.) Copy and complete the chart below, putting the words and phrases where you think they belong.

| Dialect | Colloquial | Slang |
|---|---|---|
| kid | I never took no | tell off |
| didn't think nothing | right snobbish | talk black |
| have a go at | there was | she never |
| thump | lads | on account of |
| what they done | mum or dad | and that |
| gear | skint | fancied |
| wasn't much to look at | get on with | and all |

☞ 6 **a** Why do you think the writer has chosen this register for the story? Do you agree with his choice?
**b** Why do you think it is written in the first person ('I first went to school . . .') rather than the third person ('He first went to school . . .')?

✑ ☞ 7 Rewrite the passage in Standard English. Compare your version with the original. Is anything lost or gained? Explain your opinion.

116

Now look at this poem, which is written in Jamaican dialect.

**Harassment**
One evenin, me a com from wok,
An a run fe ketch de bus,
Two police start fe run me dung,
Jus fe show how me no hav no luck,
Dem ketch me and start to mek a fus
Sa, a long time dem a watch how me
A heng, heng, round de shop

Me say What? Heng round shop?
From morning me daa work,
Me only jus stop,                                    10
And if onoo tink a lie me a tell,
Gwaan go ask de Manager.

Dem insisted I was a potential thief,
And teck me to de station,
Anyway, dem send and call me relations,
Wen dem com it was a big relief,
Fe se som one me own colour,
At least, who would talk and laugh wid me,

An me still lock up ina Jail,
So till me people dem insist that            20
Dem go a me wok to get som proof,
The police man dem nearly hit the roof,
Because dem feel dem was so sure,
That is me dem did have dem eyes on
Boy, I don't know what's rong
With these babylon men,
But dem can't tell one black man,
From de other one.

Anyway, when me reach me wok place,
Straight away de manager recognize me face,   30
And we go check me card,
Fe se sa me dis clock out

So me gather strength and say to de coppers,
Leggo me, onoo don't know wey onoo on about,
You want fe se dem face sa dem a apologize,
But wen me look pon how me nearly face disgrace,
It mek me want fe kus and fight,
But wey de need, in a babylon sight,
If yu right yu rong,
And wen yu rong you double rong,              40

So me a beg onoo, teck heed
Always have a good alibi,
Because even though yu innocent
Someone always a try
Fe mek yu bid freedom goodbye.

*Frederick Williams*

☞ **8**    Sum up briefly what the poem is about.

☞ **9**    **a** Write a glossary of dialect words and phrases (similar to the one you did on the Lawrence passage in assignment **2**).
**b** Discuss why you think the poet chose to use these particular phrases in the poem:

> *A heng, heng* (line 7)
> *insisted I was a potential thief* (line 13)
> *nearly hit the roof* (line 22)
> *Boy, I don't know . . .* (line 25)
> *If yu right yu rong* (line 39)

**c** What other parts of the poem strike you, and for what reasons?
**d** What does the use of dialect suggest about the man's feelings towards the police and towards the society he lives in? Would the poem be as effective if it were written in Standard English?

**10**    Write your own poem, play or short story about two people who do not relate very well to one another. Emphasise their poor relationship by making them speak in different registers. Perhaps one register could be the dialect local to your area or the colloquial expressions and slang you use with your friends. Some ideas:

a husband and wife; a policeman and a member of the public; a social worker and a client; a boss and a worker; a teacher and a pupil.

**11**    Act out a scene like that described in **10**.

**12**    **a** The definitions and examples on page 113 may be considered as working definitions only, rather than rigid categories. For instance, if you look up 'nosy' in some dictionaries you will find it listed as *slang*, rather than colloquial language. What other variations can you find?
**b** Why do you think these variatic ns occur?
**c** Using large dictionaries and books about the history of English, can you find any words which were once slang or dialect, but which are now accepted as Standard English?

118

Here are Simon Rae's own thoughts about the two versions of his poem on pages 70–71.

❛ In the first draft I compare leaves to moths. Leaves hitting the windscreen were a part of the experience I'm trying to capture in the poem. Night driving in the summer involves the windscreen being struck by moths, attracted to the headlights – I used 'inaccurate' there to indicate the fact that they'd missed, but later changed it to '*crippled* moths' (to suggest the curled up, twisted state of the leaves). It was only at the last minute that I ditched this image. There was something too elaborate about it.

I changed 'a sergeant . . . directs us' to 'a sergeant . . . leaps out' because I wanted something more active, more startling, more in keeping with the ghost-train idea of things suddenly appearing before your eyes that I develop in the next few lines.

I changed 'the incline tilts us' to 'as we climb' because the latter is simpler. Also, I thought it better to follow 'and the engine says "Aargh"' with something else, rather than a full-stop. The 'Aargh' is probably the boldest part of the image, and often with something striking, the mind needs something easy and undemanding immediately afterwards, so it can go on thinking about, and savouring it. 'As we climb' lets the reader down very gently, leaving him or her ready for the next thing.

I changed 'the ghost train hits the straight' because I felt the reader might begin to wonder whether it was in fact a car journey that was being described. And I keep the idea of the ghost-train, which I think quite powerful for evoking the way things suddenly loom up as you drive along minor country roads at night, in the 'ghost-train facade' bit that follows.

'The road's ill-repaired punctures' is an example of a paradoxical[1] image with the road taking on the qualities of the car's tyres ('punctures'); but on review, it seemed over-elaborate, so I cut it.

The changes involving the hanging moon are basically to do with the form of the poem. The long baggy lines of the first draft were never intended to be the final shape of the poem. Line endings are of great importance, and a great deal of my revision time is spent on them. In this poem I was helped by the decision to employ a loose form of rhyme (back/doc(tor's); engine/then; luminous/us, etc). So the 'moon' lines were rearranged so that I got 'from' and 'elm' rhyming, and 'tragically' and 'easily'. 'Arthritic' was added to give a sense of the branch's weird shape – bent, crooked, twisted.

I changed 'powdered' to 'ground' partly because 'ground' gets more of the grittiness, the underfootness, of the frost. Also, because this is a light, jokey poem, I liked the pun. 'Confetti' might be overdoing it, but I liked the two 'c's in the line (balanced by the two 'g's in the last line), and needed a rhyme for 'we'. ❜

*1 seems to be absurd*

☞ **3** **a** Which of Simon's comments here do you find interesting and why?
**b** On which points would you want to disagree? State your reasons.

☞ **4** What have you learnt from this unit which might help you redraft your own written pieces?

# U·N·I·T 31 *Keeping it fresh*

---

**Cliché** – any expression which has been used so often that its freshness has worn out and its meaning is no longer clear. Similarly, cliché can also refer to an idea or situation which has been used too often to be effective.

---

Certain types of writing and speaking often seem to be full of clichés. The three examples given below are: an extract from a romantic novel; a newspaper article; and a party political broadcast.

## A    Romantic novel

Ralph turned towards her, his firm gaze slowly meeting her ocean-deep blue eyes. He placed one of his strong yet sensitive hands on her shoulder. Ann quivered as his touch sent her tingling. 'I have to go now,' he said. 'I have a board meeting at three o'clock.' Gently, she straightened his elegant tie and removed one of her caramel golden hairs from his well-tailored sleeve.

'Will you be back?' she questioned tremulously. His tanned features burst into a wide smile revealing his even gleaming teeth.

'What do you think?' he laughed. Her look was serious, appealing – hardly daring to hope.

'But you're always so . . . so . . . busy . . .,' she stammered.

'Not too busy for you,' he replied, his husky voice suddenly serious and intense. 'Ann, I don't know how to say this,' he continued, 'but I want you to know . . . that is . . . you've taught me what love really is. Since I've met you I'm a changed man. I . . . oh God, I . . .'

His words ebbed away like a quietly flowing tide as the classical beauty of Ann's radiant features rendered him speechless. Suddenly, she was in his arms. His lips touched hers, gently at first like the touch of a butterfly's wing or a silken rose petal. Her heart gave a leap and her breath was stopped at the magic of that mouth-to-mouth contact. Then his eyes were blazing with passion and as he held her firmly against him she could feel the steady strong beat of his heart and the warmth and fervour of his love for her.

## B Newspaper article

SWIMMER JAN TO TAKE THE PLUNGE

Amid mounting speculation over the past few days, lovely swimmer turned model Janice Crippen announced yesterday that she is to take the plunge and marry her long time live-in lover, football's Mr Soccer Rex Peters. Shapely Janice, 22, quipped, 'Well, he can't play the field for ever, can he?' Only two months ago rugged six-footer Peters, 25, was to be seen with actress and one time debutante Jane Parmenter as his constant companion. Sources close to Janice then described her as heartbroken.

But last week Janice's anguish turned to joy as Rex finally made his peace and named the day.

The radiant fun-loving bride-to-be gave us an exclusive interview and confided in our reporter: 'When Rex was seeing Jane it was like living a lie. I was devastated and thought I would never be the same again. But now that's all behind us. We've put it all down to experience – that's the name of the game.'

Looking bronzed and fit, redhead Janice says they are to tie the knot in August at a quiet ceremony in the heart of the Sussex countryside. After the nuptials she will take a honeymoon and a well deserved rest with ex-playboy centre-half Rex – her Mr Right who nearly got away.

## C Party political broadcast

Friends, it is in no uncertain terms that I speak to you today about the no-win situation confronting this great land of ours. At this moment in time raging unemployment and galloping inflation threaten to rock the grass roots of our caring society. Everywhere there is a decline in the quality of life. As I go up and down the country and I look about me, I see things I find totally unacceptable and completely outrageous. When we return to power we will not fail in our duty. It is our stated objective to explore every avenue and to leave no stone unturned in seeking to right these wrongs. It is clear that we need to engage in meaningful dialogue across the table to build a better and a brighter future.

But, when all is said and done, at the end of the day, how will you use your cross on polling day? This is not a time to sit on the fence. Now more than ever before is the time for us to stand shoulder to shoulder, to speak out for what is right and to stand up and be counted. In all honesty, it is only when the rank and file of this country does its little bit that each and every one of us will reap the rewards. The wind of change is blowing and, although we fight against overwhelming odds, if we ignore the gloom and doom mongers amongst us we can put our shoulders to the wheel and face the future together. In the last analysis it needs us all to pull together if we are to see the light at the end of the tunnel.

# Assignments

☞ **1**  **a**  List all the words and phrases in extract **A** which strike you as typical of the language used in romantic novels.
**b**  Put a cross by the ones which you feel are clichés.
**c**  Now look at the characters. Do you think there is anything predictable about: their appearance? their actions? their dialogue? Explain your answers.
**d**  From this extract, what can you deduce about the plot of the story? Do you suspect that it could be rather stale? Give reasons for your answer.

☞ **2**  **a**  In example **B** there are many expressions which are used repeatedly by journalists. List as many as you can.
**b**  What kind of person is the newspaper trying to suggest that Janice is?
**c**  What kind of person is Rex presented as?
**d**  Do you think this article conveys their real personalities, or is the newspaper merely projecting an 'image' for each of them?

☞ **3**  **a**  Read example **C** and list the expressions which you have heard politicians use many times.
**b**  Put a cross by the ones which seem to mean nothing or almost nothing.
**c**  Judging from what this politician says, sum up briefly what you think his party's policies are. Or is it impossible to tell?
**d**  What kind of person do you think the politician is? Is it likely that you would be influenced by what he says? Or would it depend?

☞ **4**  **a**  In what other types of written or spoken English would you expect clichés to occur frequently? Give some examples.
**b**  Suggest reasons why writers and/or speakers use clichés.

✍ **5**  Rewrite each of the examples above, trying to use no clichés at all. How do your versions compare with the originals?

✔✍ **6**  A humorous effect can be obtained by deliberately exaggerating the predictable features of a certain kind of writing. Compose a piece of writing or your own (about 400 words) in which you deliberately use as many clichés as possible. You may choose a romantic novel, a newspaper article, a politician's speech, or some other idea of your own (detective story; teenage magazine article; episode of a soap opera; Western; children's television programme; interview with a pop star . . .)

✔ ○ **7**  Perform a speech, sketch or short play along the same lines as **6** above.

# U·N·I·T 32 Writing for an audience

This is an extract from *Silas Marner* by George Eliot, a novel written in the nineteenth century (as you might guess from the rather difficult vocabulary). The passage here describes how Silas, a middle-aged weaver, begins to look after Eppie, a toddler he has adopted. As you read it, look for signs that the book was written for an adult audience.

It was clear that Eppie, with her short toddling steps, must lead father Silas a pretty dance on any fine morning when circumstances favoured mischief.

For example. He had wisely chosen a broad strip of linen as a means of fastening her to his loom when he was busy: it made a broad belt round her waist, and was long enough to allow of her reaching the truckle-bed,[1] and sitting down on it, but not long enough for her to attempt any dangerous climbing. One bright summer's morning Silas had been more engrossed than usual in 'setting up' a new piece of work, an occasion on which his scissors were in **requisition**. These scissors, owing to an especial warning of Dolly's, had been kept carefully out of Eppie's reach; but the click of them had had a peculiar attraction for her ear, and watching the results of that click, she had derived the **philosophic** lesson that the same cause would produce the same effect. Silas had seated himself in his loom, and the noise of weaving had begun; but he had left his scissors on a ledge which Eppie's arm was long enough to reach; and now, like a small mouse, watching her opportunity, she stole quietly from her corner, secured the scissors, and toddled to the bed again, setting up her back as a mode of **concealing** the fact. She had a distinct intention as to the use of the scissors; and having cut the linen strip in a jagged but effectual manner, in two moments she had run out at the open door where the sunshine was inviting her, while poor Silas believed her to be a better child than usual. It was not until he happened to need his scissors that the terrible fact burst upon him: Eppie had run out by herself – had perhaps fallen into the Stone-pit. Silas, shaken by the worst fear that could have befallen him, rushed out, calling 'Eppie!' and ran eagerly about the unenclosed space, exploring the dry cavities into which she might have fallen, and then gazing with questioning dread at the smooth red surface of the water. The cold drops stood on his brow. How long had she been out? There was one hope – that she had crept through the stile and got into the fields where he habitually took her to stroll. But the grass was high in the meadow, and there was no **descrying** her, if she were there, except by a close search that would be a trespass on Mr Osgood's crop. Still, that **misdemeanour** must be committed; and poor Silas, after peering all round the hedgerows, traversed the grass, beginning with **perturbed**

*1 low bed on wheels*

123

vision to see Eppie behind every group of red sorrel, and to see her moving always farther off as he approached. The meadow was searched in vain; and he got over the stile into the next field, looking with dying hope towards a small pond which was now reduced to its summer shallowness, so as to leave a wide margin of good adhesive mud. Here, however, sat Eppie, **discoursing** cheerfully to her own small boot, which she was using as a bucket to convey the water into a deep hoof-mark, while her little naked foot was planted comfortably on a cushion of olive-green mud. A red-headed calf was observing her with alarmed doubt through the opposite hedge.

Here was clearly a case of **aberration** in a christened child which demanded severe treatment; but Silas, overcome with **convulsive** joy at finding his treasure again, could do nothing but snatch her up, and cover her with half-sobbing kisses. It was not until he had carried her home, and had begun to think of the necessary washing, that he recollected the need that he should punish Eppie, and 'make her remember.' The idea that she might run away again and come to harm, gave him unusual **resolution**, and for the first time he determined to try the coal-hole – a small closet near the hearth.

'Naughty, naughty Eppie,' he suddenly began, holding her on his knee, and pointing to her muddy feet and clothes – 'naughty to cut with the scissors and run away. Eppie must go into the coal-hole for being naughty. Daddy must put her in the coal-hole.'

He half-expected that this would be shock enough, and that Eppie would begin to cry. But instead of that, she began to shake herself on his knee, as if the proposition opened a pleasing novelty. Seeing that he must proceed to extremities, he put her into the coal-hole, and held the door closed, with a trembling sense that he was using a strong measure. For a moment there was silence, but then came a little cry, 'Opy, opy!' and Silas let her out again, saying, 'Now Eppie 'ull never be naughty again, else she must go in the coal-hole – a black, naughty place.'

The weaving must stand still a long while this morning, for now Eppie must be washed, and have clean clothes on; but it was to be hoped that this punishment would have a lasting effect, and save time in future – though, perhaps, it would have been better if Eppie had cried more.

In half an hour she was clean again, and Silas having turned his back to see what he could do with the linen band, threw it down again, with the reflection that Eppie would be good without fastening for the rest of the morning. He turned round again, and was going to place her in her little chair near the loom, when she peeped out at him with black face and hands again, and said, 'Eppie in de toal-hole!'

This total failure of the coal-hole discipline shook Silas's belief in the **efficacy** of punishment. 'She'd take it all for fun,' he observed to Dolly, 'if I didn't hurt her, and that I can't do, Mrs Winthrop. If she makes me a bit o'trouble, I can bear it. And she's got no tricks but what she'll grow out of.'

# Assignments

☞ **1**  First make sure that you understand the extract. Some of the more difficult words have been printed in bold type. They are listed below on the left and their meanings (as used in the passage) are in a muddled list on the right. Which meanings go with which words?

| | | | |
|---|---|---|---|
| 1 | requisition | a) | lecturing |
| 2 | philosophic | b) | wrong |
| 3 | concealing | c) | logical |
| 4 | descrying | d) | troubled |
| 5 | misdemeanour | e) | effectiveness |
| 6 | perturbed | f) | determination |
| 7 | discoursing | g) | finding |
| 8 | aberration | h) | demand |
| 9 | convulsive | i) | hiding |
| 10 | resolution | j) | lapse |
| 11 | proposition | k) | suggestion |
| 12 | efficacy | l) | feverish |

☞ **2**  These are the answers to questions on the text. Read them carefully and then write down what you think the questions are. Write the questions in the *best* form possible. Don't be satisfied until you are sure that you have expressed them as clearly and accurately as you can.

**a** First, he was very involved in his work, second the loom was noisy and third Eppie was very discreet in the way she escaped.

**b** We know this because it describes Eppie's escape as 'the worst fear that could have befallen him.'

**c** Silas becomes almost delirious as he searches for Eppie, imagining he sees her when she is not there.

**d** At first he is too over-joyed to do anything but hug and kiss her, but then he feels that Eppie should be punished for her own good.

**e** He is surprised because instead of looking upset, she seems excited by the idea of going in the coal-hole.

**f** We know this because we are told that Silas has 'a trembling sense that he was using a strong measure'.

**g** It says this because Silas is rather puzzled that Eppie does not seem particularly upset at her punishment.

**h** He probably thinks that now she has learnt her lesson she will not need to be restrained again.

**i** This comment confirms what he had suspected – that Eppie thinks the coal-hole is fun.

**j** The 'moral' of the episode is that Silas learnt that punishment is often ineffective and a waste of time.

**3** Rewrite this incident as a story for young children. As you do this, bear in mind the advice in the box.

If you like, you may use this opening:

*Once there was a little girl called Eppie. She lived a long time ago with her daddy who was a weaver. She was often quite naughty and got up to all sorts of mischief. Are you like that too? Let me tell you what she did on one bright summer's morning.*

---

**Writing for young children**

- Stories often address the children directly
- Everything is seen from the child's point of view
- Vocabulary must be words which children will easily understand
- An appropriate register must be used (see page 113)
- Main points can be exaggerated (eg how worried Silas is, how naughty Eppie is)
- Children's books usually have short sentences
- The 'moral' of the story may well be emphasised
- Children's books often use repetition

---

If your children's version turns out well, perhaps you could arrange a visit to a local primary school to read it to some young children. It would be a good idea to have some illustrations, too.

 **4** Write an argument essay (see page 245) entitled 'Punishment rarely achieves the desired effect.'

In your essay you could refer to: parents bringing up both young children and teenagers; schools disciplining pupils of all ages; society punishing criminals of all types.

# U·N·I·T **33** *Judging the tone*

When someone speaks to us, we judge his or her attitude and feelings not just from the words used but also from the way they are spoken. For instance, it is usually possible to tell from the tone of voice whether a person is joking or serious, angry or excited.

When the word *tone* is applied to the written word, it really means the same thing. When we look at the words on the page, we have to try to 'hear' the voice of the author or the character saying them – and judge how they would be spoken.

If you assess the writer's *tone* and look at the *register* he uses (see pages 113–119), you will learn a good deal about the writer's intentions.

---

**Some words to describe tone**

| | | |
|---|---|---|
| jovial | stern | humorous |
| indignant | gossipy | humble |
| serious | outraged | formal |
| sardonic | comic | (un)sympathetic |
| emotional | informal | cynical |
| sentimental | restrained | factual |
| solemn | persuasive | rhetorical |
| grand | facetious | urgent |
| frightened | dignified | intense |
| passionate | tense | morbid |
| sombre | angry | sarcastic |
| bitter | excited | ironic |
| grovelling | contemptuous | mild |
| reasonable | embarrassed | tongue-in-cheek |
| surprised | casual | incredulous |
| confidential | astonished | proud |
| haughty | friendly | informative |
| instructional | matter-of-fact | straightforward |
| dull | reassuring | questioning |
| | polite | emphatic |

---

## Assignments

○ ☞ **1** Find a word or words to describe the tone of each of the passages **i–xiv**. The words in the box may help you, but add your own words too. (Most passages can be described by more than one word.) You will probably need a dictionary to help you.

**i**  You know, my dears, that your mother was an orphan, and an only child; and I dare say you have heard that your grandfather was a clergyman up in Westmorland, where I come from. I was just a girl in the village school, when, one day, your grandmother came in to ask the mistress if there was any scholar there who would do for a nurse maid; and mighty proud I was, I can tell ye, when the mistress called me up, and spoke to my being a good girl at my needle, and a steady honest girl, and one whose parents were very respectable, though they might be poor. I thought I should like nothing better than to serve the pretty young lady, who was blushing as deep as I was as she spoke of the coming baby, and what I should have to do with it. However, I see you don't care so much for this part of my story as for what you think is to come, so I'll tell you at once.

**ii**  ## DULL FOLKS DON'T WRITE TRAVEL BOOKS

First, because dull folks don't write books. They may draft the odd postcard from Margate or thankyou note in reply to a thankyou note. But never something as interesting as a book. Let alone one called, *I Rode With the Bulgars East of Kathmandu*.

Second, because dull folks don't travel. Of course, they commute back and forth to work. They may even sneak a package holiday to say, Mallorca (the built-up side) or a furtive listen to the long-range weather forecast. But you'd never catch a dull person on a transglobal expedition, crossing the Gobi Desert on a pogo stick or fording the South China Seas in a Squeezy bottle.

**iii**  When you contemplate the overwhelming evidence of the case, you can hardly fail to find Bates guilty. Is it any coincidence that a gun went missing on August 9th? Is it any coincidence that the shirt he was wearing that day cannot be found? Is it any coincidence, readers, that Bates broke down in the dock when Ella Knight's name was mentioned? I think not. I think not, but I am not on the jury. As the case continues tomorrow, I only hope that the jury considers the facts unemotionally.

**iv**  Dear Mrs Baker,
Thank you for your letter of 15th May. We were sorry to hear of your family and financial problems, and can understand the difficulty you have had in repaying what you owe us. Under the circumstances, we will be prepared to accept £5 a month until the debt is repaid.

**v**  Church-Peveril is a house so beset and frequented by spectres, both visible and audible, that none of the family which it shelters under its acre and a half of green copper roofs takes psychical phenomena with any seriousness. For to the Peverils the appearance of a ghost is a matter of hardly greater significance than the appearance of the post to those who live in more ordinary houses. It arrives, that is to say, practically every day, it knocks (or makes other noises), it is observed coming up the drive (or in other places). I myself, when staying there, have seen the present Mrs Peveril, who is rather short-sighted, peer into the dusk, while we were taking our coffee on the terrace after dinner, and say to her daughter:

'My dear, was not that the Blue Lady who has just gone into the shrubbery? I hope she won't frighten Flo. Whistle for Flo, dear.'

(Flo, it may be remarked, is the youngest and most precious of many dachshunds.)

**vi**   1   How could you tell the difference between **a** a compound of iron and sulphur and **b** a mixture of iron and sulphur?
2   How can a mixture of oxygen and hydrogen be separated? How can the compound water be separated into hydrogen and oxygen?
3   Group the following into **a** mixtures and **b** compounds: sea water, air, common salt, rock salt, gold chloride, aluminium oxide, ink.

**vii**   Sir,

What in God's name can be done about the way the public highways are frequently abused, contaminated and defiled by that lowest breed of life – litter louts! When I see a stinking, decaying chip paper or a slimy, germ-infested cigarette carton it makes me so angry that I could immediately seize the person concerned and stuff him bodily into the nearest litter receptacle. When I think of the way these 'people' treat England . . .

**viii**   Dear Friends,

I know that you will join me today in grieving the sad loss of a very dear friend. Annie was a woman seen not only as generous, not only as brave, but also as a true saint and one whom we shall miss greatly. Many's the time my wife and I have looked out from our little cottage window to see that bright, loving face smiling at us across the rose bushes, the sun gleaming on her kindly features. On those occasions we had not the remotest idea how her frail form was suffering.

**ix**   James I slobbered at the mouth and had favourites; he was thus a Bad King. He had, however, a very logical and tidy mind, and one of the first things he did was to have Sir Walter Raleigh executed for being left over from the previous reign. He also tried to straighten out the memorable confusion about the Picts, who, as will be remembered, were originally Irish living in Scotland, and the Scots, originally Picts living in Ireland. James tried to make things tidier by putting the Scots in Ulsters and planting them in Ireland, but the plan failed because the Picts had been lost sight of during the Dark Ages and were now nowhere to be found.

**x**   **USING FOOD TABLES**

If your study has brought you to the point of looking at RDA, you will then want to go further and find out more precisely what is in the foods you eat. Many foods have now been analysed. Countries and nutrition authorities throughout the world publish tables of food composition. They include a very wide range of foods available to people in the area where they are compiled. Many such publications are available.

For in-depth study it is recommended that you consult the tables printed in the most recent edition of *The Manual of Nutrition*, published by her Her Majesty's Stationery Office.

xi     Of course, many of those agony aunts on the problem pages are just voyeurs who positively enjoy the concept of smirking at the real life tragedies their poor correspondents find themselves in. Some of them stoop so low as to encourage their problem page to be seen as light entertainment — something for the punters to giggle at over breakfast. What a deplorable mode of journalism.

xii     Well, my dears, if I told you what sort of a week I've had you just wouldn't believe me. You get so used to reading about my awful wrecked recipes and disastrous D-I-Y attempts that you will nearly choke on your chicken at the thought that little old me has done something right for a change. Yes, loves, I've had a one-in-a-million week.

xiii     The tears welled up in his eyes. A passing waiter noticed that his glass was empty and came back with a gin bottle.

He took up his glass and sniffed it. The stuff grew not less but more horrible with every mouthful he drank. But it had become the element he swam in. It was his life, his death, and his resurrection. It was gin that sank him into stupor every night, and gin that revived him every morning.

xiv     Feliks watched anxiously. The blaze was spreading too quickly. Already large areas of the first floor were burning — he could see the glow in the windows. He thought: Come out, you fools. What were they doing? He did not want to burn everyone in the house — he wanted them to come out. The policeman in the portico seemed to be asleep. I'll give the alarm myself, Feliks thought desperately; I don't want the wrong people to die.

☞ **2** What sort of writing do you think each of the extracts comes from? This is a list of muddled-up sources. Try to match each of them to one of the passages.

  **a** novel about one man's struggle against an oppressive government
  **b** business letter to a customer
  **c** journalist's personal view of news story
  **d** church magazine
  **e** weekly column in woman's magazine
  **f** weekly column in national newspaper
  **g** the old nurse's story
  **h** home economics textbook
  **i** a 'thriller'
  **j** chemistry textbook
  **k** letter to a newspaper
  **l** humorous book about modern behaviour
  **m** humorous look at history
  **n** author's account of a family he knows who live in a haunted house.

  Write down how you decided on the source of each passage.

**3** **a** Choose at least two of the passages and try to rewrite them, using a different tone but keeping the meaning the same.
  **b** Have you had to change many words? Give examples.
  **c** Would you say that if the *tone* changes then the *register* also has to change? Or is it not that simple? Try to summarise your findings in **a** and **b** above.

**4** Give a talk or oral performance in an *inappropriate* tone. Some suggestions might be: a demonstration of how something works – spoken in a contemptuous tone; a love story – read in a humorous tone; a history lesson – given in a rhetorical tone . . .

**5** Write a 15-minute radio play, paying particular attention to the *tone* in which lines should be spoken. (Why is this especially important for radio?) Some suggestions: a family argument; an awkward customer in a shop; a sudden shock or surprise.

---

### Scripts – adding tone

When you write a play the tone of voice goes immediately before the words spoken, eg
Bill: (*Emotional*) Oh no! United have lost!
Eric: (*Incredulous*) No!
If it is obvious from the words themselves how they are to be spoken there is no need to describe the tone of voice used.

---

**6** Tape record or give a performance of the play you wrote for **5** above.

# U·N·I·T 34 *What's said where*

## *Assignments*

☞ **1** The paragraphs below are in no particular order. Each of them can be summed up in one sentence. Scan the paragraphs and match each of them to one of the sentences **1–10**.

*Do not read every word of all the paragraphs yet; try to do this exercise as quickly as possible.*

**1** Women try to be like the very thin models they see in the media.
**2** Perhaps people are more willing to criticise their own body than their own personality.
**3** Thinking about calories actually makes us overeat.
**4** Since 1960 millions of women have become obsessed with trying to be thin.
**5** Many Americans have an unnatural fear of becoming fat.
**6** It is surprising that slimness has been in fashion for so long.
**7** Designers have claimed that clothes only look good on thin women; this is unfair.
**8** We cannot do much about worldwide problems but we can change our body size.
**9** The emphasis is now beginning to be on fitness rather than on thinness.
**10** Princess Diana has lost a good deal of weight and others try to copy her.

**a**
There are encouraging signs that the tide may be turning after all. Even the goddess of fitness, Jane Fonda, says its OK to be fat as long as you are also fit. And among health-conscious Americans, where all these crazes start, this message is gaining popular currency.

**b**
Since the 1960s millions of women in Britain and the rest of the Western world have tortured themselves with the insane desire to conform to the supposed perfect size 8, 10 or 12. Millions upon millions of women have become obsessed with 'correcting' the shape they were born with and have grown up hating their natural selves and making millionaires of everyone who has ever had something apparently 'new' to say on dieting.

**c**
In doing so, they demand that fashion models are one step up from skeletal, making the rest of us feel ashamed of our more natural curvaceous shapes. The models have to starve themselves to appear fashionably lean and waiflike and women in their millions seek to emulate them because the media promotes the image as desirable.

**d**

What is surprising perhaps, is that the lean look inspired by Twiggy in the Sixties has lasted so long. No doubt it has been bolstered by the dieting industry which has continued to hammer home the message that thinness equals elegance and style and wealth.

**e**

What is certain is that the minute you actually start to think about the number of calories you are consuming, food suddenly becomes something to be either guiltily enjoyed or martyrishly denied. Either way, you end up eating far more than usual. Hence the bingeing and fasting see-saw which characterises the lives of so many women who have become victims of this self-laid psychological trap.

**f**

There are various reasons why this happened. High fashion is one of them, and designers do women a disservice when they claim – as some do – that they cannot make clothes look good on a woman larger than a size 12. Surely the art of a good designer is to make clothes look good on anyone, disguising the 'bad' features and emphasising the 'good' ones?

**g**

Perhaps too, it is a sign of our impotence in terms of the world we live in. We cannot change much that goes on around us, nor, except by plastic surgery, much of what we were born with, but by exercising willpower, we can move up and down the size charts and feel we are in control of something. The nuclear war may

not happen after all, but the body we live in is inescapable.

**h**

So obsessive has the desire to be slim become that when 500 men and women were recently stopped on the streets of San Francisco and asked what things they feared most of all in the world, about 200 of them named 'getting fat' before nuclear war, violent crime, poverty or unemployment.

**i**

Under this pressure the quite normal shaped, even bosomy Lady Diana was transformed into a sometimes painfully thin Barbie Doll for the whole world to marvel at. As she did it, millions of women were persuaded that if she could undergo such a dramatic change in so short a time, surely they could do the same? Intentionally or otherwise, she symbolised their self-imposed struggle.

**j**

Women who are entirely happy about their shape – even very slim ones – are hard to find these days. Perhaps it is just that it is socially acceptable to air your concern about weight and shapes. In which case how shallow we must have become if its okay to wail 'my hips are too large' but definitely not okay to say you suspect there is something more fundamentally wrong with you. But perhaps it is easier to deal with flabby thighs and spare tyres and podgy shoulders than with personality defects, especially if the perceived physical defect is not apparent to others.

**2** For this exercise you will need to read the paragraphs more closely. They are all taken from an article about the fashion for women to look slim. Arrange the paragraphs in what you think is the correct order.

**3** Write a letter to a dieting friend explaining the content of the article. Your letter should state clearly:

- the reasons the article gives for women wanting to be slim;
- the reasons suggested for the slimness craze continuing so long;
- some examples of people's obsession with thinness;
- the evidence that things may be changing;
- your advice to your friend, based on what the article says.

**4** **a** Invent a slogan encouraging people not to worry about their weight.
**b** Design a poster encouraging people not to worry about their weight.

**5** Hold a formal debate (see box) on the motion 'We believe that being fat is not important'.

---

### Holding a debate

To run a debate you need a chairperson, two speakers to propose the motion, two speakers to oppose it, and an audience. The order of events is as follows:

**1** 1st speaker proposes (5 minutes)
**2** 1st speaker opposes (5 minutes)
**3** 2nd speaker proposes (3 minutes)
**4** 2nd speaker opposes (3 minutes)
**5** Audience discusses the issue. Chairperson controls the discussion (The first four speakers are not allowed to say anything now.)
**6** 1st opposer sums up his/her main points (2 minutes)
**7** 1st proposer sums up his/her main points (2 minutes)
In the second speeches and the summing up, the speakers try to answer points made either by the opposition or by the audience.
**8** Audience votes on the motion. Chairperson announces how many people are in favour of it, how many against, and how many abstentions there are.

# U·N·I·T 35 *Same subject, different lives*

When you're thinking about a particular topic, it's possible to gain insights from very different types of material on the same theme. Take the topic of the relationship between parents and children, for instance.

First, here is an extract from Shakespeare's *King Lear*. Lear, now an old man, wants to divide his kingdom between his three daughters: Cordelia, Goneril and Regan. (Goneril and Regan are married.) Before he does this, though, he asks: 'Which of you shall we say doth love us most?'

| | | |
|---|---|---|
| **Lear** | Goneril, Our eldest-born, speak first. | |
| **Goneril** | Sir, I love you more than words can *wield* the matter; | express |
| | Dearer than eye-sight, space and liberty; | |
| | Beyond what can be valued rich or rare; | |
| | No less than life, with grace, health, beauty, honour; | |
| | As much as child e'er lov'd, or father found; | |
| | A love that makes breath poor and speech unable; | |
| | Beyond all manner of so much I love you. | |
| **Cordelia** | (*aside*) what shall Cordelia do? Love, and be silent. | |
| **Lear** | (*indicating on a map*) Of all these *bounds*, even from this line to this, | boundaries |
| | With shadowy forests and with *champains rich'd*, | plains enriched |
| | With plenteous rivers and wide-skirted *meads*, | meadows |
| | We make thee lady: to thine and *Albany*'s issue | Goneril's husband |
| | Be this perpetual. What says our second daughter, | |
| | Our dearest Regan, wife of *Cornwall*? Speak. | (Regan's husband) |
| **Regan** | I am made of that *self* metal as my sister, | same |
| | And prize me at her worth. In my true heart | |
| | I find she names my very deed of love; | |
| | Only she comes too short: that I profess | |
| | Myself an enemy to all other joys | |
| | Which the most precious square of sense possesses | |
| | And find I am alone *felicitate* | made happy |
| | In your dear highness' love. | |

| | | |
|---|---|---|
| Cordelia | (*aside*) Then, poor Cordelia! | |
| | And yet not so; since, I am sure, my love's | |
| | *More ponderous* than my tongue. | worth more |
| Lear | To thee and thine, hereditary ever, | |
| | Remain this ample third of our fair kingdom, | |
| | No less in space, validity, and pleasure, | |
| | Than that conferr'd on Goneril. Now, our joy, | |
| | Although our last, not least; to whose young love | aristocrats courting Cordelia |
| | The vines of *France* and milk of *Burgundy* | |
| | Strive to be interess'd; what can you say to *draw* | earn |
| | *A third more opulent* than your sisters? Speak. | a richer share |
| Cordelia | Nothing, my lord. | |
| Lear | Nothing? | |
| Cordelia | Nothing. | |
| Lear | Nothing will come of nothing: speak again. | |
| Cordelia | Unhappy that I am, I cannot heave | |
| | My heart into my mouth: I love your majesty | |
| | According to my *bond*; nor more nor less. | duty as a daughter |
| Lear | How, how, Cordelia! Mend your speech a little, | |
| | Lest you may *mar your fortunes*. | lose your inheritance |
| Cordelia | Good my lord, | |
| | You have begot me, bred me, lov'd me: I | |
| | Return those duties back as are right fit, | |
| | Obey you, love you, and most honour you. | |
| | Why have my sisters husbands, if they say | |
| | They love you all? Haply, when I shall wed, | |
| | That lord whose hand must take my *plight* carry | wedding vow |
| | Half my love with him, half my care and duty: | |
| | Sure I shall never marry like my sisters, | |
| | To love my father all. | |
| Lear | But goes thy heart with this? | |
| Cordelia | Ay, my good lord. | |
| Lear | So young, and so untender? | |
| Cordelia | So young, my lord, and true. | |

# *Assignments*

☞ **1**    Answering these questions will help you understand the passage:

**a** How do Goneril and Regan answer their father's question?
**b** What is Lear's response to their answers?
**c** What do we learn about Cordelia from her aside comments?

**d** Without Cordelia's aside comments, what impression of her would you have formed from her reply, 'Nothing, my lord.'?

**e** How does Cordelia go on to explain her views?

**f** Can you predict what Lear's response will be? (See page 81.)

**g** Why do you think Cordelia responds in this way? Do you think she is right?

**h** Do Goneril and Regan's answers strike you as sincere? Give reasons for your opinion.

Now read these comments made by modern teenagers – two brothers and a sister – about their parents.

**John** (19) 'I have quite a good relationship with Mum but I can't relate to my Dad at all. He's always very hard on me. Usually he won't help me or give me any money or anything like that. On the rare occasions he does slip me a fiver he expects me to be eternally grateful. Months later he'll still bring it up. But Mum often lends or gives me cash and then forgets it. She's really generous.

Dad says I don't understand his feelings. He gets upset if I don't sit and talk to him much but he makes no attempt to understand me. He's always been closest to Lisa. I think it's because she's a girl and the youngest. He can be a bit more affectionate with her. With Paul and me he acts like showing any affection would be a weakness. Yet he still wants us to be thoughtful to him!

When I compare myself to my mates and their Dads I think I'm good to my Dad but he never appreciates it. No matter how many times I mow the lawn or wash the car it would never be enough to satisfy him. I love him, I suppose, and he loves me but neither of us can show it.'

**Paul** (17) 'Dad finds it hard to show his feelings. He does care, though. I remember when John had really bad glandular fever Dad was very worried. He kept buying him things like car magazines and a record. He even put the telly in John's room because he thought it would cheer him up. He never tells you he likes you, though. I was upset when I got good exam results and Dad hardly said anything. I'd worked really hard, too – it wasn't like I'd just strolled through them with no effort. I know Mum's proud of us all but with Dad you never know.

I suppose sometimes we're a bit thoughtless about Dad. He often gets in late from work so he misses out on things we tell Mum. When you've already discussed the day's events once you can't be bothered to go through it all again. So sometimes he doesn't know what's happening. He shouldn't take this as an insult, though, the way he does. It seems like he's always wanting to play the hard-done-by father. You know – "You don't realise how lucky you are . . . other kids don't have good parents like you . . ." and all that stuff. Mum's a good parent too but she doesn't keep reminding us.'

**Lisa** (14) 'I get on all right with Mum and Dad. Dad takes me around a lot because he doesn't like me catching buses on my own, especially in the evenings. He treats me a bit like his little girl, but I don't mind that really.

I like making a fuss of him, like buying him a chocolate bar sometimes or making the cakes he likes.

He has terrible rows with John and Paul sometimes, especially John. He is hard on them really. It's like he wants to keep being thanked all the time, just for being their father. He's always on to them about "doing their share" but they do a lot of things like work on the car and helping Dad with jobs about the place. Paul's studying hard, too, so it's not fair to get him to do too much. Some of their mates treat their homes like a hotel, but John and Paul aren't like that at all. They're nice lads really!

I suppose I get quite a bit of money spent on me one way and another and both Mum and Dad accuse me of taking it for granted. That's not true though. I may not always be thanking them but I am grateful. One day I'll pay it back. When they're old they'll need my support, won't they? They'll get it too. That's the way life is, isn't it? Parents do what they can for their kids and then when they get old their kids should look after them.'

☞ ◊ **2**   **a** Copy out this table and write down in note form the positive and negative points which John, Paul and Lisa make about their father. (The table has been begun for you, starting with John. Finish off the points he makes, then do the same for Paul and Lisa.)

| | Positive | Negative |
|---|---|---|
| 1 | | 1 Hard on sons |
| 2 | | 2 Won't help John |
| 3 | | 3 Won't lend money |
| 4 | | 4 Wants lasting gratitude for any presents |
| . . . | | . . . |

**b** Based on your table, write a short account of what John, Paul and Lisa's father is like, according to his three children.

◊ **3**   If their mother and father were asked to write down their feelings about relationships with the three children, what do you think they would say? Write down what you think each would say about John, Paul and Lisa.

✔ ◊ **4**   Write a discussion essay (see box) entitled 'Parents and children'. You may use any examples you wish to support the points you make, including the extract from *King Lear* and the comments made by the three teenagers.

138

## Discussion essays

- This type of essay can be similar to an argument essay (see page 246) but in a discussion essay you need not put forward a particular point of view.
- You should discuss different aspects of the subject you are writing about in as interesting a way as possible.
- You may arrive at a conclusion if you wish, but your aim is to interest, rather than to persuade, your readers.
- Plan your essay carefully first.
- Have one main point per paragraph.
- Expand on each main point by introducing examples to support it. (These might include references to: your own experiences; experiences of people you know; books or articles you have read; programmes on radio or television; events from the past; any facts and figures you know about the subject.)
- Discuss each of your examples fully before moving on to the next point.
- Organise your paragraphs in a logical way, bearing in mind how one paragraph can be linked to the next.
- Ensure that the opening of the essay immediately captures the reader's interest and that the ending leaves him/her with something to think about.

○ ◇ **5**  You are to carry out a survey on relationships between parents and teenage children. Prepare two questionnaires – one aimed at parents and one aimed at teenagers. Each should have 20 questions, which can be answered by only one of the following simple responses:

*a*   *b*   *c*   *d*   Yes   No   Agree   Disagree

You could ask some questions about how parents and teenagers think of one another. Then perhaps you could think of some specific situations where conflict might arise (coming in late; being lazy; what clothes to wear . . .) and ask about those. Looking at questionnaires in magazines might give you some more ideas.

Carry out your survey – interview at least 10 parents and 10 teenagers.

✔ ◇ **6**  **a** Write a report (see page 19) on the findings of your survey. Choose a style suitable for your school magazine.
**b** Work out some kind of chart, graph or table to accompany your report.

✔ ○ **7**  **a** In a group, devise a discussion-type radio or television programme on this topic. Both parents and teenagers should be represented. For instance, if there are five of you, one person could chair the discussion, two could take the parts of parents and two the parts of teenagers.

Questions and answers need to be carefully prepared first, so that no one 'dries up'. (See **Unit 51** for an example of this type of discussion.)
**b** Present the programme to the rest of your class, or tape record it and let other classes see it.

**8**　**a** Design a simple board game called 'Kids and parents' which is about children growing up. The idea of the game is to travel from square 1 to square 100 by throwing the dice and moving counters. If you wish, you can include lucky dip cards.

For instance, the game could begin and end like this:

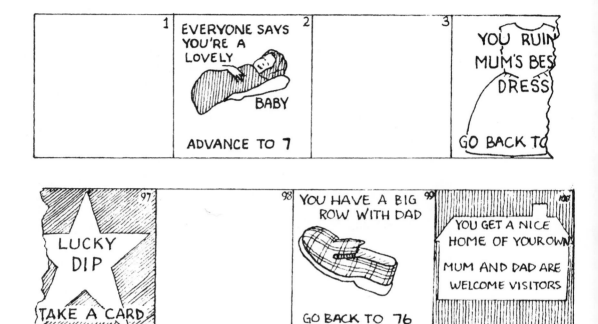

**b** Play the game to see if it works!

**ALL BUT EMPTY**
Part 4

Then he went on speaking, his voice gaining strength and calmness. 'I had just put down the borax for the black-beetles that morning. How could I have guessed? I must have been very angry coming downstairs. The clock struck two, and there he was, smiling at me. I must have sent it to be reground when I had the joint of pork for Sunday dinner. Oh, I was angry when he laughed: the knife trembled. And there the poor body lay with the throat cut from ear to ear,' and hunching up his shoulders and dropping his bearded chin towards his hands, the old man began again to cry.

It needed courage to stand up and press by him into the gangway, and then turn the back and be lost in the blind velvet folds of the curtains which would not part, knowing that he might have the knife still with him. I got out into the grey afternoon light at last, and startled the girl in the box with my white face. I opened the door of the kiosk and shut it again behind me with immeasurable relief.

'The police station,' I called softly into the telephone, afraid that he might hear me where he sat alone in the cinema, and when a voice answered, I said hurriedly, 'That murder in Seymour Terrace this morning.'

The voice at the other end became brisk and interested, telling me to hold the line.

Is the old man the murderer? How will the story end? (Turn to page 239)

# U·N·I·T 36 *Clear instructions*

When you're telling someone how to do something, it is best if your language is clear and simple. This passage on using a video camera assumes that the reader knows little or nothing about the subject.

With the camera, the first requirement is that you _____1_____ yourself with it completely. You want to find a comfortable way of holding it and fitting the eyepiece to your face, and to get used to moving about with it in a shooting position. If you are going to be doing _____2_____ shooting with the recorder on your shoulder, you need to familiarise yourself with carrying this around too.

Get the feel of all the _____3_____ and_____4_____ so that it becomes second nature for you to go for the right ones. The on/off switch is easiest, because it lies under your trigger finger as you hold the camera.

If you have an electrically driven zoom lens, it is fairly simple to use and does your _____5_____ for you. If you have a manual one, you need to practise going in and out smoothly on the zoom. Record your practice shots on the zoom lens and then look at them critically on the monitor to see if you are doing them smoothly and without _____6_____.

Then there's the focus. Your left hand has to get used to finding the focusing ring and pulling the focus to just the required spot in the picture. If you're on the wide angle part of the zoom lens there may be no problem; almost everything is sharp. It is when you zoom in that trouble may start, for if you aren't _____7_____ focused the shot looks more and more out of focus as you zoom in, whereas ideally it should become even _____8_____.

One of the tricks _____9_____ by professional cameramen in getting focus sharp is to zoom tight on to the central subject, be it a person or an object; twirl the focus ring until the picture is quite sharp; then go back on the zoom to the wider frame that they need to shoot the shot. Then they can count on sharp focus if they need a tight shot. Meanwhile on each wider part of the zoom they are bound to be sharp, because the more wide angle the shot, the less _____10_____ the point of focus is.

Practise with your camera and do dummy shooting runs, recording them as you go, until you feel really familiar with the _____11_____. Once you are satisfied that you are using the equipment well and that your shots are smooth and sharply focused, you can erase your practice tapes and use them for more serious shooting.

There is no necessity to carry the camera around all the time; it is useful for _____12_____ shots, but there are many occasions when it is more _____13_____ and every bit as effective to have the camera on a tripod.

Again you want to get yourself into a comfortable stance so that you can catch anything that happens and don't feel tired and stooped after a bit. The best kind of tripod has a fluid head; you cannot move it jerkily either when panning or tilting, it won't let you. Fluid heads can be both _____14_____ and heavy but there are now cheaper tripods that have similar qualities and these help you to operate the camera smoothly and easily.

A good tripod is a great _____15_____. You want one that is light to carry around and yet sturdy enough to hold the camera steady. The balance of the camera on the tripod wants to be right so it is easy to operate. And a fluid head, or imitation fluid head, is the most desirable feature.

# Assignments

○ ☞ **1** For each of the gaps in the passage, three words are suggested below. Decide in each case which you think is the best word to fill the gap and give a reason for your choice.

  **1** familiarise, trust, involve
  **2** much, mobile, frequent
  **3** knobs, levers, equipment
  **4** switches, parts, items
  **5** work, job, task
  **6** fuss, jerking, thinking
  **7** properly, well, accurately
  **8** nicer, closer, sharper
  **9** employed, known, tested
  **10** critical, important, bother
  **11** equipment, environment, knobs
  **12** on-the-move, professional, trying
  **13** simple, static, restful
  **14** awkward, expensive, light
  **15** expense, blessing, encumbrance

✐ **2** Rewrite this passage in a form which would be suitable for a magazine. Your editor has asked you to write it in the form of questions and answers. The questions should act as sub-titles, with the answers forming the main body of the article. You may illustrate the article if you wish. Remember to use your own words where possible – do not simply copy from the passage.
   Here is an example of how you could start:

**Q:** *I've got my new video camera. Where do I start?*
**A:** Well, first of all you need to get to know your camera and feel comfortable with it. Practise holding it and using the eyepiece. Then get used to moving about with the camera. If you are going to carry the recorder on your shoulder, you need to get used to this too.
**Q:** *What about all the knobs and buttons?*
**A:**

**Q:** *How do I get used to the zoom lens?*
**A:**

**Q:** *What about focusing?*
**A:**

**Q:** *How do I keep the picture steady?*
**A:**

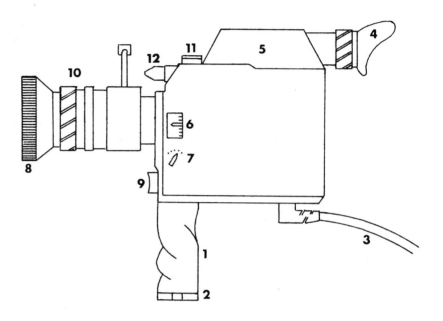

○ ☞ **3**  Look at the diagram of a typical video camera. Match the labels **A–L** to what you think are the appropriate numbers on the diagram.

**A**  The *rubber eye-cup* is the part the camera operator looks through
**B**  The *zoom lens* is the part through which photos are taken
**C**  On the end of the zoom lens is the *rubber lens hood*
**D**  Protruding slightly above the zoom lens is the *omnidirectional micro-phone*
**E**  A small button underneath the zoom lens is the *stop/start trigger* associated with a video recorder
**F**  On the side of the camera is a small button which is the *colour temperature adjustment control*
**G**  Next to the temperature adjustment control is the *colour temperature meter*
**H**  The camera is held by a *pistol grip*
**I**  At the bottom of the pistol grip is a small *socket* to attach the camera to a tripod
**J**  The *cable* from the camera links to a video recorder or to a mains power unit
**K**  Level with the eye-cup is the *viewfinder*
**L**  Next to the viewfinder is a *shoe* for a high quality directional microphone.

**4** Choose an interest or hobby which you know something about. Assume that your reader knows nothing about this subject:

   **a** Write a clear account of how to carry out some activity associated with your chosen subject.
   **b** List the main terms and items of equipment associated with your chosen subject and write a brief, simple definition of each of them.
   **c** Draw a clearly labelled diagram to illustrate your account.

**5** Prepare notes for a talk similar to the written assignment **4** above. Again, assume that your audience knows nothing about your chosen subject. Give the talk to a small group of friends or to the whole class.

---

**Giving a talk**

- Think about your audience. What will they want to know? What will they know already?
- Plan the best order for your points.
- Use notes but don't read your talk.
- Use pictures, diagrams or visual aids whenever this is possible and helpful.
- Say everything clearly, especially technical terms.
- Spell out and explain any technical or difficult words.
- Add interest to your talk by varying the pace of what you say and the tone and volume of your voice.

# U·N·I·T 37 *Looking forward to the big event*

All the assignments in this unit relate to planning a sponsored walk and run. Study the map and all the other information carefully before you begin writing. (If you are to complete the assignments under timed conditions, allow two hours.)

Beverley Green Nature Park is a forested area of great beauty, popular with families enjoying a peaceful day out and with scientists studying nature. This year, for the first time, on Sunday May 9th 2000 people will be taking part in a sponsored walk and run around the park in aid of children's charities. The route will start and end at *The Laughing Pixie* pub and will take in five other checkpoints as follows:

Checkpoint 1 *The Laughing Pixie* pub
Checkpoint 2 *Woodside* café
Checkpoint 3 Golf club
Checkpoint 4 Youth hostel (lunch for walkers)
Checkpoint 5 *The Good, the Bad and the Ugly* pub
Checkpoint 6 Nature study centre
Checkpoint 7 *The Laughing Pixie* (tea and cakes for everyone)

## Assignments

**1** Study the map carefully and use it to help you write a clear description of the route. This description will be issued to all participants and should include all the landmarks to be seen en route, details of roads crossed, etc.

(15 marks)

**2** When a meeting of the organising committee was held, the secretary made the notes you see on the right.
**a** The notes are rather muddled. Write down the numbers of the points which refer to:

- how to enter for the event
- what entrants should do on the day
- food and hygiene
- safety
- collecting sponsor money
- other points (if any)                                                  (5 marks)

**b** Write an information sheet on the walk entitled *The Beverley Green sponsored event – what every walker and runner should know*
   Use your notes from **a** to help you organise your material. Put in appropriate headings.

(25 marks)

146

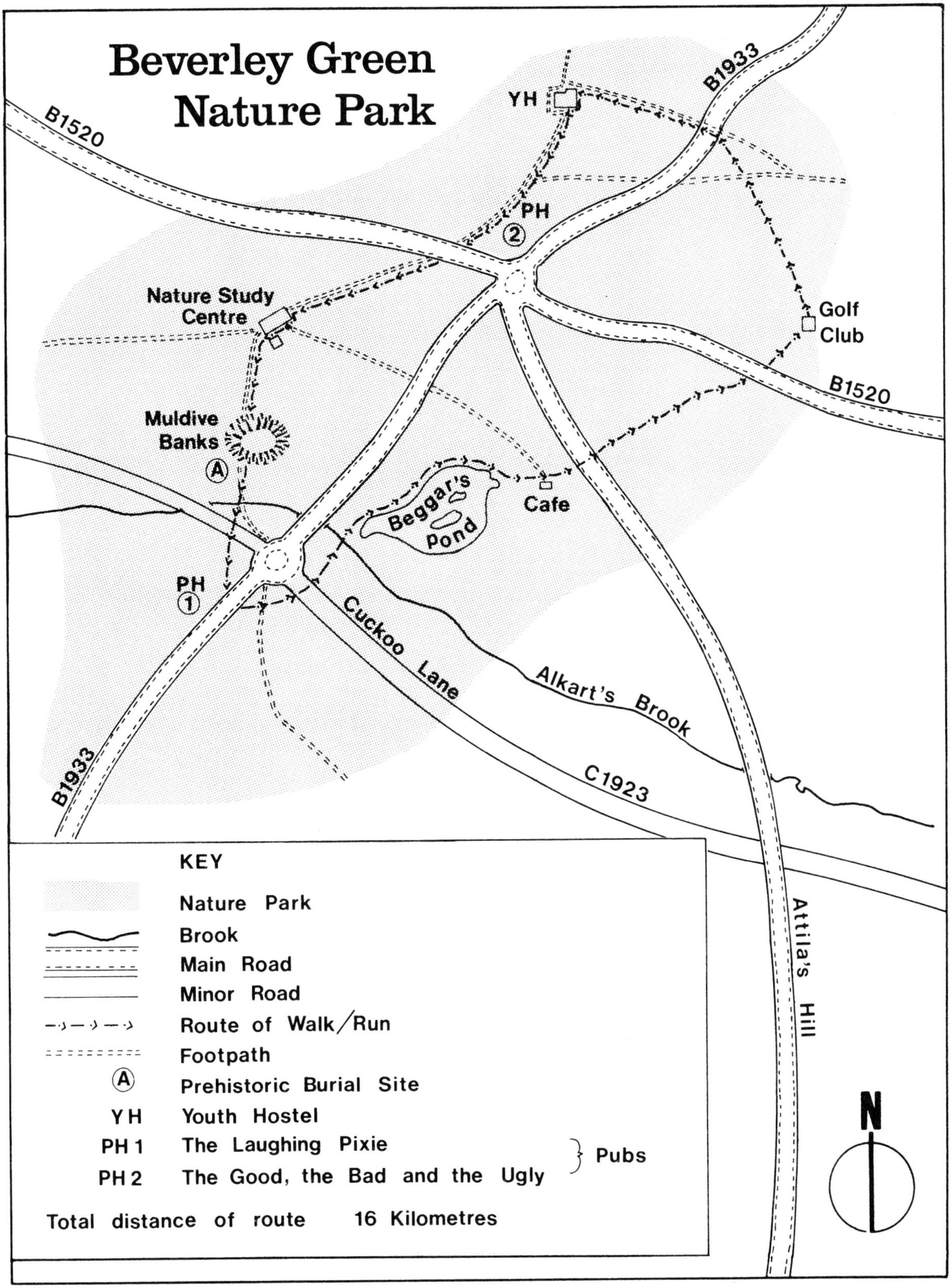

Beverley Green
Nature Park
B1520
YH
B1933
PH
2
Nature Study
Centre
Golf
Club
B1520
Muldive
Banks
A
Beggar's
Pond
Cafe
PH
1
Cuckoo Lane
Alkart's Brook
C1923
B1933
Attila's Hill
KEY
Nature Park
Brook
Main Road
Minor Road
Route of Walk/Run
Footpath
A Prehistoric Burial Site
YH Youth Hostel
PH 1 The Laughing Pixie
PH 2 The Good, the Bad and the Ugly
Pubs
Total distance of route 16 Kilometres
N

# Sponsored Walk Committee Meeting          February 27th

1. Lunch for walkers at YH. Tea for all at LP
2. Police will patrol all roads crossed by walkers and runners
3. 1st aid crews at all checkpoints and wherever route crosses road
4. Great care needed crossing roads — only at supervised crossing points
5. Cold drinks available at all checkpoints
6. Litter to be placed in giant bins at all checkpoints — important
7. All entrants will receive sponsor card and registration number
8. Must check in at all checkpoints and have card signed — vital
9. Must all register by April 30th. Send age, name & address to committee
10. Registration number in large figures on chest and back
11. Have to be aged 12+ to walk, 16+ to run
12. Remember to say in letter whether running or walking
13. All under 16s to be accompanied by adult
14. All sponsor money to be collected and given to committee by June 30th — vital
15. Organisers reserve right to expel from park anyone creating any nuisance
16. Must make sure card is signed at LP pub at end of route — proof route completed
17. Cash prizes for 1st 3 runners back
18. Toilet facilities available at checkpoints. Extra portable ones too.
19. Marshals to stop traffic and help entrants across roads
20. Route to be marked by yellow posts on the day

**3** Rosie Ward, the committee secretary, will be sending the map, description of the route and information sheet to all entrants. Write the informal letter which she sends out with it.

Her address is: Nature Study Centre, Beverley Green Park, Near Catchmore, Dorset.

The *tone* of the letter (see page 127) should be bright and friendly. The organisers wish to stress the fact that this is the first time they have held an event of this kind. If it is successful, they hope to make it an annual occurrence. (15 marks)

**4** A local television reporter was asked to present an item about one of the entrants for the event, 64-year-old Joan Butcher from Clacton. Joan loves raising money for charity and is hoping to get into the *Guinness Book of Records* for the number of sponsored walks she has been on. Joan originally intended to walk the Beverley Green route, but on this occasion all her sponsors have agreed to double their donation if she runs. For several weeks now she has been training hard, because she has never done any running before.

Write the entire script for the item, as it appeared on the local television news. You may include: snatches of film of Joan doing various things; an interview with Joan; introductory and linking comments by the reporter. (20 marks)

---

**Setting out a TV script** – example

(*Film of Joan skipping and doing press-ups*)
*Interviewer*: Well, Joan has been training hard like this for weeks now, and she's beginning to look quite fit.
(*Joan stops exercising and joins interviewer*)
How are you feeling now, Joan?
*Joan*: Worn out!

# U·N·I·T 38 *Reading between the lines*

*Flight* is a story in which much more is implied than is actually said. For the time being, ignore the symbols which appear alongside the text. As you read the story, try to work out how the people in it are feeling – both about one another and about their situation in life.

**FLIGHT**
**by Doris Lessing**

### I

Above the old man's head was the dovecote, a tall wire-netted shelf on stilts, full of strutting, preening birds. The sunlight broke on their grey breasts into small rainbows. His ears were lulled by their crooning, his hands stretched up towards his favourite, a homing pigeon, a young plumpbodied bird which stood still when it saw him and cocked a shrewd bright eye.

'Pretty, pretty, pretty,' he said, as he grasped the bird and drew it down, feeling the cold coral claws tighten around his finger. Content, he rested the bird lightly on his chest, and leaned against a tree, gazing out beyond the dovecote into the landscape of a late afternoon. In folds and hollows of sunlight and shade, the dark red soil, which was broken into great clods, stretched wide to a tall horizon. Trees marked the course of the valley; a stream of rich green grass the road.

His eyes travelled homewards along this road until he saw his granddaughter swinging on the gate underneath a frangipani tree. Her hair fell down her back in a wave of sunlight, and her long bare legs repeated the angles of the frangipani stems, bare, shining-brown stems among patterns of pale blossoms.

She was gazing past the pink flowers, past the railway cottage where they lived, along the road to the village.

His mood shifted. He deliberately held out his wrist for the bird to take flight, and caught it again at the moment it spread its wings. He felt the plump shape strive and strain under his fingers; and, in a sudden access of troubled spite, shut the bird into a small box and fastened the bolt. 'Now you stay there,' he muttered; and turned his back on the shelf of birds. He moved warily along the hedge, stalking his grand-daughter, who was now looped over the gate, her head loose on her arms, singing. The light happy sound mingled with the crooning of the birds, and his anger mounted.

'Hey!' he shouted; saw her jump, look back, and abandon the gate. Her eyes veiled themselves, and she said in a pert neutral voice: 'Hullo, Grandad.' Politely she moved towards him, after a lingering backward glance at the road.

'Waiting for Steven, hey?' he said, his fingers curling like claws into his

150

palm.

'Any objection?' she asked lightly, refusing to look at him.

He confronted her, his eyes narrowed, shoulders hunched, tight in a hard knot of pain which included the preening birds, the sunlight, the flowers, herself. He said: 'Think you're old enough to go courting, hey?'

The girl tossed her head at the old-fashioned phrase and sulked, 'Oh Grandad!'

'Think you want to leave home, hey? Think you can go running around the fields at night?'

Her smile made him see her, as he had every evening of this warm end-of-summer month, swinging hand in hand along the road to the village with that red-handed, red-throated, violent-bodied youth, the son of the postmaster. Misery went to his head and he shouted angrily: 'I'll tell your mother!'

'Tell away!' she said laughing, and went back to the gate.

He heard her singing, for him to hear:

'I've got you under my skin,
I've got you deep in the heart of . . .'

'Rubbish,' he shouted. 'Rubbish. Impudent little bit of rubbish!'

Growling under his breath he turned towards the dovecote, which was his refuge from the house he shared with his daughter and her husband and their children. But now the house would be empty. Gone all the young girls with their laughter and their squabbling and their teasing. He would be left, uncherished and alone, with that square-fronted, calm-eyed woman, his daughter.　i)

He stooped, muttering, before the dovecote, resenting the absorbed cooing birds.　**C**

II

From the gate the girl shouted: 'Go and tell! Go on, what are you waiting for?'

Obstinately he made his way to the house, with quick, pathetic persistent glances of appeal back at her. But she never looked around. Her defiant but anxious young body stung him into love and repentance.　ii)
He stopped. 'But I never meant . . .' he muttered, waiting for her to turn and run to him. 'I didn't mean . . .'

She did not turn. She had forgotten him. Along the road came the young man Steven, with something in his hand. A present for her? The old man stiffened as he watched the gate swing back, and the couple embrace. In the brittle shadows of the frangipani tree his grand-daughter, his darling, lay in the arms of the postmaster's son, and her hair flowed back over his shoulder.

'I see you!' shouted the old man spitefully. They did not move. He stumped into the little whitewashed house, hearing the wooden veranda creak angrily under his feet. His daughter was sewing in the front room, threading a needle held to the light.

He stopped again, looking back into the garden. The couple were now sauntering among the bushes, laughing. As he watched he saw the girl escape from the youth with a sudden mischievous movement, and run off through the flowers with him in pursuit. He heard shouts, laughter, a scream, silence.

'But it's not like that at all,' he muttered miserably. 'It's not like that. Why can't you see? Running and giggling, and kissing and kissing. You'll come to something quite different.'

He looked at his daughter with sardonic hatred, hating himself. They were caught and finished, both of them, but the girl was still running free.

'Can't you *see*?' he demanded of his invisible grand-daughter, who was at that moment lying in the thick green grass with the postmaster's son.

His daughter looked at him and her eyebrows went up in tired forbearance.

'Put your birds to bed?' she asked, humouring him.

'Lucy,' he said urgently. 'Lucy . . .'

'Well what is it now?'

'She's in the garden with Steven.'

'Now you just sit down and have your tea.'

He stumped his feet alternately, thump, thump, on the hollow wooden floor and shouted: 'She'll marry him. I'm telling you, she'll be marrying him next!'

His daughter rose swiftly, brought him a cup, set him a plate.

'I don't want any tea. I don't want it, I tell you.'

'Now, now,' she crooned. 'What's wrong with it? Why not?'

'She's eighteen. Eighteen!'

'I was married at seventeen and I never regretted it.'

'Liar,' he said. 'Liar. Then you should regret it. Why do you make your girls marry? It's you who do it. What do you do it for? Why?'

'The other three have done fine. They've three fine husbands. Why not Alice?'

'She's the last,' he mourned. 'Can't we keep her a bit longer?'

'Come, now, dad. She'll be down the road, that's all. She'll be here every day to see you.'

'But it's not the same.' He thought of the other three girls, transformed inside a few months from charming petulant spoiled children into serious young matrons.

'You never did like it when we married,' she said. 'Why not? Every time, it's the same. When I got married you made me feel like it was something wrong. And my girls the same. You get them all crying and miserable the way you go on. Leave Alice alone. She's happy.' She sighed, letting her eyes linger on the sun-lit garden. 'She'll marry next month. There's no reason to wait.'

'You've said they can marry?' he said incredulously.

'Yes, dad, why not?' she said coldly, and took up her sewing.

His eyes stung, and he went out on to the verandah. Wet spread down over his chin and he took out a handkerchief and mopped his whole face. The garden was empty.

### III

From around a corner came the young couple; but their faces were no longer set against him. On the wrist of the postmaster's son balanced a young pigeon, the light gleaming on its breast.

'For me?' said the old man, letting the drops shake off his chin. 'For me?'

'Do you like it?' The girl grabbed his hand and swung on it. 'It's for you, Grandad. Steven brought it for you.' They hung about him, affectionate, concerned, trying to charm away his wet eyes and his misery. They took his arms and directed him to the shelf of birds, one on each side, enclosing him, petting him, saying wordlessly that nothing would be changed, nothing could change, and that they would be with him always. The bird  v) was proof of it, they said, from their lying happy eyes, as they thrust it on him. 'There, Grandad, it's yours. It's for you.'

They watched him as he held it on his wrist, stroking its soft, sun-warmed back, watching the wings lift and balance.

'You must shut it up for a bit,' said the girl intimately. 'Until it knows this is its home.'

'Teach your grandmother to suck eggs,' growled the old man.

Released by his half-deliberate anger, they fell back, laughing at him. 'We're glad you like it.' They moved off, now serious and full of purpose, to the gate, where they hung, backs to him, talking quietly. More than anything could their grown-up seriousness shut him out, making him alone; also, it quietened him, took the sting out of their tumbling like  vi) puppies on the grass. They had forgotten him again. Well, so they should, the old man reassured himself, feeling his throat clotted with tears, his lips trembling. He held the new bird to his face, for the caress of its silken feathers. Then he shut it in a box and took out his favourite.

'*Now* you can go,' he said aloud. He held it poised, ready for flight,  **D** while he looked down the garden towards the boy and the girl. Then, clenched in the pain of loss, he lifted the bird on his wrist and watched it soar. A whirr and a spatter of wings, and a cloud of birds rose into the evening from the dovecote.

At the gate Alice and Steven forgot their talk and watched the birds.

On the veranda, that woman, his daughter, stood gazing, her eyes shaded with a hand that still held her sewing.

It seemed to the old man that the whole afternoon had stilled to watch his gesture of self-command, that even the leaves of the trees had stopped shaking.

Dry-eyed and calm, he let his hands fall to his sides and stood erect, staring up into the sky.

The cloud of shining silver birds flew up and up, with a shrill cleaving of wings, over the dark ploughed land and the darker belts of trees and the bright folds of grass, until they floated high in the sunlight, like a cloud of motes of dust.  **E**

They wheeled in a wide circle, tilting their wings so there was flash after flash of light, and one after another they dropped from the sunshine of the upper sky to shadow, one after another, returning to the valley and the shelter of night.

The garden was all a fluster and a flurry of returning birds. Then silence, and the sky was empty.

The old man turned, slowly, taking his time; he lifted his eyes to smile  vii) proudly down the garden at his grand-daughter. She was staring at him. She did not smile. She was wide-eyed, and pale in the cold shadow, and he saw the tears run shivering off her face.

# Assignments

Questions **1–3** are intended to familiarise you with the characters and events of the story. Questions **4–5** ask you to probe a little more deeply. (Questions **1–5** are best discussed in small groups.)

☞ **1**  Look at Section **I** of the story.
**a** List five words or phrases which suggest the mood of: the old man; the girl.
**b** Suggest why each of them is feeling this way.

☞ **2**  **a** List five words or phrases from Section **II** which reveal how the old man's daughter feels about him.
**b** Section **II** shows us a slightly different side to the old man's character. Note down any new insights we learn about him in this section.

☞ **3**  **a** What impression of the girl do you form from Section **III**?
**b** What change takes place in the old man's attitude, and how does it come about?
**c** In what way is the situation at the end of the story a reversal of the way the story started?

☞ **4**  **a** The numbers **i–vii** alongside the text direct your attention to some interesting parts of the story which you may have missed so far. Study these sections carefully. Do they offer you any new understanding of the story?
**b** Do any phrases in these sections puzzle you? Write them down, then attempt to explain them.

○ ☞ **5**  **a** The letters **A–E** alongside the text direct your attention to some of the passages about the pigeons. Look at these sections carefully. Why do you think the pigeons are in the story at all? Do they 'represent' something? If so, what?
**b** Find a phrase in Section **III** which describes the old man's feelings about his pigeon, but could also refer to his reaction to his grand-daughter's marriage.
**c** In a few words, suggest what you think the *theme* of the story is. (Is the title a clue?)

✔ ✎ **6**  Having discussed the story, write about it in any way you choose. You could begin by referring closely to the story itself, and the things you talked about for questions **1–5**. You may then like to discuss wider issues which reading the story has set you thinking about.

✔ ✎ **7**  Write the old man's diary for the day described in the story. (If you like, you could extend it for several days.)

✔ ✎ **8**  Write Alice's diary for this day or for several days.

154

**9** Write a conversation either between Alice and Steven or between Alice and her mother, which takes place after the events in this extract. Their discussion should include their concern for the old man and his feelings.

**10** Write a paragraph explaining your thoughts as if you were:

   **a** Alice
   **b** Steven
   **c** The old man
   **d** His daughter

You should explain your feelings about the marriage, about the others and about life in general. If you choose the words and phrases carefully, you may be able to make this into a poem.

# U·N·I·T 39 *At home and abroad*

Save the Children Fund is a charity which works to protect the rights of children all over the world. On pages 158–159 you can read about some projects run by SCF in the United Kingdom. Pages 160–161 deal with the kinds of problems SCF are helping to overcome in some selected countries overseas. Taken all together, this section gives a fairly representative picture of the scope of SCF's work at home and abroad.

## Assignments

☞ **1** Read pages 158–159 carefully and then make out a table like the one below. (An example of how you could fill in the table has been provided.)

| Problems faced in UK | SCF's solution |
|---|---|
| 1 Children in hospital may be alarmed by unfamiliar circumstances | 1 Playschemes to help children cope with their fears through games |
| 2 . . . | 2 . . . |

☞ **2** **a** Look at the table of statistics on page 161. What do these figures suggest about the general problems existing in Fiji, Mozambique, Colombia, Ethiopia and Bangladesh?
**b** Which of these countries seem to be worst off and in which respects?

☞ **3** Now read the accounts of SCF's work in these five countries (pages 160–161). Make out a table like the one you did for **1** above, listing the types of problems that may occur and their possible solutions.

✔ ◌ **4** Your school is organising a charity week to raise money for Save the Children Fund. You have been asked to prepare a four-page leaflet to make other pupils more aware of what SCF does. The information you need can all be found on the next four pages. (Your answers for assignments **1–3** should also help you here.)
  This is how your four pages should be organised:

*Page 1* should be eye-catching and include a slogan which you have invented for the charity week;

*Page 2* should give a general outline of the type of work SCF is doing in the United Kingdom;

*Page 3* should give a general outline of the type of work SCF is doing overseas;

*Page 4* should be a letter addressed to pupils, asking for their support during the fund-raising week and giving them advice on how to help raise money.

---

**Writing a pamphlet**

- Plan your pamphlet carefully, in note form. A good deal of work needs to be done before you can write out a final, neat version.
- Include as much information as you can, but don't make people feel they are being bombarded with facts.
- Keep your written style clear so that even the youngest pupils can understand it.
- Use charts, diagrams and pictures where appropriate, but *do not simply copy information given here.*

---

**5** **a** In groups of 2–6, prepare a lively ten-minute radio programme about the school's fund-raising week and the work of Save the Children Fund. You may include reports, interviews and anything else which will make your programme interesting.

**b** Tape record your programme so that other classes may hear it, or present a 'live' performance.

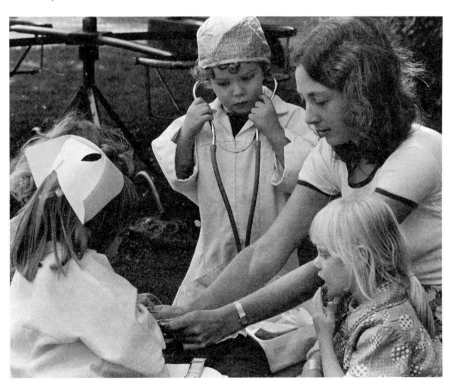

SAVE THE CHILDREN FUND IN THE
UNITED KINGDOM

### Hospital Play
SCF led the way in starting playschemes in general hospitals to help children cope with unfamiliar and often alarming experiences there. The value of these specialised play-schemes is now widely accepted, and SCF encourages the setting up of new schemes.

An SCF hospital play specialist explains her work: 'Play is vital to every child's development but in hospital it's even more important. Helped by experienced staff, children can work through their fears and fantasies. We prepare all children who come in for planned surgery; if a four-year-old is having a squint operation, for example, we dress a Teddy bear in hat and gown, put him on a stretcher, give him a pre-med and anaesthetic and apply an eye patch.

Children shocked and hurt in road accidents are helped to play through fears and anxieties using road maps, model cars and dolls. Children facing repeated unpleasant treatments come to terms with them better if they can give the same treatment to a doll; they feel they have some control of the situation. In our playroom we have all the familiar play activities like painting, clay, dressing up and cooking. These activities can also be taken to the bedside or into the ward and even children too ill to play are encouraged by seeing activities around them and knowing they are still possible.'

### Vietnamese Children's Home
SCF's centre for Vietnamese children is the only one of its kind in Europe because of its predominantly Vietnamese staffing. Most children there are 'Boat People' refugees who arrived in the UK unaccompanied by parents or relatives able to care for them, often after traumatic experiences. We hope most will eventually be reunited with their families if they can come to the UK.

The idea of a Vietnamese home for unaccompanied children, with Vietnamese houseparents, was worked out by SCF in consultation with the refugees themselves. The aim is to keep children in contact with their cultural roots through Vietnamese language, customs, food and festivals, like Full Moon and New Year, so they can settle back easily into their families if they are reunited. At the same time, they learn about living in England, joining in activities with local children and enjoying English festivals like Christmas as well as observing their own traditions. They attend nearby schools and colleges and receive extra help with learning English.

### Crumlin Road
With father in prison, mother under tremendous stress and home a depressed, bitterly divided province, a sense of security for children is not easily built up. Many find the refuge they desperately need at Crumlin Road Family Centre in Belfast. It is used by families visiting men in HM Crumlin Road Prison or attending the nearby court. The Centre is run jointly by SCF and the Northern Ireland Association for the Care and Resettlement of Offenders and used by people from all parts of Northern Ireland, many having to make a long journey.

At Crumlin Road, which opens every day except Sundays, Christmas Day and Good Friday, when the prison is closed, SCF's playleader and her two helpers look after up to 60 children during a day. Their colourful playroom has something for all ages, from mobiles for babies to paints, toys, books and craft materials for older children. Stimulating activities and the company of other children and of caring adults in a relaxed atmosphere, give children a break from tension and the chance to develop skills, confidence and knowledge.

There is friendly, practical support for mothers too, some very young and devastated by their husbands' imprisonment. The Centre offers storage and toilet space, help with cheap rail travel, reasonably priced food, a quiet room, information on housing, benefits and health and a chance to meet others with the same problems.

### Overstream House
Canoeing down a Scottish river through gale force winds and snow and taking responsibility for camp equipment and organisation is a challenge for city teenagers; when they come through it successfully, their self confidence receives a considerable boost.

Cambridge Expeditions is one of many activities managed by SCF at its Overstream House project in Cambridge. It offers teenagers, many referred by the Intermediate Treatment Scheme or social services, a stimulating outdoor activity not otherwise available to them. The Riverside Club, also based there and run in partnership with local community and special schools, gets out and about too, catering for a different though mixed group of young people, many with special educational needs. Other youth work includes the pioneering Befriending Scheme which matches an adult volunteer with a young person, aiming to build a long-term supportive friendship.

Overstream House forms a base for youth work and child care and a launching pad for new initiatives. Over 140 volunteers from town and university work beside its small professional team.

### Trinity House
Childminders are very important influences in the lives of many under-fives but they can find their job lonely and restricting. To give them support and practical help and so benefit the children they care for, SCF set up its Childminding Project in 1976. This is now part of SCF's Trinity House Family Centre in the Rusholme district of Manchester, offering training courses for childminders, legal advice and the loan of toys and safety equipment like fireguards. There are regular drop-in sessions when minders can consult staff over coffee or simply relax and compare notes.

The Family Centre reaches out to the multicultural community around it with a very wide range of services. Its day nursery takes up to 60 children full or part time each week, while 20 children needing more individual attention are each matched with an approved childminder. There are thriving mother and toddler groups, youth clubs, a handicraft class with a creche and local activities ranging from a councillors' advice surgery to an informal pensioners' club. All help bring the community closer together and so provide a rich, stimulating environment in which young children can develop fully.

### The Matchbox
The Matchbox Project, in the Burdett Estate Community Centre in the East End is in the heart of one of London's more rundown and neglected areas. It got its name because its ever-expanding programme constantly threatens to burst the seams of its squat little hall. It provides five clubs for children of different ages, summer and Easter playschemes, football training for girls and English language classes, as

well as being home to local groups like the Bengali youth club and mother-tongue groups.

'Children can come to The Matchbox with their families from the earliest age and find something of interest, right through to adulthood,' says its project leader. 'Young people can then learn to mix and later support others growing up in a tough and testing environment.

This is a multiracial, culturally mixed but generally poor community that struggles hard against the disabling effects of disadvantaged inter-city life. We aim to work alongside local people to improve the quality of life here, as the most effective way of helping the children. Gradually we are handing over control of the Centre to a locally elected management committee.'

### Playtrac

The bright red Playtrac van is fitted out with racking and crates of exciting toys, paints, junk materials, musical instruments, equipment for sand and water play, and a parachute which has many uses – even if not dropping from the sky!

Playtrac is the Play, Leisure, Advice and Resources Mobile Centre, and the advantage of being mobile is that it can go to hospitals, hostels, schools, adult training centres and parent groups, bringing information, displays and practical training to their doorstep.

Playtrac offers the opportunity to try out many different kinds of play equipment, including commercial items not normally seen in toy shops and DIY toys which can be made by individuals or community groups. Practical sessions enable parents and staff to experience a wide range of play activities and explore their use with mentally handicapped people.

The first Playtrac unit took to the roads in 1981, with the aim of bringing play to children living in mental handicap hospitals by training staff in play methods and helping them to develop an awareness of the vital role of play in all children's lives. Playtrac II was launched in 1985, building on past experience but also reflecting the changing policy in care for mentally handicapped people, in particular the move away from hospital and into the community.

Mentally handicapped people are often withdrawn and lack curiosity to explore their surroundings and make contact with other people; they need to get the most out of toys and activities . . . and to experience the biggest benefit of all, fun and spontaneity. The completion of a simple jigsaw can become much more than a routine task as two people share the enjoyment of playing together.

### Ladymuir

When, in 1981, the Ladymuir Youth Project opened in two converted ground floor flats, in Pollok, Glasgow, project workers were besieged by young people desperate for a place to go and something positive to do. They included the young jobless – unemployment here is running at 48% – and many younger children who needed a break from the damp, substandard housing and the pressures of large or single-parent families.

For the young unemployed the task was to give them back a sense of purpose and self-esteem which had been eroded by long periods on the dole and the lack of any brighter future prospects. Today Ladymuir offers them the chance to discover that they *have* got a contribution to make, whether it's organising a group outing or helping to run activities for the younger ones. Such experience is also a big plus in the continuing search for jobs.

But the heart of the project is helping children and young people (and their families) to cope with conditions in Pollok. Mothers who bring their children to the under fives group are gaining in confidence; at the after-school clubs craft sessions are very popular and bring a real sense of achievement, particularly for children who may not be doing very well at school. Such activities also help the children to build up a rapport with the staff and give them an opportunity to chat informally about anything that is worrying them.

A gang of older girls asked for their own group in 1984. They have grown up in a violent, mainly male-dominated environment; and many cope by giving as good as they get and tend to be aggressive and anti-authority. The group is centred around personal development; as well as outings and discussions it provides opportunities for regular contact with stable adults, freedom to talk and build trust.

The project's three full-time staff are helped by volunteers from the community and one of them, who has been involved almost from the start, sums up Ladymuir's achievement in one sentence: 'It's wonderful to see the good coming out in kids you thought were impossible.'

## SAVE THE CHILDREN IN FIJI

Save the Children Fund's involvement in Fiji began in 1972 with a sponsorship programme to help children from poorer families to take up places they had won at secondary school by paying fees and other costs.

In 1981–83 financial support was given to the local Salvation Army organisation to establish clubs for children, designed to keep them off the streets and out of trouble. But the main focus of SCF's work in Fiji today is a programme for the early identification and treatment of cerebral palsy, with a budget in 1986/87 of some £30,000.

*Cerebral Palsy* is a general term used to describe some chronic injury or damage to a child's developing brain which has led to problems in controlling movement and posture. It therefore covers a variety of different disabilities affecting different parts of the body and to varying degrees, sometimes accompanied by problems with sight, hearing, speech or learning. The causes are equally numerous, ranging from genetic defects or illness in the mother during pregnancy, through difficulties during birth (with premature and low birth weight babies particularly at risk), to illness (eg meningitis) or accident after birth.

Cerebral palsy is the main cause of physical handicap in Fiji, where the incidence seems to be much higher than would be expected from the size of population. One survey found some 2000 cases in the island group as a whole – a rate five times higher than the UK one of just over two per thousand children of school age. At present, especially in rural areas, many disabled children are not brought to the attention of the education or health authorities until they reach the age of seven or eight, by which time it may be too late to help them. Early identification and treatment are important because children learn and develop most quickly during the first 18 months of life, and it is during this period that the opportunity for adjusting to cerebral damage is greatest.

*SCF Support*. Since 1982 Save the Children has been working closely with the Fijian authorities and the Crippled Children's Society of Fiji to establish a nationwide system for the early identification and treatment of handicapped children. The most effective treatment is usually physiotherapy, and ideally parents should be involved and taught simple techniques so that this can be done regularly at home. But Fiji has few trained physiotherapists to provide the necessary expertise and several years will be needed to train additional staff. SCF currently provides one expatriate physiotherapist, who works closely with the Fijian government's advisor on cerebral palsy.

Efforts to improve the identification of affected children have concentrated on teaching doctors, medical students, physiotherapists, physio aides, nurses, community health workers, teachers and members of other voluntary organisations to recognise the various signals that can give an early warning of the need for treatment.

## SAVE THE CHILDREN IN COLOMBIA

Through the Fundacion Colombo-Britanica (FCB) Save the Children Fund has for several years been supporting a day nursery for 70–80 children aged between two and six in the capital Bogota. Without the centre, most of these children would be left alone at home or in the streets because their mothers have to go out to work. The centre provides supervision of the children for ten hours every day, three good meals and medical checks twice a year. Parents are also given lessons on diet and other relevant topics.

The day centre relies heavily on its own fundraising efforts and SCF support, especially since official grants have remained static while inflation has eroded their value and increased running costs.

In the aftermath of the volcano disaster of November 1985, which destroyed the town of Armero and killed an estimated 23,000 people, the centre took in 25 children who had become separated from their families. Part of the centre was turned into a dormitory and staff were on hand round the clock to look after the children until their families or other relatives could be traced. In fact, with the help of television, the whole operation took only three weeks, a tribute to the efficiency with which the situation was handled by all concerned. The extra costs involved were paid out of emergency funds by SCF.

## SAVE THE CHILDREN IN ETHIOPIA

SCF's work in Ethiopia began in Wollo Province during the famine of 1973/74, in which 200,000 people are believed to have died. After the famine, programmes were developed to assist in the establishment of mother and child health services in various parts of the country, but the focus of SCF's work was the training of nutrition field workers. Their role was to monitor the nutritional status of local communities, as well as changes in food prices and harvest prospects. It was the information they supplied which formed the basis for the warnings of impending famine in the region made by several organisations as early as 1982 – two years before television reports galvanised the international community into action.

*Famine Relief*. Because of its involvement in Wollo, one of the regions worst hit by the drought, as the famine in the region worsened Save the Children was quickly drawn into relief operations, including emergency feeding and medical care.

By the middle of 1986 the emphasis had shifted to longer-term rehabilitation and development programmes. For example, with £25,000 raised by the RAF base at Lyneham in Wiltshire, SCF has been able to respond to a local initiative for an irrigation project at Bulbulo; enabling up to 130 families to improve their diets by growing more fruit and vegetables.

*Unaccompanied Children*. One of the main problems which faced relief workers as the feeding centres closed was the question of how to help the hundreds of children who had been orphaned or separated from their families. In conjunction with the International Red Cross, an SCF team set about tracing relatives, and by October 1986 all but 600 children had been reunited with their families or other relatives. Most of those remaining were brought together at a centre in Bati, and many more found places in residential homes.

*Wollo Transport Operation*. SCF/Oxfam's fleet of trucks (most of them four-wheel drive for rough roads) is already being used for non-emergency purposes, carrying seed and tools as well as food supplies to outlying areas, and there are plans to ensure that it is maintained in some form as a resource for the general development of the region. Communications have long been a problem in this respect, because the mountain roads are often only passable by specially equipped lorries and the difficult conditions demand regular servicing and large stocks of spare parts.

One possibility may be to establish the operation with its workshops and stores in Dessie as a transport pool for all the government departments in the region, distributing everything from books and medicines to food and fuel.

## SAVE THE CHILDREN IN MOZAMBIQUE

Save the Children has been working in Mozambique since 1984, establishing close contacts with health, education and child welfare authorities both at national level and in the province of Zambezia.

*Immunisation.* Save the Children's longest established programme in Mozambique is its support for the country's Expanded Programme of Immunisation (EPI), which aims to protect children against the six main killer diseases of childhood (polio, measles, tuberculosis, whooping cough, tetanus and diphtheria). An SCF doctor works at the EPI department in the Ministry of Health, helping to manage and evaluate the programme, train personnel and promote health education not just in Maputo but in the provinces as well. Material support for the programme is given in the form of cold-chain equipment (refrigerators and cold boxes to keep vaccines fresh), syringes, teaching aids and loudspeakers for publicity. The Fund will also be providing a technician to help with cold-chain management.

### Zambezia

In line with Save the Children's commitment to education and training, and at the request of the provincial health authority, a new project was initiated in March 1986 to establish a training centre for health workers from all over Zambezia. Prefabricated buildings are to be erected in the provincial capital Quelimane to provide a library, classrooms and hostel facilities, but already the two SCF teaching staff in the city have begun holding one-month refresher courses for qualified health workers, as well as giving classes for students at the Quelimane Institute of Health Sciences. One problem, however, is that health workers can face difficulties and dangers in reaching the city or returning to their posts in outlying areas, so the possibility of providing transport or correspondence courses is under consideration.

*Child Welfare.* War and drought have forced entire communities to leave their homes in search of food and security. In the process literally thousands of children have been orphaned, lost or abandoned. Often their only refuge was an institution, but the government is now anxious to get as many children as possible back into the community. With the tradition of the extended family there are usually some relatives able to care for such children – the problem is tracing them or finding foster families. SCF's social worker is helping to improve the chances of reunion.

By 1987 the conflict in Mozambique meant that hundreds of thousands of people had been forced to leave their homes, taking nothing with them. These refugees needed food, seeds, tools, cloth, basic utensils and medical supplies – and the government needed lorries to transport emergency supplies. Save the Children joined with other aid agencies to mount a relief operation.

## SAVE THE CHILDREN IN BANGLADESH

Save the Children Fund began its work in Dhaka in 1974, setting up an emergency centre for the care and treatment of the many severely ill children to be found on the streets of the city as a result of widespread flooding and famine. Particular priority was given to the care and rehabilitation of severely malnourished children, and the centre became known as the Children's Nutrition Unit (CNU). Despite the unit's success, there is now a great need for a purpose-built clinic which will provide better facilities for both treatment and training. The present building is too small to cope with the increasing demands on it, and the fact that the building is rented places a strain on the budget. A site has now been purchased, and it is hoped that the new CNU will be finished and in use soon.

### River Project

The River Project was originally set up at the beginning of 1975 as a disaster relief programme in response to the famine which has followed the severe floods of 1974. The project area lies on the east bank of the Jamuna river in the northern districts of Jamalpur and Gaibandha. It is a poor and relatively remote rural area, which frequently suffers from flooding, erosion or drought. The people are mostly poor, heavily dependent on agriculture and, in many cases, landless.

Over the years the project has developed into a comprehensive rural health care programme with a strong emphasis on educational development as well. There are four main objectives: to provide clinic and village based health facilities to the local population; to provide facilities for the care and feeding of malnourished children; to encourage the acceptance of primary education among the rural poor by giving assistance to the children or poor families; and to encourage community participation in the project work through representative village committees.

### Khulna

The Khulna programme, established in 1974, aims to provide three services: primary health care for children under five among the poor communities in and around the city, as well as ante-natal care, family planning and health education for mothers; day care facilities and treatment for severely malnourished children, together with practical training and advice for their mothers; and community-based health services within selected slum areas.

| Comparative Statistics | UK | Fiji | Mozambique | Colombia | Ethiopia | Bangladesh |
|---|---|---|---|---|---|---|
| Population (millions) | 55.6 | 0.7 | 13.4 | 27.5 | 42.2 | 95.8 |
| Population growth (per year) | 0.2% | 2.0% | 2.6% | 1.9% | 2.7% | 2.4% |
| Infant death rate (0–1) | 10/1000 | 31/1000 | 155/1000 | 50/1000 | 172/1000 | 130/1000 |
| Child death rate (1–4) | 0.4/1000 | 5/1000 | 22/1000 | 3/1000 | 39/1000 | 18/1000 |
| Life expectancy at birth (years) | 74 | 73 | 46 | 65 | 44 | 48 |
| Adult literacy (% male/female) | 99+ | 84/74 | 44/12 | 86/84 | 10/5 | 40/18 |
| GNP per capita[1] (US dollars) | 9200 | 1810 | 230 | 1390 | 110 | 130 |

[1] Total value of all goods and services produced by a nation in a year divided by the number of people in the country.

# U·N·I·T 40 Choosing the right words

All writers – perhaps especially poets – have to choose their words very carefully in order to make sure they say what they mean. As we read, without being aware of it, we often try to guess which words the writer will use next.

**'Out, Out—'**
The buzz saw snarled and rattled in the yard
And made dust and dropped stove-length sticks of wood,
Sweet-scented stuff when the breeze drew across it.
And from there those that lifted eyes could count
Five mountain ranges one behind the other
Under the sunset far into Vermont.
And the saw ___1___ and ___2___ , ___3___ and ___4___ ,
As it ran light, or had to bear a load.
And nothing happened: day was all but done.
Call it a day, I wish they might have said
To please the boy by giving him the half hour
That a boy counts so much when ___5___ from work.
His sister stood beside them in her apron
To tell them 'Supper'. At the word, the saw,
As if to prove saws ___6___ what supper ___7___ ,
___8___ out at the boy's hand, or seemed to ___9___ –
He must have given the hand. However it was,
Neither refused the meeting. But the hand!
The boy's first outcry was a rueful ___10___ ,
As he swung toward them holding up the hand
Half in appeal, but half as if to keep
The life from ___11___ . Then the boy saw all –
Since he was old enough to know, big ___12___
Doing a ___13___ 's work, though a ___14___ at heart –
He saw all spoiled. 'Don't let him cut my hand off –
The doctor, when he comes. Don't let him sister!'
So. But the hand was gone already.
The doctor put him in the dark of ether.
He lay and ___15___ his lips out with his breath.
And then – the watcher at his pulse took fright.
No one believed. They listened at his heart.
Little – less – ___16___ ! – and that ___17___ it.
No more to build on there. And they, since they
Were not ___18___ ___19___ ___20___ turned to their affairs.

# Assignments

☞ ○ ✔ **1** Imagine that the writer of the poem, Robert Frost, is having difficulty deciding which words should go in the numbered gaps.

   **a** Choose the best word for each gap.
   **b** Give a reason for each choice. (For instance, does it seem necessary for the poem's 'story'? Does it repeat a previous word or idea? Does it describe a sound in an appropriate way? Does it fit in with a sequence? Is it correct grammatically?)

   To find out which words Frost actually chose, turn to page 255.

**2** **a** Quote one line from the poem which suggests:

   - the practical, day-to-day work of the saw
   - that wood is pleasant to work with
   - that the scenery round about is impressive
   - that the boy's first reaction is one of shock
   - that the boy is really very inexperienced
   - that the witnesses of his death do not make a fuss
   - that the saw has human qualities
   - a family atmosphere
   - that something awful is going to happen

   **b** If you had to write a recipe for this poem, what would the list of ingredients be? Do you feel that the various aspects of the poem are well combined? Explain your view.
   **c** What makes this a poem rather than a short story? (Not an easy question!)

✎ **3** The boy's sister has to inform a close family member of what has happened. Write the letter she sends, remembering to convey her feelings and the sense that she finds the letter hard to write. (See pages 75–76 for an example of a letter to a family member.)

✔ ✎ **4** Write a newspaper account of the incident, which appeared in the *Vermont Daily Herald*. (See page 80 for reminders of how to write a newspaper article.) Your report should include:

   - what happened;
   - an interview with the boy's sister;
   - details about the boy's age, work, school record and interests;
   - an interview with someone else who knew him well, eg a friend, an old teacher or a youth club leader.

   Make up the boy's name and other personal details which are not supplied in the poem.

**5** Choose another poem (perhaps one you have written yourself) and cross out some key words. Give it to a friend or group of friends to see whether they can supply appropriate words to fill the gaps. Compare their suggestions with the original.

This poem has even more gaps than the previous one!

**Title**?

Beneath the oaks the _____

In sombre woodland _____

_____ sad as _____

All I knew _____

_____ never to be told _____

Crushed like flower petals _____

_____ stamped on _____

_____ uncaring.

Growing older _____

Life was a dream _____

Mirrored reflections like _____

_____ silently thinking.

Large spots of rain _____

Slow realisation _____

_____ gripping _____

Life is really _____

_____ never knew before.

_____ trusting now _____

Echoing _____

_____ as the clock chimes

_____ all I know

_____ happy like _____

_____ in sombre woodland

_____ beneath the oaks.

## Assignments

☞ **1** Imagine that you are the poet and are struggling to complete this poem.
Find something to fill all the gaps and make sense of the poem. Then supply
a title.
   Asking yourself these questions may help you to complete the poem:

- Should the poem have some sort of rhyme?
- Should all the lines contain the same number of syllables?
- Does the poem have any kind of pattern?
- What is the poem about?
- What is the mood of the poem?
- Where might it be appropriate to use comparisons? (See page 39) and
  which comparisons?

(When you've finished, turn to page 255 to see how close your version is to
the original)

# U·N·I·T 42 *More than words can tell*

Sometimes an idea can be put across without words, or by using only a few words. This unit looks at some of the ways this can be done. For questions **1–4** you will need a partner to work on each section **a**).

## *Assignments*

☞ **1** **Describing a process**

**a** Without the book in front of you, describe clearly to a friend what is happening in Fig 1. Then let him/her describe Fig 2 to you.
**b** Write down in words what is happening in each of Figs 1 and 2. (This time you may use the book.)

Coloured crystals added to water

Colour spreading

Coloured solution

**Fig. 1 Crystals dissolving**

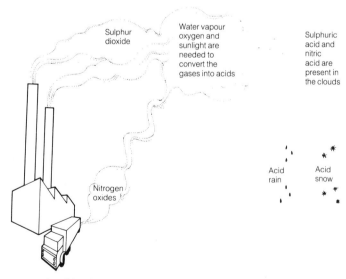

Sulphur dioxide

Water vapour oxygen and sunlight are needed to convert the gases into acids

Sulphuric acid and nitric acid are present in the clouds

Acid rain

Acid snow

Nitrogen oxides

**Fig. 2 Sources of acid rain**

166

☞ **2    What does it look like?**

**a** Study the two Pyramid diagrams for a few minutes, then close the book and describe as accurately as possible to a friend the ground plan of Cheops' pyramid. Then let your partner describe the cross-section to you.
**b** Write a description of the layout of Cheops' pyramid, including as much detail as possible. (There is no need to try to do this from memory.)

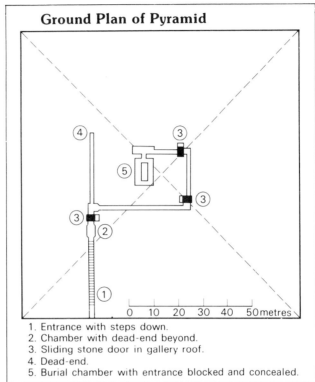

**Ground Plan of Pyramid**

1. Entrance with steps down.
2. Chamber with dead-end beyond.
3. Sliding stone door in gallery roof.
4. Dead-end.
5. Burial chamber with entrance blocked and concealed.

**Fig. 3**

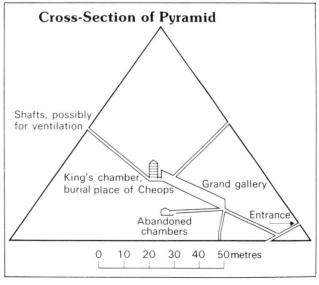

**Cross-Section of Pyramid**

Shafts, possibly for ventilation

King's chamber, burial place of Cheops

Grand gallery

Abandoned chambers

Entrance

**Fig. 4**

☞ **3  Raising a laugh**

**a**  Tell these jokes to a friend without looking at the book or referring to the pictures at all. If you prefer, your partner could tell one or more of the jokes to you.
**b**  Write the jokes out in words.

"WHY SHOULD I HAVE BEEN HERE AT NINE MISS? ... WHAT HAPPENED?"

"SORRY MISS, I'VE NO DOGS GOING CHEAP – ALL OURS SAY **WOOF**."

"WHAT DO YOU MEAN HAVE I TAKEN A BATH?, — IS THERE ONE MISSING?"

**Conveying facts and figures**

(One partner should do **a** and the other **c**. Either or both of you may do **b** and **d**.)

**a** Study the piechart and then, without looking at the chart, tell a friend how fuels obtained from oil are used in the UK.
**b** Write this information down in a few sentences.

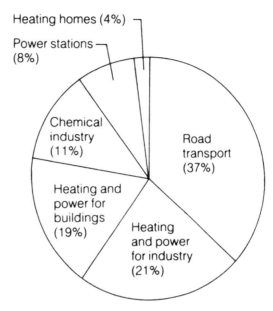

Heating homes (4%)

Power stations (8%)

Chemical industry (11%)

Road transport (37%)

Heating and power for buildings (19%)

Heating and power for industry (21%)

This is how the fuels obtained
from oil are used in the UK

**c** Study the figures below for a few minutes and then give a brief talk to your friend on what you think are the most significant things the figures show.
**d** Write a clear report (see page 19) on what these figures show about the preferences for evening classes in Lympington.

**Student enrolment at Lympington Evening Institute**

| Evening class | Men | | | | | Women | | | | |
|---|---|---|---|---|---|---|---|---|---|---|
| | aged 15–20 | aged 21–40 | aged 41–59 | aged 60+ | total | aged 15–20 | aged 21–40 | aged 41–59 | aged 60+ | total |
| Art | – | 4 | 3 | 2 | 9 | 1 | 9 | 7 | 8 | 25 |
| Badminton | 11 | 10 | 8 | 4 | 33 | 6 | 11 | 9 | 1 | 27 |
| Cake decorating | – | 1 | – | – | 1 | 1 | 10 | 6 | 3 | 20 |
| Cookery | 4 | 4 | 1 | – | 9 | 6 | 13 | 10 | 3 | 32 |
| Do-it-yourself | 4 | 14 | 8 | 2 | 28 | – | 4 | 2 | – | 6 |
| Literature | – | 7 | 7 | 8 | 22 | – | 9 | 13 | 8 | 30 |
| Motor mechanics | 9 | 7 | 4 | – | 20 | 2 | 3 | 2 | – | 7 |
| Needlework | – | – | – | – | – | 1 | 10 | 9 | – | 20 |
| Typing | 4 | 4 | – | – | 8 | 13 | 8 | 2 | 2 | 25 |
| Yoga | 2 | 6 | 2 | – | 10 | – | 15 | 10 | 7 | 32 |

**5** After completing assignments **1–4**, work with your partner to copy out and fill in the chart below.

**a** First decide jointly how effective each of the three methods – visual, oral and written – is for communicating each of the listed items. Award each a mark from 1–10 accordingly (1 if it is very poor, 10 if it is very good). For the oral and written categories your mark should take into account both how difficult the task was to perform and how well the listener/reader was able to understand the information communicated.

| | Visual | Oral | Written |
|---|---|---|---|
| Fig 1 – crystals dissolving | | | |
| Fig 2 – sources of acid rain | | | |
| Pyramid – ground plan | | | |
| Pyramid – cross-section | | | |
| Joke *i* | | | |
| Joke *ii* | | | |
| Joke *iii* | | | |
| Piechart – oil | | | |
| Table of figures – evening classes | | | |

**b** Which item worked best: visually? Orally? In written form?
**c** For which item(s) did the method not seem too important? Why was this, do you think?
**d** Give an example of a situation where using two of the methods together might seem a good idea. Explain why.
**e** Is it possible to make any generalisations about the best way to communicate:

- a process?
- the layout of a place?
- jokes?
- facts and figures?

Or does it always depend? On what?
**f** For what type of communication(s) would you *never* want to use:

*i* a visual representation? *ii* an oral account? *iii* a written account?

Why not?

**6** Select a subject of your own choice which you think can be communicated in all three ways. (It can be anything you think would work.) Make a visual, an oral and a written representation of your subject. Write a paragraph saying which representation you feel is most successful and why.

# U·N·I·T 43 It all depends

A number of teenagers were asked about their attitudes to and experiences of crime. Here are extracts from what 13 of them said:

**a** 'They're out to rook you first, I mean the employers, ain't they? Docking this and that off your money? No, I don't reckon there's much wrong with pinching at work.' (18, *storekeeper*)

**b** 'I've knocked off things from work – spare parts, light switches, mirrors and given them to people or sometimes sold them.'

**c** 'I work a fiddle if I ever get the chance. Say a load of material comes in, and it's marked on the ticket 45 metres. After a few days that ticket may come away and the governor may say, "What's the length?" You tell him you don't know, so you measure it on the machine and you find that it's 50 metres. You look in the book and you find that it's supposed to be 45 metres. You've got five metres over, haven't you? If you tell the governor about it, he'll keep it for himself. He's not going to send it back to the mills and tell them they've made a mistake. So what I do, I take it myself. I don't see any reason why I shouldn't. To take off your governor is the usual practice, I should say. Governors fiddle, don't they? And they cheat each other. So why shouldn't you do the same?'

**d** 'The way I see it is this – the governor's on the fiddle and he's making it out of you anyway. No matter what you do, if you're making something on the side, the governor's making more.' (17, *labourer*)

**e** 'If someone pinches something from a big shop or from the back of a Rolls-Royce, or something like that, and they get away with it, I say good luck to them. What does it matter? It's only a crime against society, so who cares? It's not at all the same thing as knocking down some poor little old lady who's walking along leaning on a stick and with a big purse in her hand. I don't like to think that people around here would knock an old lady like that down for her purse.' (19-year-old)

**f** 'If you steal off someone who's a friend of yours, someone you know, that's bad. I don't see as there's anything wrong with stealing from a big shop or from a bank or somewhere like that. Ordinary people don't have to find the money out of their own pockets – it's all covered by insurance anyway.' (17-year-old)

**g** 'I started with scooters. You know, you come home from school and you see a scooter parked there. You've found out how to get it started from your mates and you think "I'd just like to ride one of those things around the block". If it's dark and there's no one about you get on and ride away on it. If nothing goes wrong, you're tempted to do the same thing the next day and the day after that.' (18-year-old)

**h** 'It's very common round here – more common to take scooters than cars. The girls go for the scooter boys and they don't care whether the boy owns the scooter or whether he's pinched it. They don't know and they don't care.' (17-year-old)

**i** 'I've done my share of "borrowing" cars and scooters in the past. I don't think it's right, particularly sometimes. Two blokes from round here came out of the Lyceum ballroom one night and pinched a Mini to get home because they reckoned there weren't any more buses running. Well, this car belonged to a young out-of-work actor, who's got polio. It puts him in a right fix. The police find this car abandoned down Bethnal Green and someone grasses about these two blokes and they get pinched. Then the story comes out. Of course the two chaps say they're sorry about the polio bloke and all that, but the beak says they're only sorry because they got caught. Still they only got fined. The point is it just shows how you can hurt people who haven't done anything to you. It's daft really, thoughtless.'

**j** 'I've never really knocked anything off – nothing important. I might have pinched a pencil from school or something like that, but I've never done a job, you know – broken into somewhere and smashed it all up or anything like that. I know people who do do that sort of thing, but I've never done it. I mean, if I'd done it I'd have had the fear my mother would find out and smack me. I've always known my parents disapproved of that sort of thing.' (17-year-old)

**k** 'When this copper started shoving my friend around, I hit him with a bottle. I was put on probation for two years for that. My old man said, "Jolly good luck – sod the coppers." He don't like the coppers because he's a lorry driver; and before he drove lorries he was pinched lots of times for being a street trader.' (17-year-old)

**l** 'My dad's done some jobs in his time – years ago, you know, when the family was hard up. He let it drop once that he'd done some warehouses. He said, "The only time I've ever done something was when I done it for my wife and children." But he went straight off the subject after that – he kind of jumped on to something else. No, I think he'd rather kill me than see me up in court. Anyway, it's all more or less forgotten now. I've got enough sense now not to get caught.'

**m** 'Look at my family – everyone goes inside from time to time. One of my uncles has just come out after doing six years. Another uncle goes in now and then for three months. Another one is selling stolen goods – he's been doing that for two years and he ain't been caught. He's making loads of money. It runs like that in the family.' (16-year-old)

# Assignments

☞ **1** How do you respond to these comments? Do you have any sympathy with these teenagers? Do you agree with their views, or is there no excuse for any of these crimes?

☞ **2** **a** Make a list of the different words and phrases meaning 'steal' which the teenagers use.
**b** How do these different words reveal the teenagers' attitudes? For instance, do some words make the crime sound worse than others?

 ☞ **3** Analyse the kinds of crime mentioned and the teenagers' reactions. Copy out the chart below and fill in the boxes (a few have been done for you) – note that you will not be able to complete every box for every crime.

| Crime | Against whom | Does teenager think this crime is acceptable? | Reason |
|---|---|---|---|
| **a** Stealing | Employer | Yes | Employers cheat – they dock pay |
| **b** Stealing parts etc | | | |
| **c** | | | |
| **d** | | | |
| **e** Stealing | Shop or rich | | |
| **f** Stealing purse | Old lady | No | She's weak and poor |

 ☞ **4** Use your chart to help you write a magazine article entitled *The Young Offenders*. The article is for a Sunday newspaper supplement, read by people of all ages. Use this rough plan for your article:

- types of crime committed and against whom;
- reasons why crimes committed;
- what types of crimes the teenagers try to justify and how;
- what crimes they cannot justify and why not.

Your article should be 300–450 words long.

> **Remember**
> - your article deals mainly with opinions, not facts
> - your style should be fluent – do not be tempted to copy lists from the chart

**5** Consider the following examples of theft and decide how 'wrong' you think they are. Grade each of them on a scale of 1–10 (1 as the least serious and 10 as the worst).

**a** Breaking into the home of someone wealthy and stealing £2000 worth of antiques.
**b** Mugging a poor old lady and stealing £2 from her.
**c** Finding £5 in the street and keeping it.
**d** Taking home pens and sellotape from the office where you work.
**e** Breaking into a house in a poor district and stealing a radio.
**f** Going for a joyride in a car found unlocked.
**g** Stealing clothes from a large shop.
**h** Stealing £3 000 000 in an armed robbery from a bank.
**i** Stealing 20p from your friend's pocket.
**j** Stealing a dress from a small local shop.

Compare the way you have graded the crimes with some of your friends' opinions. Are there big differences?

**6** Imagine that each of the above crimes is committed by these four people:

**Fred** (aged 42)  Has already been to prison twice for long spells. When not in prison he drives a Mercedes and lives in a mansion.
**Jeanette** (aged 19)  Has stable family but parents and two brothers are all unemployed. She has not found a job since leaving school.
**Mark** (aged 16)  Both parents dead. Has lived in six different foster homes.
**Elise** (aged 51)  Recently divorced, three grown-up children all living a long way away. Has very comfortable home but has not worked since she was married.

If you were the magistrates, what sentences would you pass on each of them? Set your answers out in a chart:

| Crime | Suggested sentences | | | |
| --- | --- | --- | --- | --- |
| | **Fred** | **Jeanette** | **Mark** | **Elise** |
| **a** | | | | |
| **. . .** | | | | |

The sentences you can choose from include: fine (how much?); prison or youth custody (how long?); suspended sentence; probation (how long?); community service (what kind?); no punishment at all.

If you feel that any of your sentences needs more explanation, write notes on them underneath your chart.

**7** Your form is to hold a formal debate (see page 134) on the motion 'We believe that stealing is always wrong'. Write a speech either proposing or opposing this point of view.

**8** Hold the debate mentioned in **7**.

This article describes the lifestyle of an 18-year-old debutante. A debutante is a young lady from an upper-class background who has recently been presented to wealthy society for the first time, usually at a formal ball.

As you read it, try to decide what you think the writer's attitude towards Anastasia is.

She isn't really like other young girls of 18. For one thing there's her *glorious* name – Natasha Anastasia Cooke. For another, money, jobs and the future seem to hold no problems at all. Finally, there's a little matter of a *really super* honour likely to come her way soon – being named Deb Of The Year, in case you missed it. The Season, an annual round of balls, cocktail parties and other social thrashes, kicked off last month with the Berkeley Dress Show. Anastasia, as she prefers to be known, was chosen to wear the bride's dress in the grand finale – a great honour which was rewarded by getting her picture in the papers the following morning. She couldn't be more pleased – Anastasia loves to be the centre of attention and that is what being a deb is all about.

Until the late Fifties, the climax of the debutante's year was to be presented at Court and curtsy before the Queen. Today's deb, however, is more likely to be at boarding school studying for University or a career but the good old days are far from over. Money still talks, sometimes it shouts, and University degree or not, jobs are gained by friends . . . especially *Daddy's*.

Anastasia, the youngest of three children, has everything it takes. A family with wealth and property, a nine-bedroom house in the right part of Wimbledon, where home-helps and gardeners tread a respectful path and where the most important household accessory is a burglar alarm.

What *really* sets debs apart is attitude. They seem programmed to be charming and adept at social chit-chat, but to know what they really think – or *if* they really think about much beyond their own lives – you have to be one of them.

From an outsider's point of view, it seems that having fun is what growing up is all about. Accordingly they put a remarkable amount of energy into this pastime. But while they know they're lucky – 'I do feel I'm very, very privileged,' admits Anastasia – they don't seem to understand what being *un*lucky really means. True, they might help with charity work but they also seem totally detached from the nitty-gritty of normal life which, according to your point of view, could be blatant ignorance, arrogance or simply genuine naivete.

Today, Anastasia is home from her boarding school, St Mary's, Ascot. She wakes up in her green bedroom with its *perfect* doll's house, china horses and cuddly gorilla, pulls on a pair of jeans and a sweater and goes down to the kitchen for a light breakfast of juice, cereal or toast and reads the paper – a choice of The Daily Telegraph, The Times or the Financial Times. Blinking back the excesses of the night before – debs tend to go out *every* night – Anastasia takes the family dogs, a mastiff and a bassett-hound, for a walk before trying to find time for some study.

It's not *quite* all fun for a deb and Anastasia, working for her A levels, still tries to put in three hours study a day. With 9 O levels and one A level already under her belt, she needs two more with decent grades to get into Bristol University to read Psychology and Sociology. But before she does that, she hopes to take a year off modelling, working and travelling.

'I'm with Gavin Robinson, the model agency – Mummy was there, too – and I'm to get an assignment in Japan for two months,' she explains. 'Then I'm going to do a short course in typing and speedwriting, after which I'd really like to go to Australia in January. A friend of mine lives in Sydney and I could either work for her father or she could find me a job elsewhere. Another friend's father owns a radio station in Florida and he could give me a job, too.' It is, as they say, most definitely who you know not what, and perhaps for some debs, that's just as well.

While she plays tennis, her mother prepares lunch for the family and friends. Because of the holiday, organisation is slightly more of a problem than usual, not helped by the fact that: 'There's no daily help on Saturday and the gardener is having a new hip put in. Oh well,' she says *stoically*. 'It's what everybody else manages on.'

About an hour into lunch, Anastasia moves down the table to talk to me about her life and her future. She's chatty and helpful, tries to answer all the questions and obviously enjoys the attention without any hint of embarrassment.

Asked about her long-term future, she confides she would like to work in television journalism, or try her hand at acting. Her mother went to RADA and she is thinking of doing a post-graduate drama course herself. 'Yes, of *course* I want to be famous,' she says confidently, as if it were the most natural thing in the world. 'I want to have a good career, then marry when I'm about 26. I'd like three or four children but if I have a career I'd like to carry on working – which makes me hesitant about having too many – if any.'

It's all neatly mapped out. Maybe it's because many 18-year-olds think it's all there for the taking or maybe it's because Anastasia is used to getting what she wants.

At seven o'clock Anastasia disappears upstairs to change for the fifth time that day, and returns wearing a pink and black outfit. She changes again into a frothier black dress before changing back into the first outfit, which her mother thinks is more suitable.

Armed with her addressbook, *because you never know*, we return to Knightsbridge for a drinks party at a friend's flat.

From the drinks party a group of *young things* in cars go to dinner at L'Escargot in Soho. Over steamed chicken, vegetables and white wine, Anastasia talks about her life. What class would she describe herself as? 'Middle?' she suggests, hesitantly. 'I don't know, I think I'm average.' She pauses. 'Well, maybe a bit more.'

At the coffee stage of the meal, Anastasia moves round the table, sits on laps, hugs her friends and makes arrangements for future evenings. The only dampener on their evening is contributing to the £173 bill. The young rich, it would appear do not like being parted from their money.

# Assignments

**1** Some words and phrases have been italicized. What do you think would be the effect of replacing them with the following words and phrases?

| In passage | Replace with |
| --- | --- |
| glorious | unusual |
| really super | great |
| Daddy's | her father's |
| perfect | beautiful |
| stoically | brightly |
| because you never know | in case she needs it |
| young things | friends |

---

**2** **a** List any statements you can find in the passage which seem to be the author's *opinion* rather than the *facts* (see page 218).
**b** List any details which you feel are included not because they are strictly relevant but because they create a certain impression of Anastasia. What is this impression?
**c** What would you now say is the author's attitude to Anastasia?
**d** Are there any statements in the text which would make you reconsider your answer to **c**?
**e** Would you say the article presents a balanced view? What is the *tone* (see page 27)?
**f** Is it a good idea to write an article like this from a certain point of view? What is to be gained? What is to be lost?

---

**3** Choose a character, either real or imaginary, to write a magazine article about. Write one version of the article sticking simply to the relevant facts, told in a straightforward way. Then write a second version which you make biased either towards or against the character, by including:

- a biased vocabulary
- opinion written as though it were fact
- unnecessary details added to support your point of view.

Finally, write a paragraph explaining what you think the good and bad points of your articles are.

# U·N·I·T 45 *The rules of the game*

Maureen Shaw is compiling a book of wordgames which can be played by anyone over 14. She is considering including both *Ghost* and *Target Word* in the book, but a little research into the two games needs to be done first. She would like to know: first, whether the games are successful; second, the best way to present the instructions. Here, *Ghost* is explained in the form of a flow-chart and *Target Word* as a list of numbered points.

## Assignments

(Numbers **1–3** are best carried out in small groups.)

**1**
  **a** Play both games briefly to see whether the instructions are clear.
  **b** What alterations, if any, would you make to the instructions?
  **c** Do you find the flow-chart or the numbered points easier to follow?

**2** Work out and then write instructions for *Ghost* in the form of numbered points.

**3** Work out and then draw instructions for *Target Word* in the form of a flow-chart.

**4** Write a report (see page 19) for Ms Shaw, giving your findings about the two games. Organise your report as follows:

- Are both games straightforward to play? (Point out any drawbacks or advantages)
- Do the instructions need any alteration?
- Which type of instructions seems best for each game? (Give reasons)
- Would you recommend that Ms Shaw includes these two games in her book? (Give reasons)

**5** Choose another game which you think would be suitable for the book. Write instructions for it – either as a flow-chart or in numbered points, or both.

178

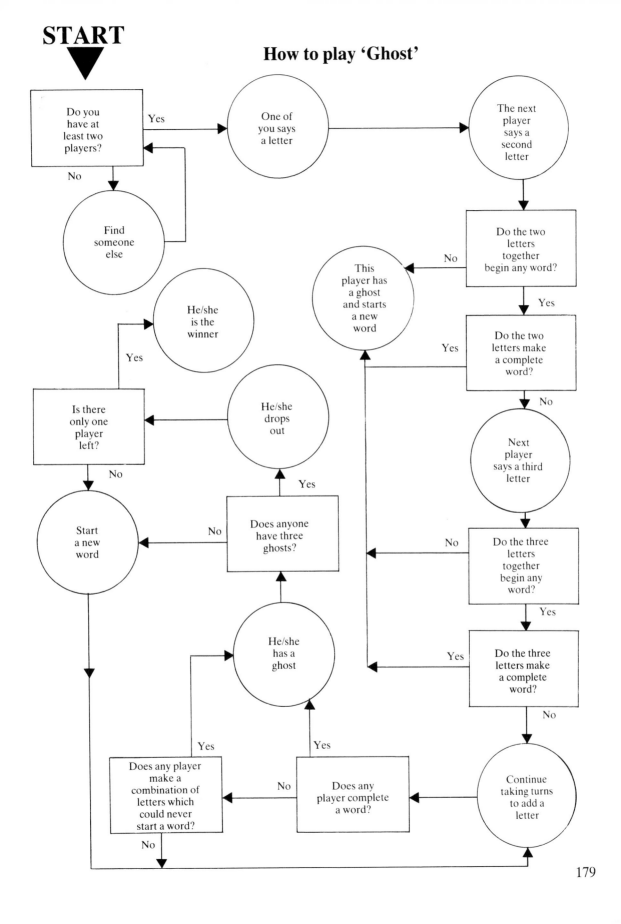

START

# How to play 'Ghost'

179

## How to play 'Target word'

1. This game is played by two teams with at least three players in each. A referee is also needed to conduct the game.

2. The referee calls one player from each team and tells them a word, which another member of their team then has to guess.

3. The player from team one gives her/his partner a one-word clue to the target word (eg a clue for the word 'yellow' might be 'daffodil').

4. The partner is allowed one guess at the word.

5. If the guess is correct, the referee gives two different players a new word for two different partners to guess. This time team two goes first.

6. If the guess is wrong, the player from team two gives her/his partner a different one-word clue.

7. The two players continue taking turns to give their partners a clue to the target word until it is guessed.

8. If the word is guessed after the first clue, the team that guesses scores ten points; after the second clue nine points; after the third clue eight points, and so on.

9. If neither team has guessed the target word after ten clues have been heard (five from each team) then the referee gives everyone the answer and moves on to a new word.

10. When an agreed number of words have been guessed, the scores are added up and the team with the most points wins.

# U·N·I·T 46 *Contrasting registers*

A *register* is a form of language which is especially appropriate for a certain situation (see Unit **31** on page 120). Sometimes, interesting effects can be achieved by using two contrasting registers. The following poem by Henry Reed is about an unwilling soldier listening to a lecture from a superior officer.

**I. Naming of Parts**

Today we have naming of parts. Yesterday,
We had daily cleaning. And tomorrow morning,
We shall have what to do after firing. But today,
Today we have naming of parts. Japonica
Glistens like coral in all of the neighbouring gardens,
    And today we have naming of parts.

This is the lower sling swivel. And this
Is the upper sling swivel, whose use you will see,
When you are given your slings. And this is the piling swivel,
Which in your case you have not got. The branches                    10
Hold in the gardens their silent, eloquent gestures.
    Which in our case we have not got.

This is the safety-catch, which is always released
With an easy flick of the thumb. And please do not let me
See anyone using his finger. You can do it quite easy
If you have any strength in your thumb. The blossoms
Are fragile and motionless, never letting anyone see
    Any of them using their finger.

And this you can see is the bolt. The purpose of this
Is to open the breech, as you see. We can slide it               20
Rapidly backwards and forwards: we call this
Easing the spring. And rapidly backwards and forwards
The early bees are assaulting and fumbling the flowers:
    They call it easing the Spring.

They call it easing the Spring: it is perfectly easy
If you have any strength in your thumb: like the bolt,
And the breech, and the cocking-piece, and the point of balance,
Which in our case we have not got; and the almond-blossom
Silent in all of the gardens and the bees going backwards and forwards,
    For today we have naming of parts.               30

# Assignments

○ ☞ **1**  **a**  Some of this poem consists of the officer's lecture and some of it is the thoughts of the soldier as he listens to the lecture. Decide which parts are which; make a note of the line references.
  **b**  Briefly summarise the subject matter of: the officer's lecture; the soldier's thoughts.
  **c**  How would you describe the *language* of the soldier's thoughts? For instance, is it gentle or harsh? Do these lines of the poem flow or are they stilted and clumsy? Pick out examples to support your views.
  **d**  Now look at the language the officer uses. Note down examples of phrases which you think sound clumsy. Note down any phrases which seem dull or technical. Do his lines flow or are they stilted?
  **e**  Would you agree that the registers used for the officer and the soldier are related to the subject matter? Explain your answer.

○ ☞ **2**  **a**  With what is each of the following contrasted: the branches (line 10); the blossoms (line 16); the bees (line 23)?
  **b**  Why do you think these contrasts are made? Is the poet suggesting something about war and nature?

○ **3**  **a**  Now that you have a fairly clear idea of how the poem works, practise reading it aloud in a way which brings out all its most important features.
  **b**  Read it aloud to the rest of the class, or tape record it.

✔ ◇ **4**  Write a similar poem of your own describing a different situation. For example, instead of the army lecturer you could have a schoolteacher giving a lesson. Remember to use words which are typical of a particular subject, and use a different register for your own thoughts, which could be about anything (whatever you usually daydream about during lessons!)

# U·N·I·T 47 *Facing the future*

All the work on the next four pages relates to the development of a small village.

Lower Tinksbury until recently was a village of 800 inhabitants. It is now being developed, however, with new housing and other new buildings to cater for 2000 inhabitants. Of the present inhabitants, about half are over 60 and only 30 under five. When the new housing is occupied, it is anticipated that there will be 100 more under-fives and a further 100 under-tens.

At present there are three thriving industries on the outskirts of the village and a new soft toy factory is being built. There are six shops: a small supermarket, a butcher's, an ironmonger's, a post office and newsagent's, a children's clothes shop and an antique shop. Other existing facilities are shown on the map. The village is in a rural area. Public transport is poor and the nearest town of any size is 12 miles away.

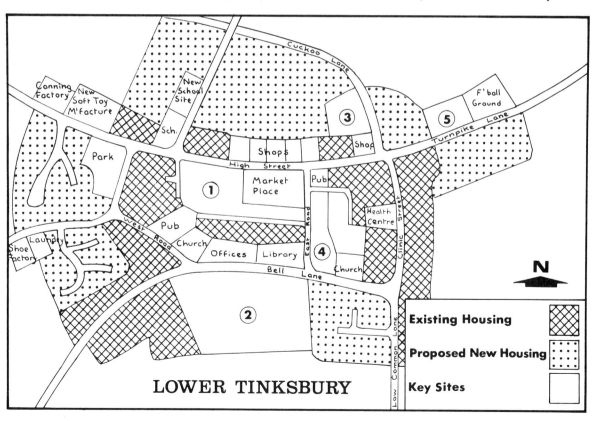

LOWER TINKSBURY

Existing Housing

Proposed New Housing

Key Sites

Some Lower Tinksbury residents were interviewed on local radio about their views on the new development. Here are some extracts from what they said:

*Development? Well, it'll be chaotic if we don't get a bigger health centre. Older people and young children make most use of healthcare facilities and we're overstretched as it is.*

(Dr Sayad, Lower Tinksbury Health Centre)

*I'm glad there are more children coming to the village. At last we're getting a new school and now they'll have to do something about providing a nursery school too. The tiny tots are so important!*

(Carol Tills, Headteacher)

*I suppose we old'uns will get a rough deal as usual. This village will change overnight. It used to be so quiet and peaceful. Now it'll be like a bloody new town. Full of snivelling brats. I hear they'll get a nursery school. What about our over-sixties' social centre we've wanted for twenty years? They can't walk over us just because we're old.*

(Christine Phillips, 76)

*More young people? Great! Things might liven up round here. This is a dead hole – nothing to do. I hope there'll be some entertainment for young people.*

(Judith Hackett, 15)

*Certainly the character of the village will change and I've got my doubts about that. Still, let's hope we get a nice new library. I guess we'll need a much larger children's section, too.*

(Tom Luxton, Chief Librarian)

*A larger congregation – wonderful! I do hope for a large new parish hall. We hope to hold more clubs for the young and old then, too.*

(Reverend Mike Gilly)

*A bigger village means a better football team! We need a new stand and a whole new complex – gym, bar etc if the team's really going to take off.*

(Robert Messenger, Manager of Lower Tinksbury FC)

# Assignments

○ ☞ **1**  Look back at the details on the map and the facts about Lower Tinksbury, then make a list of all the problems you think will arise as this new development takes place. What new facilities will be needed? (Bear in mind the needs of all age groups and both existing and new residents.)

_____

✔ ◇ ☞ **2**  The map shows five key sites which are to be developed in the village. The local council's planning department has drawn up alternatives for the uses of the five sites (see diagrams for the suggestions that have been put forward.) Write a report (see page 19) on these proposals, to be given to everyone attending the public meeting.

Mention each of the sites (**1–5**) in turn. State the different uses which could be made of each site, and indicate which section(s) of the community would benefit. Be careful to write in a clear, matter-of-fact way, without letting your opinions influence what you say.

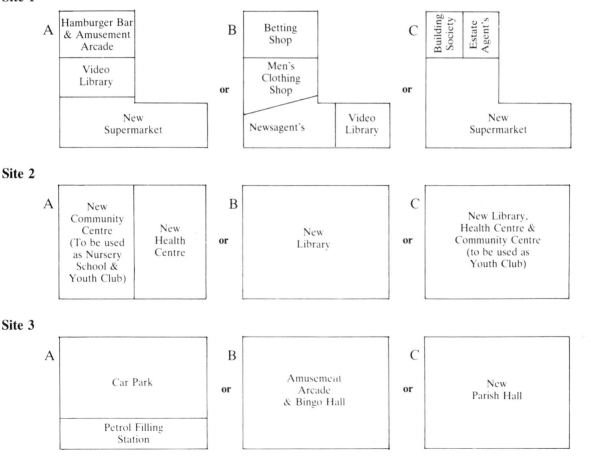

**Site 1**

A
| Hamburger Bar & Amusement Arcade |
| Video Library |
| New Supermarket |

or

B
| Betting Shop |
| Men's Clothing Shop |
| Newsagent's | Video Library |

or

C
| Building Society | Estate Agent's |
| New Supermarket |

**Site 2**

A
| New Community Centre (To be used as Nursery School & Youth Club) | New Health Centre |

or

B
| New Library |

or

C
| New Library, Health Centre & Community Centre (to be used as Youth Club) |

**Site 3**

A
| Car Park |
| Petrol Filling Station |

or

B
| Amusement Arcade & Bingo Hall |

or

C
| New Parish Hall |

**Site 4**

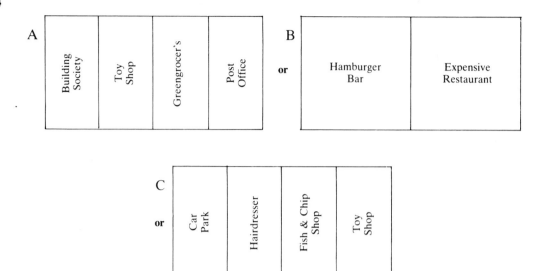

**Site 5**

✔ ○ ☞ **3**   **a** Act out the meeting at which it is decided how the key sites **1–5** are to be used. (Note that if the old library, health centre or church are no longer needed, you may suggest a new use for these buildings.) Each member of the class should take one of the roles listed below. (You do not necessarily need *all* the people listed.) Spend about ten minutes thinking about your role and deciding your views on the key sites. Make notes to help you argue for your point of view at the meeting.

**People at the meeting**

- Mayor(ess) who chairs and controls the meeting
- Five local councillors who sit on the platform with the mayor(ess). They may ask for specific information to help them make decisions about the key sites and they should take careful notes at the meeting
- Revd Gilly
- Dr Sayad
- Robert Messenger
- Carol Tills
- Tom Luxton
- Christine Phillips
- Judith Hackett
- Youth leader, newly appointed to Lower Tinksbury

186

- Two engineers from the local council who offer advice on traffic, roads, carparks etc
- Two planning officers from the local council who offer advice on the size and type of buildings and how to create an attractive environment
- District Recreation Officer, who is concerned with providing enough entertainment for local residents
- Representative of the Heritage Trust, who feels that all new developments should be in keeping with the old, traditional character of the village
- Local resident who runs the County Anti-gambling Association
- Representative from Moneygrow Building Society
- Representative from Surefull Supermarkets
- Representative from Betabet Gambling Games Ltd
- Young parents
- Elderly people
- Teenagers
- Local shopkeepers

**b** After the public meeting, the Mayor(ess) and councillors meet to make final decisions on how the five sites will be used. These decisions will immediately be passed on to local newspapers (see **4**).

**4** Write a full-length feature for the *Tinksbury District Gazette* about the new development. This is big news in an area like Tinksbury, so the local paper will cover it in detail, taking several pages. Half your article should explain what will be built and where, while the other half should be about how local residents will be affected. If you wish, you may include interviews, pictures and plans.

**5** The *Tinksbury District Gazette* has the following advertisement in its *Jobs* column a year after the meeting:

| | |
|---|---|
| **CANTEEN SUPERVISOR** | required for soft toy factory opening shortly. Good pay for experienced and go-ahead applicant. Qualifications an advantage.<br>Apply: Monttoys Ltd, Lower Tinksbury, Shropshire, SH61 4NF. |

**a** Write five other advertisements for new jobs in Lower Tinksbury. (Look back at the description of the development to help you forecast which jobs will now be available.)
**b** Write a letter from a very suitable applicant applying for one of the jobs.
**c** Write a letter from a very unsuitable applicant applying for one of the other jobs. (See page 69 on writing formal letters.)

This short story by Heinrich Böll has been translated from German. But sometimes words can be wrongly translated. How can we tell if the translation is correct? Read the story straight through once, to get a 'feel' for it.

**CHILDREN ARE CIVILIANS TOO**

'NO, you can't,' said the sentry cheerily.

'Why?' I asked.

'Because it's against the rules.'

'Why is it against the rules?'

'Because it is, chum, that's what; patients aren't allowed outside.'

'But,' I said with pride, 'I'm one of the wounded.'

The sentry gave me a scornful look: 'I guess this is the first time you've been wounded, or you'd know that the wounded are patients too. Go on, get back in.'

But I persisted.

'Have a heart,' I said, 'I only want to steal cakes from that little girl.'

I pointed outside to where a pretty little Russian girl was standing in the whirling snow peddling cakes.

'Get back inside, I tell you!'

The snow was falling softly into the huge puddles on the black schoolyard, the little girl stood there patiently, calling out over and and over again: 'Khakes . . . khakes . . .'

'My God,' I told the sentry, 'my mouth's watering, why don't you just let the child come inside?'

'Civilians aren't allowed inside.'

'Good God, man,' I said, 'the child's just a child.'

He gave me another scornful look. 'I suppose children aren't civilians, eh?'

It was comical – the empty, dark street was wrapped in powdery snow, and the child stood there all alone, calling out 'Khakes . . .' although no one passed.

I started to walk out anyway, but the policeman grabbed me by the sleeve and shouted furiously: 'Get back, or I'll call the sergeant!'

'You're a bloody fool,' I snapped back at him.

'That's right,' said the sentry with satisfaction. 'Anyone who still has a sense of duty is considered a bloody fool by you fellows.'

I stood for another half minute in the whirling snow, watching the white flakes turn to mud; the whole schoolyard was full of puddles, and dotted about lay little white islands like icing sugar. Suddenly I saw the little girl wink at me and walk off in apparent unconcern down the street. I followed along the inner side of the wall.

'Damn it all,' I thought, 'am I really a child?' And then I noticed a hole in the wall next to the urinal, and on the other side of the hole stood the little girl with the cakes. The sentry couldn't see us here. May the Führer bless your sense of duty, I thought.

The cakes looked marvellous: macaroons and cream slices, buttermilk twists and nut squares slimy with oil. 'How much?' I asked the child.

She smiled, lifted the basket towards me, and said in her piping voice: 'Two marks fifty each.'

'All the same price?'

'Yes,' she nodded.

The snow fell on her fine blonde hair, powdering her with fleeting silver dust; her smile was utterly betwitching. The dismal street behind her was empty, and the world seemed dead . . .

I took a buttermilk twist and bit into it. It was delicious, there was marzipan in it. 'Aha,' I thought, 'that's why these cost as much as the others.'

The little girl was crying.

'Good?' she asked. 'Good?'

I nodded. I didn't mind the cold, I had a thick bandage round my head that made me look very romantic. I tried a cream slice and let the delectable stuff melt slowly in my mouth. And again my mouth watered . . .

'Here,' I whispered, 'I'll take the lot, how many are there?'

She began counting, carefully, with a delicate, rather dirty little forefinger, while I devoured a nut square. It was very quiet, it seemed almost as if there were a soft, gentle weaving of raindrops in the air. She counted very slowly, made one or two mistakes, and I stood there quite still eating two more cakes. Then she raised her eyes to me suddenly, at such a startling angle that her pupils slanted upwards and the whites of her eyes were the thin blue of skim milk. She twittered something at me in Russian, but I shrugged my shoulders with a smile, whereupon she bent down and with her dirty little finger wrote a 45 in the snow; I added my five, saying: 'Let me have the basket too, will you?'

She nodded, carefully handing me the basket through the hole, and I passed a couple of hundred-mark bills through to her. We had money to burn, the Russians were paying seven hundred marks for a coat, and for three months we had seen nothing but mud and blood, a few whores, and money.

'Come back tomorrow, O.K.?' I whispered, but she was no longer listening, quick as a wink she had slipped away, and when I stuck my head sadly through the gap in the wall she had vanished, and I saw only the silent Russian street, bright and empty; the snow seemed to be gradually entombing the flat-roofed houses. I stood there for a long time, like a raging animal looking out through a fence, and it was only when I felt my neck getting stiff that I pulled my head back inside the prison.

And for the first time I noticed the revolting urinal stench from the corner, and all the nice little cakes were covered with a light sugar-icing of snow. With a sigh I picked up the basket and walked towards the building; I did not feel cold, I had that romantic-looking bandage round my head and could have stood for another hour in the snow. I left because I had to go some place. A fellow has to go some place, doesn't he? You can't stand around and let yourself be buried in snow. You have to go some place, even when you're wounded in a strange, black, very dark country . . .

# Assignments

**1**
**a** Now read the story a second time. This time, look out for details which seem out of keeping with the rest of the story. Ten words have been altered. How many of them can you find? How did you spot the mistakes?
**b** Suggest how the mistakes could be corrected.
**c** Which mistake is the most important one, in your opinion? Why? Put the ten mistakes in order of how important you think they are to the story. (Explain your reasons)

**2**
**a** What do you think the story is about?
**b** What difference would it make if you replaced

- the snow with sunshine?
- the little girl with a middle-aged woman?
- Russia with Britain?
- the cakes with a bottle of brandy?
- the fussy sentry with a kind, easy-going sentry?

**c** Do your answers for **b** make you reconsider your answer to **a** in any way?

# U·N·I·T 49 *We are what we say*

This is a *transcript* (a written version) of a radio programme about friendship. Four 20-year-olds, Helga, Janice, Joe, and Wayne were invited to the studio to discuss the friendships they'd made and lost during their teens. Mark is the interviewer. Begin by reading the transcript aloud, either in class or in your discussion group.

| | |
|---|---|
| Mark | Well, we're moving on now to think about friendships in the teenage years. Is it true that they're harder? |
| Helga | Yes, well in my experience at any rate. I always found friendships terribly intense when I was about thirteen. I can remember that the girls at school were always arguing and making up. It was all so upsetting at the time. |
| Janice | Yes, I remember that too – one girl I'd been friends with for years suddenly started being really rotten to me and I cried for ages. |
| Joe | Boys are not like that, though, are they? |
| Wayne | Well, I dunno, I think my mates was always important, like, but I suppose girls get more emotional, don't they? |
| Helga | Ah, come on, boys can get pretty nasty to each other too! |
| Wayne | Oh yeah, but it's more competitive, like everyone trying to be the smoothest. Who's the tallest? Who'll be the first to get a car? Who'll be the first to get serious with a girl? |
| Joe | Yeah, and when you've got a car you're suddenly very popular! Blokes are not at all bothered about using each other for convenience! |
| Helga | Yes, but people use each other all the time, don't they? |
| Janice | Don't you think girls are more loyal, though? I don't really think my friends have used me – not my real friends. And I haven't used them either. I wouldn't. |
| Wayne | (Laughing) Aah . . . she's nice, isn't she! |
| Janice | No, I don't mean . . . like . . . I'm no saint or anything . . . I just meant that friends don't use each other. |
| Wayne | Yeah, I know what you mean. I don't think I use my mates either. |
| Joe | Oh, come on, what about when you want to drink and you want someone to drive you home? |
| Wayne | Oh, yeah, but then you take it in turns, don't you? No-one wants to drive home from a party, do they? |
| Mark | We've heard that boys can be competitive but what about girls? |
| Janice | Yes, they can be too. I think clothes are the main thing. You go through a stage when you want to be dressed exactly like all the other girls. But there always seems to be one who leads the way and the others try to compete. It's usually the one with the most money! |
| Helga | I don't think I competed. I wanted to be an individual – at least as far as clothes were concerned. I do remember, though, I had one friend who I |

|        |                                                                                                                                                                                                                                   |
| ------ | --------------------------------------------------------------------------------------------------------------------------------------------------------------------------------------------------------------------------------- |
|        | thought was terribly clever. Even at the age of 14 she used to read the most intellectual books – Jean Paul Sartre and that kind of thing. I tried to copy her but I couldn't compete. I think she's a professor now, or something . . . |
| Joe    | I think I went my own way too. I followed fashions to an extent but I wasn't bothered if other kids didn't like what I wore. |
| Wayne  | I was conscious of being short when I was about 14. So to make up for that I tried to be real trendy and smart! I thought I was the bees' knees. |
| Joe    | Yeah, it seemed to be important to be tall, didn't it? |
| Helga  | I think that's nonsense. I mean I'm tall for a girl but I never let it bother me. It certainly never affected friendships. |
| Janice | I think looks are important, though. Pretty girls always have plain friends, don't they? It's as if they don't like competition. |
| Wayne  | But don't other girls get jealous? It must be hard to get friends if you're too pretty! |
| Janice | Yeah, but the pretty girls don't always get the boyfriends! A lot of boys are half afraid of them so they go for the plain friend. |
| Joe    | Less likely to be rejected, I suppose. |
| Mark   | Are a lot of friendships spoilt once boys and girls start dating? |
| Helga  | Can be. I mean, when you're hopelessly in love you tend to forget friends of the same sex, don't you? |
| Wayne  | I don't agree. As far as I'm concerned, girlfriends come and go but I could still be seeing my mates when I'm 90. |
| Helga  | You've obviously never had a serious girlfriend. |
| Wayne  | That's a bit of an assumption! |
| Helga  | I bet you'd leave the blokes down the pub if you had a steady girlfriend! |
| Wayne  | Well, I suppose I'd see my mates less, but I'd still insist on seeing them. Definitely. I think it's important. |
| Mark   | Why? |
| Wayne  | Well, you can't pin all your hopes on one person, can you? Supposing she lets you down? |
| Joe    | I agree with Wayne. But I'm wary about blokes too. I think everyone lets you down in the end. It's best just to rely on yourself. That way you don't get disappointed. |
| Helga  | What a grim way to go through life! |
| Mark   | And on that rather solemn note I'm afraid we have to leave our discussion and move on . . . |

## Assignments

📖 ☞ 1 **a** Make notes on the characters and personalities of Helga, Janice, Wayne and Joe. For each of them consider: their opinions; the way they speak; their reactions to the others.

**b** Write up your notes to give clear, fluent descriptions of the four 20-year-olds.

**c** Imagine that you used to teach Helga, Janice, Wayne and Joe. They are all applying for new jobs and have asked you to write references for them. Copy and fill in a form like this for each of them:

*Name* _____

*Job applied for* _____

*How do you know the applicant?* _____

_____

*State applicant's strengths* _____

_____

*State applicant's weaknesses* _____

_____

*How well does s/he relate to other people?* _____

_____

*What sort of job do you think s/he is best suited to?* _____

_____

**2** Pick out five opinions (see page 218) expressed in the transcript and label them **a–e**. For each opinion, write what you would say in reply to the speaker. State whether you agree or disagree with him/her and give your reasons.

**3** The producers of this radio programme have invited listeners to write in expressing their views on friendship. (The best letters will be read out on next week's programme.) Write a letter about 400 words long in response to this invitation, clearly setting out your thoughts and feelings about friendship. The letter should go to:

> 'A Friend Indeed' mailbag,
> Radio Chinwag,
> Marlton Towers,
> Sheffield,
> SH11 TR4.

Remember to plan your letter carefully. See page 139 for advice on discussion essays which can also apply to this letter.

**4** **a** In a small group, devise a similar radio programme on the subject of friendship. One person should be the interviewer and prepare some questions, while the others should prepare their responses to the questions.
**b** Present your programme to the rest of the class, or tape record it.

# *Getting to the heart of it*

To 'get to the heart' of what you're reading often requires a good deal of thought. Usually, discussion can be a valuable way of thinking, too.

Stewart Wilkinson has gone to collect his son Phil (PS) from an American boarding school. Phil has just been expelled for cheating in a Latin exam.

Stewart Wilkinson closed the door behind him and looked at his son. He wanted to hold the boy and comfort him, but Phil looked so solid, so strong, standing there. Why isn't he crying, he wondered, and then he told himself that he wouldn't have cried, either; that the boy had had plenty of time to cry; that he would never cry in front of his father again. He tried to think of something to say. He knew that he often was clumsy in his relations with Phil, and said the wrong thing, and he wondered whether he had been that sensitive at his son's age. He looked down at the plate of cookies and the empty milk glass.

'Where did you get the milk and cookies, son?'

'Mrs Burdick brought them to me, sir.'

He never calls me 'Dad' now, Stewart Wilkinson said to himself. Always 'sir' . . . My own son calls me 'sir' . . .

'Did you thank her?'

'Yes, sir.'

Stewart Wilkinson walked over to the couch next to his son and sat down. The boy remained standing.

'Phil, son, sit down, please.'

'Yes, sir.'

Looking at his son, Stewart Wilkinson could not understand why they had grown apart during the last few years. He had always remained close to his father. Why wasn't it the same between him and the boy who sat so stiff beside him, so still in spite of the horror he must have gone through during the past few hours?

'I'm sorry, sir.'

'Yes . . . yes, son, I know you are . . . I'm terribly sorry myself. Sorry for you . . . Mr Seaton told me another boy turned you in, is that right?'

PS nodded.

'He also told me that he believes you would have turned yourself in had you been given enough time.'

'I don't know whether I would have or not. I never had a chance to find out.'

'I think you would have. I think you would have.'

He waited for his son to say something; then, realizing there was nothing the boy could say, he spoke again. 'I was talking to Dr Fairfax outside – you knew he was my Latin teacher, too?'

'Yes, sir.'

'We always used to be able to tell when the first day of spring came, because Dr Fairfax put on his white linen suit.'

'Yes, sir.'

'At any rate, that man thinks very highly of you, Phil. He is very upset that you had to be expelled. I hope you will speak to him before we go. He's a good man to have on your side.

'I want to speak to him.'

'Phil . . . Phil . . .' Stewart Wilkinson thought for a minute. He wanted so desperately what he said to be the right thing to say. 'Phil, I know that I am partly responsible for what has happened. I must have in some way pressured you into it. I wanted your marks to be high. I wanted you to get the best education that you could. V.P.S. isn't the best school in the country, but it's a damn fine one. It's a school that has meant a lot to our family. But that doesn't matter so much. I mean, that part of it is all over with. I'm sorry that you cheated, because I know you're not the cheating kind. I'm also sorry because you are going to have to face the family and get it over with. This is going to be tough. But they'll all understand. I doubt that there is any of us who have never cheated in one way or another. But it will make them very proud of you if you can go see them and look them in the eye.'

He picked up one of the cookies and began to bite little pieces out of the edge. Then he shook his head sadly, in the gesture PS knew so well. 'Ah, God, son, it's so terrible that you have to learn these lessons when you are young. I know that you don't want me to feel sorry for you, but I can't help it. I'm not angry with you. I'm a little disappointed, perhaps, but I can understand it, I think. I suppose I must appear as an ogre to you at times. But Phil, I – If I'm tough with you, it's just because I'm trying to help you. Maybe I'm too tough.' Stewart Wilkinson looked over at this son. He saw that the boy was watching him. He felt a little embarrassed to have revealed so much of himself before his son. But he knew they were alike. He knew that Phil was really his son. They already spoke alike, already laughed at the same sort of things, appreciated the same things. Their tastes were pretty much the same. He knew that, if anything, he was too much like the boy to be able to help him. And also that the problem was the boy's own, and that he would resent his father's interfering.

'Phil, I'll go speak with Mr Seaton for a little while, and then I'll come on over and help you pack. If you'd like, I'll pack for you and you can sit in the car.

'No, that's all right, sir, I'll pack. I mean, most of the stuff is packed up already. I'll meet you over there.'

Stewart Wilkinson rose with his son. Again he wanted to hold the boy, to show him how much he loved him.

'I'll be through packing in a few minutes. I'll meet you in my room,' PS said.

'Fine, son.'

# Assignments

○ ☞ **1**    This assignment is best discussed in small groups. Each of the following statements is intended to help your understanding of the passage. Put them in order of how important you think they are as ways of summing up what the passage is about.

    **a** Sometimes it takes an unpleasant event to bring family members closer to one another.
    **b** Stewart is being more honest with himself than he has been for a long time.
    **c** PS cannot communicate with his father.
    **d** Teenagers and parents often have communication problems.
    **e** In our society it is very difficult to show your emotions.
    **f** It is unfair of parents to put pressure on their children.

    At the end of your group's discussion compare your views with those of the rest of the class.

○ **2**    **a** Imagine you have chosen to include this passage in an English textbook you are writing. Write a series of questions on the passage, designed to draw pupils' attention to the writer's use of detail.
    **b** Try to answer the questions set by another pair or group.
    **c** Look at the questions written by another pair/group. How good do you think their questions are? Write an assessment of their questions, bringing out the good and bad points about them.

✔ ◇ **3**    Write some of the conversations that are going on 'outside' this passage: (They may be either in story form or as simple dialogue.)

    **a** Stewart Wilkinson talks to Dr Fairfax
    **b** Stewart talks to Mr Seaton, the Headteacher
    **c** Stewart rings his wife while waiting for PS to pack
    **d** As he packs, Phil talks to his friend Charlie
    **e** Dr Fairfax talks to Mr Seaton as they watch the Wilkinsons drive away
    **f** The Wilkinson family all talk when Stewart and Phil arrive home

✔ ○ **4**    Use the conversations from **3** as a basis for dramatic improvisation.

Both these passages are about people who have just started teaching; the first is fictional, the second fact. (If you answer these questions as a timed exercise, allow one and a half hours.)

Ursula faced her class, some fifty-five boys and girls, who stood filling the ranks of the desks. She felt utterly non-existent. She had no place nor being there. She faced the block of children.

Down the room she heard the rapid firing of questions. She stood before her class not knowing what to do. She waited painfully. Her block of children, fifty unknown faces, watched her, hostile, ready to jeer. She felt as if she were in torture over a fire of faces. And on every side she was naked to them. Of unutterable length and torture the seconds went by.

Then she gathered courage. She heard Mr Brunt asking questions in mental arithmetic. She stood near to her class, so that her voice need not be raised too much, and faltering, uncertain, she said:

'Seven hats at twopence ha'penny each?'

A grin went over the faces of the class, seeing her commence. She was red and suffering. Then some hands shot up like blades, and she asked for the answer.

The day passed incredibly slowly. She never knew what to do, there came horrible gaps, when she was merely exposed to the children; and when, relying on some pert little girl for information, she had started a lesson, she did not know how to go on with it properly. The children were her masters. She deferred to them. She could always hear Mr Brunt. Like a machine, always in the same hard, high, inhuman voice he went on with his teaching, oblivious of everything. And before this inhuman number of children she was always at bay. She could not get away from it. There it was, this class of fifty collective children, depending on her for command, for command it hated and resented. It made her feel she could not breathe: she must suffocate, it was so inhuman. They were so many, that they were not children. They were a squadron. She could not speak as she would to a child, because they were not individual children, they were a collective, inhuman thing.

Dinner-time came, and stunned, bewildered, solitary, she went into the teachers' room for dinner. Never had she felt such a stranger to life before. It seemed to her she had just disembarked from some strange horrible state where everything was as in hell, a condition of hard, malevolent system. And she was not really free. The afternoon drew at her like some bondage.

The first week passed in a blind confusion. She did not know how to teach, and she felt she never would know. Mr Harby came down every now and then to her class, to see what she was doing. She felt so incompetent as he stood by, bullying and threatening, so unreal, that she wavered, became neutral and non-existent. But he stood there watching with the listening-genial smile of the eyes, that was really threatening; he said nothing, he made her go on teaching, she felt she had no soul in her body. Then he went away, and his going was like a derision. The class was his class. She was a wavering substitute. He thrashed and bullied, he was hated. But he was master. Though she was gentle and always considerate of her class, yet they belonged to Mr Harby, and they did not belong to her. Like some invincible source of the mechanism he kept all power to himself. And the class owned his power. And in school it was power, and power alone that mattered.

Soon Ursula came to dread him, and at the bottom of her dread was a seed of hate, for she despised him, yet he was master of her. Then she began to get on. All the other teachers hated him, and fanned their hatred among themselves. For he was master of them and the children, he stood like a wheel to make absolute his authority over the herd. That seemed to be his one reason in life, to hold blind authority over the school. His teachers were his subjects as much as the scholars. Only, because they had some authority, his instinct was to detest them.

*Sheila Tobin*
*Biology teacher*
*Boys' secondary*
*school*
*North-West*

There was no formal induction at all. On my first day I merely arrived and looked in and nobody even looked up. There I was, a female, not unattractive in a male school, but nobody looked up, nobody said 'Hello', nobody said 'Who are you?', nobody said 'I'm Mr Thomas, I'm Mr Smith.' So I sort of stood around uncertainly – gathered up some books and then when the bell went, thankfully went out. Eventually the first year housemaster found me and explained what I needed to do – what the administration was, how to deal with registers and how to – in fact I had to induct a first year class into the school. I never saw the head – in the whole of the first year, I only ever saw the head if I had done something wrong which had reached his ears.

What I remember about beginning is that there seemed to be a conspiracy, right from the smallest kid, right through the staff up to the head to make life difficult for the poor young unsuspecting teacher who is coming along and doesn't really know where he is and what it's all for. And everybody seems to take terrific glee in seeing you fall into every trap that they know is there – in fact they set it up for you and they watch and they wait. And they know that you not going to be strict enough. They know that you are going to make all sorts of errors and your administration is going to be poor but they are waiting negatively and their criticisms are all negative.

The kids especially, well – the attitude of the teachers rubs off on the kids, and they know that the moment a young teacher comes in this is someone to be played with, rather like kids torturing tadpoles or squashing them or stepping on them. Every trick they can try on, they're ready to try. All the kids, it doesn't matter what IQ range, it doesn't matter what age. There are always of course the very mature boys or the frightened ones who don't do anything, but the vast majority right from the first moment are there ready to trick you.

198

Well, for example, the kids start playing up, they are giggling, they are laughing, they are farting, they are flicking stuff around and they are doing it to test your reaction. Now at this school they are used to a very authoritarian reaction – but you start reacting in the way you want to go on – you want them to stop being stupid, stop being silly, be responsible . . . for the first time you laugh you tie the halter round your neck; the first time you laugh and join in and therefore have condoned what they are doing it grows and it grows until the whole class may well be in an uproar. And the worst moment in that sort of situation is when you look up and see a very quiet, very mature child looking you straight in the eye – rather like your conscience watching you lose control of the class and control of yourself.

# Assignments

**1**  **a**  Give two examples of factual statements from either passage.
**b**  Give two examples of statements which describe feelings from either passage.
**c**  Which passage is the more factual and which is more concerned with feelings, in your opinion?
**d**  Do facts and feelings in the passages affect you in different ways? Explain. (*10 marks*)

**2**  What do you learn from these two passages about the way new teachers may be affected by other members of staff? (*10 marks*)

**3**  What do you learn from both passages about the ways pupils may react to a new teacher? (*10 marks*)

**4**  How does your own experience of *either*

**a**  being a pupil in a class taken by a new teacher
*or*
**b**  being new somewhere yourself compare with what you have read in the two passages? (Refer to both facts and feelings.) (*10 marks*)

**5**  Spend about 30 minutes writing about *one* of these alternatives:

**a**  You have been asked to give a talk to student teachers. They want you to give them a pupil's point of view on how to be a successful teacher, concentrating particularly on how to cope when new to a school. Write your talk using information from the passage and drawing on any other relevant knowledge.
*or*
**b**  Imagine that you are the new teacher in either of these passages or a new teacher at your own school. Describe a typical day at work after you have been there about a week. If you wish, you may write it in the form of a diary. (*20 marks*)

*The right candidate for the job*

**Job advertisement**

```
┌──────────────────────────────────────────────────────────┐
│                         REQUIRED:                          │
│                 HEAD OF ENGLISH                            │
│  To teach English and run a large English department at    │
│  this 1500-pupil 11–18 mixed comprehensive school. Must    │
│  have a good knowledge of modern syllabuses and have       │
│  organisational ability as well as good qualifications.    │
│  Experience of drama teaching and liaising with other      │
│  departments an advantage.                                 │
│                                                            │
│           Send curriculum vitae and reference to:          │
│                   Ms H. Sparling,                          │
│                   Topford Comprehensive,                   │
│                   Ashmanhaugh,                             │
│                   London NW 39.                            │
└──────────────────────────────────────────────────────────┘
```

TOPFORD COMPREHENSIVE

Topford Comprehensive was purpose-built for 1500 pupils in 1971. It is situated in a pleasant suburb of north-west London and enjoys good facilities, including a large modern library and a school bookshop. Examination results have been extremely good in recent years and the school prides itself on the large number of pupils who go on to university each year. Last year four sixth-formers went on to study English at Oxford. The school also has a sizeable number of pupils of Asian origin for whom English is a second language; in recent years their progress has been most impressive. The school has its own small theatre which has been the venue for many successful plays produced jointly by the English and Drama departments.

Topford is a friendly school which cares for its pupils. It is expected that the successful applicant will have a pastoral as well as an academic interest in the pupils. The staffroom is large and comfortable, and there is a warm atmosphere of co-operation among all staff.

200

# The candidates

FRED GRIGGS

Age  54

2nd class degree in English

EXPERIENCE

30 years at Lapbush comprehensive - now assistant Head of English

Has taught all syllabuses and for many years has trained sixth formers for Oxford and Cambridge entrance examinations. No experience of teaching drama but has organised many successful theatre trips. Ran the school library for five years until becoming assistant Head of English. Has recently obtained qualification in Hindi and has attended courses on timetable planning, school management and 'Literature courses - the way ahead'.

REFERENCE

Mr Griggs has long been a trusted and respected member of staff at Lapbush. He is enthusiastic in his teaching and has done a good deal to encourage a love of literature amongst the sixth form. He is held in esteem by staff and pupils alike, although at times his amiable nature has resulted in his allowing others to overrule him too easily. He has tried hard to further his knowledge of modern developments in education.

*T. P. Ward*

T. P. Ward
Headteacher

ANN JENKINS

Age: 35        2nd class degree in English

EXPERIENCE
4 years at Eggford comprehensive
2 years at South Giles 6th form college
7 years at Rotworth comprehensive

Now Head of school Library. Has taught English at all levels, including preparing students for University entrance exams. Has taught drama up to 15-year-olds and helped produce school plays. No knowledge of teaching English as a second language but as Head of Library is used to liaising with many other people in school. Has attended courses on running an English department and 'Literature courses: the way ahead'.

REFERENCE

Mrs Jenkins has been an invaluable member of staff here for seven years. She is known to pupils for her strict discipline and good teaching and to staff for her warmth and friendship. Her bright smile is a ray of sunshine in the staffroom and her fine contralto voice is an absolute asset to the school choir. She has the organisational ability to be a Head of English, although whether her sensitive nature could cope with the emotional strain of the job remains to be seen.

*R Krystopher*

R  Krystopher
(Headteacher)

JOCELYN FALLS-BURNS

1st class degree in Anthropology and Sociology

Age: 30

EXPERIENCE
2 years at Mombasa high school, Kenya
1 year at Greenlea comprehensive, Wilts
2 years at City Girls' Birmingham
2 years at City boys' school, Liverpool
1 year at Grove comprehensive, Washville, Surrey

At present teaches English and Drama. Has taught many different syllabuses in her short but varied career. Has taught English up to age 16 and Drama up to age 14. Wide experience of helping with difficult and unruly pupils. Has also taught English as second language to Asian pupils. Some experience of teaching girls' games. Has attended course on 'Social integration in a multi-cultural secondary school'. Ran school bookshop for a term.

Reference
Although Ms Falls-Burns has only been with us for one year, she has certainly made her presence felt here at the Grove. She has a very forceful (some would say charismatic) personality and has proved something of an attraction with the pupils. Sincere, intelligent and well-meaning, Ms Falls-Burns has done her best to keep abreast of evens in school. Her efforts in producing a Kenyan play last term deserve warm congratulation. She has not yet taught English to the sixth form but I feel that she may soon be ready to do so.

*Rosemary Brahms*

Rosemary Brahms
(Headteacher)

---

FRANK BOLD                    Age: 38

3rd class degree in English

EXPERIENCE
5 years at St Peter's boys' grammar
3 years at Runnymede comprehensive
2 years at Beaufort primary
6 years at Coatbrook comprehensive

At present acting Head of English during long illness (nervous exhaustion) of Head of English. Has taught English up to sixth form and Drama to first years. Also teaches English as second language to Asian pupils. Has produced several successful school plays. Has supervised running of school library during period as acting Head of English. Has attended courses on pastoral care and running an English department. Also member of County advisory body on new courses in English literature.

REFERENCE
Mr Bold is an extremely forthright and opinionated member of staff who always makes his views known at staff meetings. At times he has antagonised his senior colleagues. He has a wide experience of education although his views against university education are well known. It must be admitted that the examination results of his pupils have been excellent and that he has acquired considerable respect and popularity among some pupils. Although he has done a good job in producing school drama, his choice of play has not always been a good one.

*Barbara Pullen*

Headteacher

ANNETTE LAZENBY

Age 34

1st class degree in English

Experience
4 years at St Anne's girls grammar
2 years at Roker 6th form college
6 years at Roedean city girls' comprehensive
Currently assistant Head of English. Runs school bookshop, used to run school library. Has taught English at all levels up to university entrance examinations. Has taught drama in the lower school and English as a second language at St Anne's. Has attended courses on multi-cultural secondary schools, running an English department, timetable planning and pastoral care. Has established a new literature course for 4th and 5th forms.

REFERENCE
Miss Lazenby is a very quiet, determined and dedicated teacher. She has been a worthy and efficient assistant Head of English for two years now and has made the school bookshop an extremely successful enterprise. Her pupils fear and respect her for her meticulous discipline. Staff find her a self-effeacing and rather private colleague. During her time here she has also developed new courses in English as a second language, for which our Multi-Cultural Department was extremely grateful. Her keen intellect and organisational flair also deserve full credit.

*H. Darby*

A Darby
(Headteacher)

# Assignments

*Assignments*

☞ **1** The five applicants for the job of Head of English at Topford comprehensive are to be interviewed by the Headmaster, deputy head and three school governors. You have been asked to prepare a chart for the interview panel which shows at a glance the qualifications, experience and personal qualities of each candidate. You should approach this task as follows:

**a** Make a detailed list of all the requirements mentioned in the advertisement.
**b** Add to these all the points mentioned about the school which suggest other qualities or experience that it would be useful for the new Head of English to have.
**c** Write these in boxes along the top of your chart. The interviewees' names should go down the side. Then fill in the boxes with the relevant information.

|  | Age | Degree |  |  |
|---|---|---|---|---|
| Fred Griggs | 54 | 2nd |  |  |
| Joceln Falls-Burns | 30 | 1st (not Eng) |  |  |
| Ann Jenkins | 35 | 2nd |  |  |
| Frank Bold | 38 | 3rd |  |  |
| Annette Lazenby | 34 | 1st |  |  |

You may find that you need to make more than one chart to fit in all the relevant information. Keep the chart neat, accurate, concise and informative.

○ ☞ **2** Prepare a list of five questions which you think the Headteacher should ask each candidate at the interview. (Your questions should deal particularly with aspects of the job which you think may prove difficult for the individual concerned.)

✑ **3** Obviously the interview is crucial, but looking at the candidates *on paper* only, which one would you give the job to? Give your reasons.

○ **4** Act out what might happen at one of the interviews *or*

✑ **5** Write a script for one of the interviews.

# U·N·I·T 53 Looking at drama

This short play by Ken Whitmore was written for radio. The only characters are a husband and wife.

**'ALWAYS IN LOVE WITH AMY'**

*The* COPPELL'S *sitting room*

| | |
|---|---|
| Henry | But of course I care for you. What do you mean? I think the world of you. |
| Amy | You have a strange way of showing it, that's all I can say. Are you ready for your pudding? |
| Henry | Oh, yes, that was very nice. |

*He shoves the dinner plate away*

| | |
|---|---|
| | Lovely. |
| Amy | [*going to get the pudding*] You wouldn't care if I dropped down dead this minute. Except there'd be no one to cook and clean for you. |

*She bangs the oven door*

| | |
|---|---|
| | [*coming back*] To put your pudding in front of you when you walk in at any old time. There! Pudding! |

*She bangs the pudding down*

| | |
|---|---|
| Henry | Hang on! No need for that. |
| Amy | Eat your pudding. After all, you don't want to deprive me of my sole function. Your pudding provider. Your handmaiden and bottlewasher. |
| Henry | Look here, Amy . . . |
| Amy | Eat. |
| Henry | I don't want to eat. You've taken away my appetite. |
| Amy | Is it no good? Is the pudding unacceptable like me? Is your palate dulled? Has the salt lost its savour like me? The sugar lost its sweetness like me? |
| Henry | Now calm down. Blimey. Crikey. [*fondly*] A-mee. |
| Amy | Well where the hell have you been? Where do you go every night? Who goes with you? Do you think I'm blind? Do you think I go about in a walking trance of – of blind, sunny, suburban, domestic, cowlike acceptance? |
| ① Henry | Darling, have you taken your tablets today? |
| Amy | [*very sharp*] Do you love me? That's what I'd like to know. |
| Henry | Of course I do. What a question. |
| Amy | Well say it! Say it! Why don't you ever say it? |
| Henry | I . . . |
| Amy | Yes? Go on? |

| | | |
|---|---|---|
| | Henry | I love you. |
| | Amy | [*laughing bitterly*] It comes as easy to you . . . saying that . . . it fits in your mouth as easy as a – as a – as a giraffe in a bungalow. [*wild laughter*] As a giraffe in a bungalow! |
| | Henry | That's rather good. I see it. A giraffe in a bungalow. That's rather good. |
| ② | Amy | Where have you been tonight? I want name and date. I want pack drill. Pack drill. What's that *mean*? I'd rather have the truth. It would be a relief. Anything as long as this torment isn't continued. |
| | Henry | I've been out to Purley. To supervise a new salesman. He was delivering the pitch for the first time. I thought I mentioned it this morning. |
| | Amy | Salesman? |
| | Henry | Yes, why? |
| | Amy | Sales *man*? |
| | Henry | You can look at my book. |
| | Amy | Ha! And who filled it in? You've started using after shave. You pong of it. And shiny collars. You never used to wear shiny collars. And a knife – a knife-edge crease. And going to the barber's every week. |
| | Henry | But you said I should. I was promoted, remember? |
| | Amy | I never said you should wear after shave lotion. |
| | Henry | [*puzzled*] Oh, I *thought* it was you. |
| | Amy | Ah, there, at last, it's out! If it wasn't me, who was it? |
| | Henry | A-meee! |
| | Amy | Who was it? I said. |
| | Henry | Well, if it wasn't you, Lord knows. I'll drop it if you like. All the same to me if I smell like mountain lilacs or old shag, I'm sure. |
| | Amy | You employ sales women now, don't you. |
| | Henry | Er, a few. |
| | Amy | Why have you gone red? |
| | Henry | [*very irritated*] I've gone red because your little inquisition's put me in a false position of guilt because yes we employ sales women and yes I sometimes have to take them out to the prospects for their first bash at the sales pitch and my wife suspects me of carrying on affairs with them, so though nothing goes on I feel guilty about it. Anybody would go red! God! |
| | Amy | Don't you raise your voice to me! Now we're getting to it. Tonight. Purley. Sales man or sales woman? |
| | Henry | You can ring him up if you like. Say I'm not back yet or something. |
| | Henry | *spoons his pudding* |
| | Amy | I thought you weren't going to eat that pudding. |
| | Henry | All right. I'm not going to eat that pudding. |

*He puts the spoon down*

| | | |
|---|---|---|
| | | Darling, I asked you if you'd taken your tablets today. |
| ③ | Amy | No, I'm saving them up. |
| | Henry | Saving them up. What do you mean? Now wait a minute. |
| | Amy | And where were you on Monday night and Wednesday night? This is Friday night. |
| | Henry | Just one moment. |
| | Amy | And four nights last week. |

206

| | | |
|---|---|---|
| Henry | You say you're saving your . . . |
| Amy | Baloney. Forget it. I just said that. |
| Henry | You're hoarding them. |
| Amy | I said forget it! |
| Henry | But darling, that's why you're so wrought up. If you haven't taken them of course you're going to feel rough . . . anxious . . . and frightened and get all steamed up with me. |
| Amy | Am I a mess? Am I a hag? Do I smell stale? Have I lost my youth? Well, you took it, you know. You chewed it up and spat it out. You had all the goodness of me. You had me when I was lively and my hair was black and my skin was like cream and I laughed at things . . . and my body . . . and my body was fresh. Women are the saddest. Women are the saddest. |
| Henry | Darling, I love you. You're still wonderful to me. I remember all that. I remember. How could I forget? And you're still the same girl. To me. Age – what's that got to do with it? All right, you grow older, I grow older. But I still remember. And you're still the same. |
| Amy | Where were you on Monday? Where were you on Wednesday? Who've you been – doing it with the last six months? |
| Henry | I'll resign. |
| Amy | Resign then. Resign. |
| Henry | I will. |
| Amy | What do I care? We're finished, aren't we? |
| Henry | No. We've got troubles, that's all. And we'll get over them. It'll be the same as before. Just . . . have faith. |
| Amy | [gentle for the first time] Do you honestly believe that? Honestly? |
| Henry | Honestly. |
| Amy | [flaring up] Oh, you can't catch an old bird! You can't catch an old bird with chaff![1] |
| Henry | You're not old. Get that into your head. You're not an old bird. I swear on my oath I've been faithful. |

*Pause*

It's the damned job. It's the job.
It's being made marketing director and the new sales pitch and training the new salesmen and working all the hours God sends; and all the time, all the time when I'm out, dreading to come home to . . .

| | | |
|---|---|---|
| Amy | There! Dreading to come home! Dreading! |
| Henry | To come home and find you've done yourself harm. Dreading to find what I'll find. What do you want from me? What do any of them want? I've told you. I'll resign. We both need to relax, that's all. Calm down, go off for a holiday somewhere, good Lord, we can afford it. |
| Amy | No. |
| Henry | No? Why not? |
| Amy | It's no good. |
| Henry | Why? |
| Amy | You don't love me. |
| Henry | I do. |
| Amy | You don't love me, you don't love me, you don't love me! |

1 *The husk as opposed
to the grain of wheat*

| | |
|---|---|
| Henry | How can I prove it? What can I do? It's hopeless. It's ridiculous. How can I prove that God exists? Mm? Same species of question. |
| Amy | You could take me to bed. You could love me in bed. |
| Henry | I can't. Look, I'd do anything. I'd cut off my right arm. You're Amy. I met you when you were eighteen. You had a yellow silk dress. Parachute silk. You walked up the hill into the trees. |
| Amy | You wouldn't! I just bet you wouldn't! |
| Henry | What are you talking about? What are you referring to? |
| Amy | Your arm. You said you'd cut off your arm. Your right arm. |

(6)          *Pause*

| | |
|---|---|
| Henry | Is that what you want? Would that convince you? |
| Amy | You wouldn't even cut off your little finger. |
| Henry | My finger? Is that what you want? |
| Amy | Yes. Cut your finger off. If you love me, prove it. Cut it off. Cut it off. |
| Henry | You really want me to? |
| Amy | It was your suggestion. Of course, if you want to back out . . . |
| Henry | No. No. If it . . . makes you happy. |
| Amy | All right. |
| Henry | Right. |

(7)          *Pause*

| | |
|---|---|
| Amy | Well, what are you waiting for? |
| Henry | I don't really know the best way. |
| Amy | The knives are there. Well, what are you waiting for? |
| Henry | A knife? Yes, very well, dear. |

*He opens a drawer, a jangle of knives*

| | |
|---|---|
| | [*after a moment*] This all strikes me as being . . . a little surrealistic.[2] |
| Amy | What are you waiting for? |
| Henry | I don't know the best way to go about it? |
| Amy | Procrastination. Procrastination.[3] |
| Henry | What? Look, you'll have to hold it. |
| Amy | What? |
| Henry | The knife. I put my finger on the bread board, see? Will the left one do? |
| Amy | All right. |
| Henry | You hold the blade across the finger – like this. |
| Amy | Yes? |
| Henry | And then I . . . then I . . . |
| Amy | Yes? |
| Henry | I bash the knife down – with the rolling pin |
| Amy | Yes [*struck by an idea*] Wait a minute. Wait a minute. What was I thinking of? |

(8)          *She picks up the telephone and dials 999*

Yes. Ambulance . . . Mrs Amy Coppell – Coppell, double P, double L . . . Myrtle Bank, that's number seven, Lofting Avenue . . . My husband's had an accident – he's lost a finger. Would you please tell them to hurry? . . . Thank you.

2 *Like a strange dream*
3 *Putting it off*

208

*She hangs up*

| Henry | [*no irony*] Thank you. That was very considerate. |
| Amy | Commonsense. |

*Pause*

| Henry | Amy, I do love you, you know. Most awfully. |
| Amy | We're about to see, aren't we? |
| Henry | Yes. |
| Amy | Are you frightened? |
| Henry | I'm a bit . . . dizzy. I think I'll sit down and do it. |

⑨         *He drags up a chair*

| Amy | Procrastination, procrastination. |
| Henry | Amy? |
| Amy | Yes? You'd better hurry up or you'll have those men here and it will be a false alarm. |
| Henry | Amy, I just want you to be . . . |
| Amy | Well? |
| Henry | When I've done it, the old Amy again. The young Amy again. [*brisk*] Right. Go on. Hold the blade across the finger. |
| Amy | There? |
| Henry | A bit lower, please. |
| Amy | There? |
| Henry | Yes. Yes. |

⑩         Go on. It's the waiting that's worst.

| Henry | Yes. |

*Chop*

[*with long high keening of a wounded animal and sucking in of air through clenched teeth*] There. There. There, Amy. There.

*An ambulance approaches with siren blaring*

Now do you believe me? Now do you believe me?

| Amy | One little finger? What? One little finger? You can't catch an old bird with chaff, Henry. |

# Assignments

☞ ○ **1**  Look back at the circled numbers in the text of the play. In each case decide which of the dramatic devices listed in the box is being used. (Sometimes it may be more than one of them.)

> **Dramatic devices**
>
> **Tension** – when we feel that something momentous is about to happen.
> **Suspense** – when we're wondering what will happen next.
> **Conflict** – when two or more characters, actions or ideas are at odds with each other.
> **Relief** – when the tension, suspense or conflict is over (either temporarily or for good).
> **Mood changes** – eg from serious to light-hearted or vice versa.
> **Turning points** – times when we feel that one or more of the characters has advanced the action of the play decisively.

○ **2**  **a** How would you adapt the play to be acted on stage?
**b** How would you stage-manage chopping off Henry's finger?
**c** What would Henry and Amy look like?
**d** What would their home look like?
**e** How should their parts be acted?

○ **3**  Henry and Amy visit a marriage guidance counsellor. Write a play script for the scene.

○ **4**  Act out the scene of Henry and Amy's visit to the marriage guidance counsellor.

○ **5**  Assume that shortly after this incident Amy is admitted to psychiatric hospital. Write the story of what happens, including a visit from Henry.

○ **6**  Henry's mother telephones shortly after the finger incident. Act out the conversation.

# U·N·I·T 54 *Looking at irony*

*Irony* cannot be defined in any simple way, but the box gives you some ways of thinking about it. The context of the writing should tell you which of these definitions is most relevant.

---

**Irony**

1 Saying or writing something different from what we mean in order to emphasise our real meaning, eg *Parents enjoy the challenge of seeing who can spend the most money on a child's birthday party*, which really means 'Birthday parties are expensive and a waste of money. Parents feel they have to compete to outdo the parties given for other children.'

2 A secret shared between the author and the reader, which a character in the book or play is unaware of (usually called *dramatic irony*) eg a character dies in Act 1 of a play, but all the other characters think and talk about him as if he is still alive. Only the reader/audience knows the truth.

3 Pretending to adopt someone else's opinion in order to ridicule it, eg *Yes of course I believe you. Of course there's a ghost in your house. It's just that it doesn't appear when strangers are here, does it?* which really means 'You're talking nonsense about your house being haunted'.

4 The mildly sarcastic use of words to imply the opposite of what they usually mean – often indicated by putting extra stress on these words, or using a different tone of voice, eg *You know I love physics* which really means 'I dislike physics lessons'.

5 A situation which is totally different from what we would expect (or which has a totally different outcome), implying that Fate is against us, eg *I waited in for the gas man until 4.30. Then I had to go out, but I was sure he wouldn't come so late in the day. When I got home, there was a card to tell me he'd called at 4.35!*

6 A conflict between the way things should be, or are thought to be, and the way they really are, eg It is often stated that sport brings out the best in people, giving them the ability to win modestly or lose gracefully. In reality, sports players are often involved in violent verbal or physical disputes.

---

# *Assignments*

○ ☞ **1**  Here are some short examples which illustrate irony in different ways. Which of the definitions in the box do you think is most appropriate for each of them? (There are no right or wrong answers: some examples may fit more than one of the definitions.)

**a** 'You'd like to have a bath and something to eat before we go out, would you? Yes, fine, of course you're right. After all, we were only supposed to meet Paul and Mark an hour ago. I'm sure they'll enjoy waiting for us in the pouring rain.'

**b** In Shakespeare's *Romeo and Juliet*, Romeo takes poison because he thinks Juliet is dead. Friar Lawrence and the audience know that she is only sleeping.

**c** I've taken my umbrella every day for the last week. Today I didn't take it and it's the only day it has rained!

**d** Water, water, everywhere,
And all the boards did shrink;
Water, water, everywhere
Nor any drop to drink.
(From *The Rime of the Ancient Mariner* – the speaker and his shipmates are out at sea, dying of thirst.)

**e** 'Oh, Ruth! Have you been sick?'
'No, I was just checking what I had for breakfast!'

**f** 'I don't know why the two sisters never got on. There was a rumour once that Aggie tried to poison Emily, but I don't know if that's true. I do know, though, that they hadn't spoken for over twenty years. They absolutely detested each other.'
She looked across to where Emily was smiling bravely. Emily shook the vicar's hand and thanked him for the kind words he had spoken about Aggie and for his sermon on coping with grief. Dear Aggie's funeral, she assured him, was just as she would have wanted it.

**g** In Roald Dahl's short story, *Lamb to the Slaughter*, Mrs Maloney clubs her husband to death with a frozen leg of lamb. When four policemen arrive to investigate her husband's murder, they are puzzled that no murder weapon can be found. As they discuss the case with Mrs Maloney, she serves them a lovely meal of roast leg of lamb, which they eat hungrily.

**h** In Shakespeare's *Macbeth*, Macbeth tells Banquo, 'Fail not our feast' (Don't forget to be at our feast), knowing that he has arranged for Banquo to be murdered before the feast. Banquo's murder is carried out as planned, but his ghost still attends the feast, seen only by Macbeth.

○ **2**  Look back over the definitions and examples. For what reason(s) do you think writers and speakers might use irony? (Not a straightforward question, but it's worth thinking about!)

# A LONGER LOOK

You have looked at some brief examples of irony. Here is a longer example, taken from *Oliver Twist* by Charles Dickens.

The board, in the extract, are the men responsible for the running of the workhouse where Oliver, an orphan, has just arrived. Workhouses were places where poor and homeless people did unpaid work in return for food and accommodation. The workhouses soon became notorious for (among other things) their bad food and unhealthy conditions; the awful work that the poor had to undertake and the fact that married couples and families were separated.

The members of this board were very sage, deep, philosophical men, and when they came to turn their attention to the workhouse, they found out at once, what ordinary folks would never have discovered – the poor people liked it! It was a regular place of public entertainment for the poorer classes; a tavern where there was nothing to pay; a public breakfast, dinner, tea, and supper all the year round; a brick and mortar elysium,[1] where it was all play and no work. 'Oho!' said the board, looking very knowing; 'we are the fellows to set this to rights; we'll stop it all, in no time.' So, they established the rule, that all poor people should have the alternative (for they would compel nobody, not they), of being    10
starved by a gradual process in the house, or by a quick one out of it. With this view, they contracted with the water-works to lay on an unlimited supply of water; and with a corn-factor[2] to supply periodically small quantities of oatmeal; and issued three meals of thin gruel a day, with an onion twice a week, and half a roll on Sundays. They made a great many other wise and humane regulations having reference to the ladies, which it is not necessary to repeat; kindly undertook to divorce poor married people, in consequence of the great expense of a suit in Doctors' Commons;[3] and, instead of compelling a man to support his family, as they had theretofore done, took his family away from him, and made him    20
a bachelor! There is no saying how many applicants for relief,[4] under these last two heads, might have started up in all classes of society, if it had not been coupled with the workhouse; but the board were long-headed men, and had provided for this difficulty. The relief was inseparable from the workhouse and the gruel; and that frightened people.

For the first six months after Oliver Twist was removed, the system was in full operation. It was rather expensive at first, in consequence of the increase in the undertaker's bill, and the necessity of taking in the clothes of all the paupers, which fluttered loosely on their wasted, shrunken forms, after a week or two's gruel. But the number of workhouse inmates    30
got thin as well as the paupers; and the board were in ecstasies.

*1 Paradise*
*2 man who deals in corn*
*3 obtaining a divorce in court*
*4 State aid*

These questions are intended to help you understand the passage:

    **a** 'Philosophical' usually means reasonable or wise. What does Dickens mean by it here? (line 1)

    **b** Why would 'ordinary folks' not have discovered that poor people like the workhouse? (lines 3–4)

    **c** 'For they would compel nobody, not they.' (line 10) Apparently the board is generous in allowing the poor a choice; what is the catch?

    **d** What is ironic about the contract with the water-works? (line 13)

    **e** What do the words 'wise', 'humane' and 'kindly' seem to mean in this passage? (lines 16–17)

    **f** Why might large numbers of men have been attracted to apply for relief? (lines 21–22) What stopped them? (line 24)

    **g** What impact does the word 'frightened' have? (line 25)

    **h** Why was the workhouse system expensive at first? (lines 27–29) Why did this expense not continue? (lines 30–31)

    **i** What other examples of irony can you find in the passage?

    **j** Give two examples of contrasts between the way things were and the way they should have been.

    **k** How would you define the type(s) of irony used in this passage? (See page 211)

    **l** What do you think Dickens' purpose in writing this passage was?

    **m** How do you respond to the passage?

---

**4** Try rewriting the passage in a straightforward, literal way. How does this compare with the ironic version? What is gained and what is lost?

---

**5** Try writing a piece in an ironic style yourself. Choose any subject you like; the following suggestions may give you some ideas: school; officials and bureaucracy; men; women; nothing ever goes right. (Before you write, think about the *response* you would like to evoke from your reader – Laughter? Anger? or Sadness? something else?)

# U·N·I·T 55 *Nuts and bolts*

When you take apart something like an engine, you find a lot of nuts, bolts and other small parts. In the process you may discover how the engine works. It's also possible to take a piece of writing apart to see how it is put together – how the writing 'works'.

One woman's magazine has a regular monthly spot which gives a reader the opportunity to write on an issue she feels strongly about. One month, this article appeared:

There cannot be many people in this country today who do not know what 'Beanz meanz', which beer is 'good for you' or what comes after 'snap, crackle . . .'. The reason for this is that advertising has become part of our lives to such an extent that many slogans are now part of our common vocabulary. In fact, it would be difficult to imagine television or magazines without advertising. Indeed, bright and particularly humorous advertising can often bring a smile to our faces in the middle of the most violent film or most passionate love story.

Moreover, we are reliant on advertising to keep us informed of new products, improved products and other goods and services which we may not know about. For example, when you can't think where to take the kids at half-term or what to buy Dad for Christmas, it's sometimes useful when a voice on the screen provides all the answers.

But the advertisers are not just trying to be helpful, are they? Above all, they are trying to sell their product. And, if the product sells well, then people buy more and that keeps the prices down. Certainly that is what the manufacturers would like us to believe. However, when we go to the supermarket we find the cheapest products are those with plain labels. They are the supermarket's own brand and they are never advertised! One might conclude from this that the advertisers are deceiving us.

Despite this, some people would insist that advertising is an essential part of a free, democratic society. After all, advertising promotes competition and without competition there may be no choice. If we all had to buy the same brand of toothpaste, these people reason, that might be too much like only having one political party to vote for.

But there is nothing democratic about advertising. On the contrary. When I take my children to watch motor racing, I do not have the freedom to choose whether or not they see cigarette adverts. When they watch children's programmes on television, I can hardly stop them looking at the adverts for expensive and unnecessary toys, unhealthy desserts and unwholesome junk food which appear every fifteen minutes. What is more, advertisers know that children are their most receptive audience and they do everything possible to exploit this fact.

Similarly, they know that smoking is an extremely unhealthy habit, that alcoholism is on the increase and that too much fat in the diet can lead to heart disease. But all this does not stop advertisers promoting their unhealthy products. It seems they are totally unconcerned about our welfare. It is surely ridiculous that we can be expected to interpret this lack of responsibility on their part as democracy or our 'freedom to choose'.

Yet these are only the most obvious types of damage that advertising can do. What is even worse are the other kind of adverts which damage our lives in far more subtle ways. All the values we most cherish are cheapened by advertising. For instance, we are led to believe that a man falls in love with a girl because she wears the right perfume or hairspray. Next she is expected to trust in his love for her because he buys her the right brands of sherry and chocolates. Then, when they marry, their home will be perfect because it is purchased through the best building society. After that, the right central heating and best-made brand of furniture ensure a good home for their children. The children are happy and healthy because they wear the most watertight brand of nappies, eat the tastiest baby food and all their clothes are washed in the whitest brand of soap powder. Is all this the best we have come to expect of love and family life? It is hardly surprising that, as the children grow older, they expect their parents' love to be proved by the purchase of all the latest toys, yummiest chocolate bars and crispiest chips.

Although this picture may seem exaggerated, when you think how often we see, hear and read these adverts, it is obvious that they must have some effect on our outlook on life. Even if we do not take advertising seriously, the best we can say about it is that it is a colossal waste of money that could be better spent on putting the world right. But if we start to believe what the advertisers tell us about love and about family life, then we can only conclude that advertising is very, very wicked.

# *Assignments*

○ ☞ **1**   **a** There are eight paragraphs in this article. Sum up each of the eight paragraphs in the simplest sentence possible. (It may be a sentence copied directly from the paragraph.)

**b** Decide whether you think each paragraph could be called

- strongly in favour of
- in favour of
- neutral about
- against
- strongly against
- very strongly against advertising.

**c** Construct a diagram which shows the line of argument in the article. Use a box for each paragraph and write your sentences for **a** inside the boxes. An example of the kind of diagram you could draw is shown below. (Only two of the one-sentence summaries are included.) But don't worry if your diagram looks totally different.

**d** Does your diagram help you see the writer's line of argument?

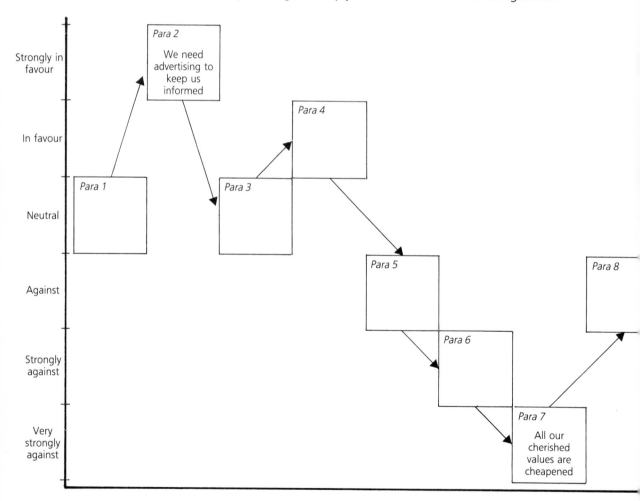

**2** One way to find out how a piece of argumentative writing is put together is to look out for 'signal words'. These are the little words and phrases which bind together the ideas in a piece of writing. Here are some of the ones to look for in this article:

*Putting ideas in order*
Next
Then
After that

*Adding to what's been said*
and
moreover

*Contrasting or balancing ideas*
however
although
but
yet
on the contrary
Despite this . . .
even if . . .

*Introducing an opinion*
It is ridiculous . . .
It is hardly surprising
It is obvious . . .
What is worse . . .

*Linking points*
similarly

*Reasons and results*
The reason is . . .
If . . . then . . .
to such an extent that . . .

*Giving examples*
For example
For instance

*Stressing a point*
particularly
in fact
above all
what is more . . .

*Persuading the reader to agree*
certainly
after all
surely

*Interpreting the facts*
It seems that . . .
One might conclude . . .
We can only conclude . . .

**a** Find as many instances of these words in the article as you can and give a line reference for each.
**b** Give an example of each of the following from the article, and explain them carefully:

- The writer clearly putting her ideas in order
- Further information being added to what has been said already
- Two ideas being contrasted with or balanced against each other
- An attempt to persuade the reader to agree
- Two points being linked
- The writer interpreting the facts
- The writer giving an opinion
- A point being emphasised

**Example** – Two ideas are contrasted in line 23. We see this as the writer introduces the paragraph with 'But'. She has just said that advertisers are helpful, but now she wants to balance this by saying that they have other motives for advertising too.

✔ ○ ☞ **3**   For this assignment each group will need one photocopy of page 215 and three coloured markers.

> **Fact and opinion**
>
> **Fact** – A statement which all available evidence suggests is true.
> eg  You are tall for your age.
>      London is a large city.
> **Opinion** – A statement which reflects a personal viewpoint. We do not know whether it is true or not because it cannot be definitely proved one way or the other.
> eg  You are the most beautiful person in the world.
>      London is a filthy, unfriendly city.

You will need to discuss each sentence in turn. Leave sentences you are unsure about and then come back to them later.

**a** Mark each sentence which you think contains a *fact* in one colour.
**b** Mark each sentence which you think contains an *opinion* in a second colour.
**c** Use the third colour for any sentences you are still unsure about after discussion.
**d** Compare your colouring with that of other groups
**e** What pattern emerges? For instance, are any paragraphs all fact or all opinion? Is a factual sentence usually followed by a sentence of opinion? What do you learn from this exercise about the balance of fact and opinion in argumentative writing?

✔ ◇ **4**   Write an argumentative piece of writing replying to this article and presenting the view that advertising is a good thing. Plan it carefully first (see box on page 245).

# U·N·I·T  56  *Efficient reading*

When you are reading information, don't take longer than you need to. There are different ways of reading, according to your reason for reading.

This unit refreshes your memory about *skimming* (see page 3), *scanning* (see page 5) and *close reading*.

## *Assignments*

☞ **1**  Begin by *skimming* the charts. *Do not read every word on the page*. Simply cast your eye quickly over the six tables of facts and figures to answer the following questions:

**a** Which table will tell you whether the Beatles had more number one hits than anyone else?

**b** Which table will tell you what position in the charts all the Beatles' hits reached?

**c** Which table will tell you (without your needing to add up) how many weeks the Beatles spent at number one?

**d** Which table will tell you most quickly how many number ones in a row they had?

**e** Which table will tell you whether they had more Top Ten hits than Elvis Presley?

**f** Which table will tell you whether they spent longer in the charts than Cliff Richard?

# BEATLES' SINGLES

| | | HIGHEST POSITION | WEEKS IN CHART |
|---|---|---|---|
| 11 Oct 62 | LOVE ME DO | 17 | 18 wks |
| 17 Jan 62 | PLEASE PLEASE ME | 2 | 18 wks |
| 18 Apr 63 | FROM ME TO YOU | 1 | 21 wks |
| 29 Aug 63 | SHE LOVES YOU | 1 | 31 wks |
| 5 Dec 63 | I WANT TO HOLD YOUR HAND | 1 | 21 wks |
| 26 Mar 64 | CAN'T BUY ME LOVE | 1 | 14 wks |
| 9 Apr 64 | SHE LOVES YOU (re-entry) | 42 | 2 wks |
| 14 May 64 | I WANT TO HOLD YOUR HAND (re-entry) | 48 | 1 wk |
| 11 Jun 64 | AIN'T SHE SWEET | 29 | 6 wks |
| 9 Jul 64 | CAN'T BUY ME LOVE (re-entry) | 47 | 1 wk |
| 16 Jul 64 | A HARD DAY'S NIGHT | 1 | 13 wks |
| 3 Dec 64 | I FEEL FINE | 1 | 14 wks |
| 15 Apr 65 | TICKET TO RIDE | 1 | 12 wks |
| 29 Jul 65 | HELP! | 1 | 14 wks |
| 9 Dec 65 | DAY TRIPPER/WE CAN WORK IT OUT | 1 | 12 wks |
| 16 Jun 66 | PAPERBACK WRITER | 1 | 11 wks |
| 11 Aug 66 | YELLOW SUBMARINE/ELEANOR RIGBY | 1 | 13 wks |
| 23 Feb 67 | PENNY LANE/STRAWBERRY FIELDS FOREVER | 2 | 11 wks |
| 12 Jul 67 | ALL YOU NEED IS LOVE | 1 | 13 wks |
| 29 Nov 67 | HELLO GOODBYE | 1 | 12 wks |
| 13 Dec 67 | MAGICAL MYSTERY TOUR | 2 | 12 wks |
| 20 Mar 68 | LADY MADONNA | 1 | 8 wks |
| 4 Sep 68 | HEY JUDE | 1 | 16 wks |
| 23 Apr 69 | GET BACK | 1 | 17 wks |
| 4 Jun 69 | BALLAD OF JOHN AND YOKO | 1 | 14 wks |
| 8 Nov 69 | SOMETHING/COME TOGETHER | 4 | 12 wks |
| 14 Mar 70 | LET IT BE | 2 | 9 wks |
| 24 Oct 70 | LET IT BE (re-entry) | 43 | 1 wk |
| 13 Mar 76 | YESTERDAY | 8 | 7 wks |
| 27 Mar 76 | HEY JUDE (re-entry) | 12 | 7 wks |
| 27 Mar 76 | PAPERBACK WRITER (re-entry) | 23 | 5 wks |
| 3 Apr 76 | STAWBERRY FIELDS FOREVER (re-entry) | 32 | 3 wks |
| 3 Apr 76 | GET BACK (re-entry) | 28 | 5 wks |
| 10 Apr 76 | HELP! (re-entry) | 37 | 3 wks |
| 10 Jul 76 | BACK IN THE U.S.S.R. | 19 | 6 wks |
| 7 Oct 78 | SGT. PEPPER'S LONELY HEARTS CLUB BAND – WITH A LITTLE HELP FROM MY FRIENDS | 63 | 3 wks |
| 5 Jun 82 | BEATLES MOVIE MEDLEY | 10 | 9 wks |
| 16 Oct 82 | LOVE ME DO (re-entry) | 4 | 7 wks |

## 2 MOST WEEKS ON CHART

The following table lists all the recording acts that spent 100 weeks or more on the British singles chart.

| | Weeks |
|---|---|
| ELVIS PRESLEY | 1098 |
| CLIFF RICHARD | 861 |

(+ 7 wks with Olivia Newton-John)

| | |
|---|---|
| BEATLES | 402 |

(+ 1 wk with Tony Sheridan)

| | |
|---|---|
| FRANK SINATRA | 391 |

(+ 18 wks with Nancy Sinatra and 9 wks with Sammy Davis Jnr)

| | |
|---|---|
| SHADOWS | 361 |

(+ 404 wks backing Cliff Richard)

## MOST TOP TEN HITS

**55** ELVIS PRESLEY
**47** CLIFF RICHARD
**25** BEATLES
**21** ROLLING STONES
**19** ABBA

## 4 MOST NUMBER ONE HITS

**17** BEATLES; ELVIS PRESLEY;
**10** CLIFF RICHARD; **9** ABBA;
**8** ROLLING STONES

## 5 MOST WEEKS AT NUMBER ONE

### a) BY ARTIST

**73** ELVIS PRESLEY
**65** BEATLES (*Paul McCartney 9 more with Wings and 3 more with Stevie Wonder. John Lennon 7 more solo and George Harrison 5 more solo*)
**35** CLIFF RICHARD
**32** FRANKIE LAINE (*one week top equal*)
**31** ABBA

### b) BY ARTIST IN ONE CALENDAR YEAR

**27** FRANKIE LAINE **1953** (*one week top equal*)
**18** ELVIS PRESLEY **1961**
**16** BEATLES **1963**
JOHN TRAVOLTA & OLIVIA NEWTON-JOHN **1978**
**15** ELVIS PRESLEY **1962**

## 6 MOST CONSECUTIVE NUMBER ONES

**11 in a row: BEATLES**
(FROM ME TO YOU through to YELLOW SUBMARINE/ELEANOR RIGBY, 1963 to 1966)

**6 in a row: BEATLES**
(ALL YOU NEED IS LOVE through to BALLAD OF JOHN AND YOKO, 1967 to 1969)

**5 in a row: ELVIS PRESLEY**
(HIS LATEST FLAME through to RETURN TO SENDER, 1961 to 1962)

**5 in a row: ROLLING STONES**
(IT'S ALL OVER NOW through to GET OFF OF MY CLOUD, 1964 to 1965)

**4 in a row: ELVIS PRESLEY**
(IT'S NOW OR NEVER through to SURRENDER, 1960 to 1961). The first number one hat-trick.

☞ **2** Now practise *scanning*. You still do not need to read every word. Concentrate on exactly what you are looking for – a word or a number, perhaps. 'See' it in your mind's eye and run your eye quickly over the page until you find what you are looking for.

*Time yourself* as you find the answers to these questions:

**a** How many weeks was *She Loves you* in the charts in 1963?
**b** What position did *Penny Lane* reach?
**c** How many weeks was *Get back* in the charts *altogether*?
**d** Which Beatles' record was in the charts for the shortest amount of time? (Exclude re-entries)
**e** How many number ones did the Beatles have in 1963?
**f** What was their highest position in the charts in 1976?
**g** Which star(s) spent more weeks in the charts than the Beatles?
**h** Who had most weeks at number one?
**i** Who had most weeks at number one if you include records by Wings, John Lennon and George Harrison in the Beatles' total?
**j** What was the greatest number of number one hits in a row the Beatles had?
**k** How many more top ten hits did Elvis Presley have than the Beatles?

Now check your answers on page 255. How long did you take? Were you fast *and* accurate?

Make up some similar questions and try them on your friends.

◇ **3** Now we come to a third type of reading: *close reading* for a specific purpose. This time you will have to read all the details carefully and interpret them in certain ways.

You have been asked to write an article about the Beatles' hit singles for your school magazine. All the information you need is in these six tables. Make your article 200–400 words long.

If you wish, you may use this plan:

- *paragraph one* – general statement of how successful the Beatles were
- *paragraph two* – particular singles and their chart performance
- *paragraph three* – the Beatles' success year by year
- *paragraph four* – time spent in charts and top ten compared with other performers
- *paragraph five* – time spent at number one compared with other performers
- *paragraph six* – were they the most successful singles performers ever?

Remember to make your article fluent and readable – do not simply quote lists of dates and figures.

As you read this story, pay attention not just to the characters, but also to the natural environment: the things growing, the animals and the seasons.

**THE GOOD CORN**
**by H E Bates**

For twenty-five years Joe Mortimer and his wife had lived in a valley, getting a living from raising hens and geese, a few cows and calves, the fruit from half a dozen cherry trees and an acre or two of corn.

Their small red brick house, surrounded by coops of wire and low wooden sheds for chickens, stood close to a railway line, and occasionally passengers could look out and see, walking about the small grass paddock or across the bare autumn stubbles, a woman with wispy fair hair and long brown arms. Sometimes she was lovingly leading a calf by a halter; sometimes she seemed to be earnestly talking to flocks of geese and hens. At times a man was with her: a tall gaunt-framed man with close-cut hair and spare knotty muscle and water-blue eyes that slowly lifted themselves and gazed absently on the windows of passing trains. In summer there were always many children on the trains, eagerly pressing faces to the glass as they travelled down to the sea, and whenever the Mortimers caught sight of them there was a sudden brightness on their faces, a great eagerness, almost an illumination, as they smiled and waved their hands.

Every Tuesday and again on Saturday the Mortimers drove in a small black truck to market. They took with them cases of eggs, half a dozen unplucked brown chickens, a few chips of cherries in their season and odd things like bunches of turnips *and* onions, a brace of pigeons, a hare, and daffodils carefully tied in dozens.

In the evenings, when they came home again, they counted out their money on the kitchen table. They laid it out in little piles of silver and copper and notes, counting it several times to make sure how much they had.

Then when the counting was finished Joe Mortimer would divide the money exactly in half. Solemnly, from the very beginning of their marriage, he would put one half into a tin cash box and then push the other across to his wife, who took it from him with long, uneager hands.

'You know what that's for,' he would say, 'put that away.'

At first they were quite sure about children. It seemed as natural to think of children coming as to think of eggs in the hen-runs and calves for cows and flowers on cherry trees. It was merely a question of time before children came. Mrs Mortimer thought of children laughing and running among flocks of hens, scattering grain, tossing it among the snapping, quarrelling brown feathers. In early spring in cold wet weather, she sometimes nursed the first yellow chicks in warm flannel, in baskets, under the kitchen stove. That was the sort of thing children always loved, she thought.

223

It was in summer, when the corn was ready, that Mortimer thought of them most. In imagination he saw boys riding in harvest carts or chasing rabbits among shocks of wheat and barley. He saw himself cutting them ash-plants from hedgerows or teaching them to thresh wheat in the palms of their hands. He saw them bouncing on piles of fresh light straw on threshing days.

Then gradually, as time went by and there were no children, he became resigned to it in a puzzled, absent sort of way. It did not embitter him. If there were no children there were no children, he thought. That was nature; that was how it was. You could not alter that. It turned out like that with some people. There was nothing you could do about it but hope and make the best of it.

But his wife could not see it like that. It was not simply that she wanted children; it was not merely a question of pride. It was a woman's duty to have children; it was all of a woman's life to give birth. Not to bear children, when her pride was deep, was something more to a woman than misfortune. It was a failure in her living. It was like a hen that did not lay eggs or a cow that was sterile or a tree that never came into blossom. There was no point in the existence of them.

As time went on she drew more and more into herself. With something more than injured pride she drew deep down into an isolation where she thought of nothing but the failure that came from sterility. The reproach of failure never left her; she could not grow used to the pain of it. It was like a gnawing physical disability, an ugly mark she wanted to hide.

All the time, waiting for children, the two of them worked very hard. They saved money. Chickens and eggs went to market every week; cherries brought good money in summer; there was always enough corn for the hens and enough hay for the cows and calves and plenty over.

Whenever a new calf came she cried a little. The mournful tender glassiness of a cow's big eyes after birth was something she could not bear. She liked to lift the soft wet heads of the new calves and hold them in her arms. She liked the smell of milk on their faces and the gluey suck of their mouths if she fed them from the bucket.

After they had been married twenty-five years she stood one morning in the small cow-shed at the back of the house and watched a calf die in her arms. It was a red heifer calf and she began to cry bitterly. The calf had been dropped in the meadow the previous afternoon, prematurely, while she and Mortimer were at market. A cold wet wind with hail in it was blowing from the west. The calf could not stand on its feet by the time she and Mortimer found it and there was a drift of wet hail along the side of its body.

She went on to grieve about the calf. The death of the calf became a personal thing. She found she could not sleep at night. She bit the edges of the pillow so that she could lay and cry without a sound. After a time there was a continuous pain in her chest: a great bony bolt that shot across her throat and made it difficult to swallow.

At the same time she began to despise herself.

'Don't come near me. I'm no good to you. You should have found someone else, not me. What have I done for you? What good have I ever been?'

224

'Don't say that. Don't talk like that,' Mortimer said. 'You're not well. You're not yourself. I'm going to get the doctor to look at you.'

The doctor spent a long time with her in the bedroom, alone, sitting on the edge of the bed, asking questions. She stared at him most of the time with pallid, boring eyes. After a time he went downstairs and gave Mortimer a pipe of tobacco and walked about the yard, among the crying geese, and talked to him.

'All she can talk about is how she's been no good to me.' Joe said. 'How I'm not to go near her. How she hates herself. How she's been a failure all the time.'

The doctor did not answer; the geese cried and squawked among the barns.

'Neither one of us is sleeping well,' Joe said. 'I can't put up with it. I can't stand it much longer.'

'Was there something that began it?'

'The calf. We lost a calf about three weeks ago. She blamed herself for that.'

'Never thought of going away from here?' the doctor said.

'Away?'

'How long have you lived here?'

'Five and twenty years. Nearly six and twenty.'

'I believe you might do well to move,' the doctor said.

'Move? Where to? What for?'

'It might be that everything here has the same association. This is where she wanted her children and this is where she never had them. She might be happier if you moved away from here.'

'She misses children. She'd have been all right with children,' Joe said.

'Think it over,' the doctor said. 'She needs a rest too. Get her to take it a little easier. Get a girl to help in the kitchen and with the hens. It'll be company for her. Perhaps she won't think of herself so much.'

'All right. It upsets me to see her break her heart like that.'

'I wish I were a farmer. If I were a farmer you know what I'd like to do?' the doctor said. 'Grow nothing but corn. That's the life. Give up practically everything but corn. With the cows and stock and birds it's all day and every day. But with corn you go away and you come back and your corn's still there. It's a wonderful thing, corn. That's what I'd like to do. There's something marvellous about corn.'

The following spring they moved to a farm some distance up the hill. All their married lives they had lived on flat land, with no view except the hedges of their own fields and a shining stretch of railway line. Now they found themselves with land that ran away on a gentle slope, with a view below it of an entire broad valley across which trains ran like smoking toys.

The girl who answered their advertisement for help was short and dark, with rather sleepy brown eyes, a thick bright complexion and rosy-knuckled hands. She called at the house with her mother, who did most of what talking there was.

'She's been a bit off colour. But she's better now. She wants to work in the fresh air for a bit. You want to work in the fresh air, don't you, Elsie?'

'Yes,' Elsie said.

'She's very quiet, but she'll get used to you,' her mother said. 'She don't say much, but she'll get used to you. She's not particular either. You're not particular, are you, Elsie?'

'No,' Elsie said.

'She's a good girl. She won't give no trouble,' her mother said.

'How old is she?' Mortimer said.

'Eighteen,' her mother said. 'Eighteen and in her nineteen. She'll be nineteen next birthday, won't you, Elsie?'

'Yes,' Elsie said.

The girl settled into the house and moved about it with unobtrusive quietness. As she stood at the kitchen sink, staring down across the farm-yard, at the greening hedgerows of hawthorn and the rising fields of corn, she let her big-knuckled fingers wander dreamily over the wet surface of the dishes as if she were a blind person trying to trace a pattern. Her brown eyes travelled over the fields as if she were searching for something she had lost there.

Something about this lost and dreamy attitude gradually began to puzzle Mrs Mortimer. She saw in the staring brown eyes an expression that reminded her of the glazed eyes of a calf.

'You won't get lonely up here, will you?' she said. 'I don't want you to get lonely.'

'No,' the girl said.

'You tell me if you get anyways lonely, won't you?'

'Yes.'

'I want you to feel happy here,' Mrs Mortimer said. 'I want you to feel as if you was one of our own.'

As the summer went on the presence of the girl seemed occasionally to comfort Mrs Mortimer. Sometimes she was a little more content; she did not despise herself so much. During daytime at least she could look out on new fields, over new distances, and almost persuade herself that what she saw was a different sky. But at night, in darkness, the gnaw of self-reproaches remained. She could not prevent the old cry from breaking out:

'Don't come near me. Not yet. Soon perhaps – but not yet. Not until I feel better about things. I will one day, but not yet.'

Once or twice she even cried: 'You could get someone else. I wouldn't mind. I honestly wouldn't mind. It's hard for you, I know it is. I wouldn't mind.'

Sometimes Mortimer, distracted too, got up and walked about the yard in summer darkness, smoking hard, staring at the summer stars.

All summer, in the afternoons, after she had worked in the house all morning, the girl helped about the yard and the fields. By July the corn was level as a mat of thick blue-green pile between hedgerows of wild rose and blackberry flower. In the garden in front of the house bushes of currant were bright with berries that glistened like scarlet pearls from under old lace curtains.

The thick fingers of the girl were stained red with the juice of currants as she gathered them. Her fingermarks were bright smears across the heavy front of her cotton pinafore.

As the two women knelt among the bushes, in alley-ways of ripe fruit, lifting the bleached creamy curtains in the July sun, Mrs Mortimer said:

'I'm glad of another pair of hands. I don't know what I should have done without another pair of hands. Your mother will miss you back home I reckon.'

'She's got six more to help,' the girl said. 'She don't need me all that much.'

'Six? Not children?'

'When I was home there was seven. Eight before the baby went.'

'Before the baby went? Whose baby? What happened to the baby?'

'It was mine. I gave it away,' the girl said. 'I didn't know what to do with it no sense, so I gave it away. My sister adopted it. They all said it was best like that. I gave it to my married sister.'

'Gave it away?' Mrs Mortimer sat on the earth, between the bushes, feeling sick. 'Gave it away? A baby? You gave it away?'

'Yes,' Elsie said. 'It's no bother to me now.'

Towards the end of the month the first corn began to ripen. The sheen of olive on the wheat began to turn pale yellow, then to the colour of fresh-baked crust on bread.

As he looked at it Mortimer remembered what the doctor had said. 'You go away and you come back and your corn's still there. It's a wonderful thing, corn. There's something marvellous about corn.'

Now as he looked at it he could not help feeling proud of the corn. It helped him too as he thought of his wife. It hurt him to hear her cry that he must keep away from her, that the pride in her was still tortured, the love in her not smoothed out. The corn helped to soothe him a little. The wind that ran darkly across it on cloudy days had a beautiful twist as if long snakes were slipping among the ears.

In the evenings, after supper, while the two women washed the dishes, he was often alone with the corn. And one evening as he stood watching it he did something he had always liked to do. He broke off an ear and began to thresh it in his hands, breaking the husk from the grain with the pressure of the balls of his thumbs.

While he was still doing this the girl came down the hillside from the house with a message that a man had called to deliver a sailcloth. Mortimer blew on the grain that lay in his cupped hands, scattering a dancing cloud of chaff like summer flies.

'I'll be up in a minute,' he said. 'Here – tell me what you think of that.'

'The wheat?' she said.

She picked a few grains of wheat from the palm of his hand. She did not toss them into her mouth but put them in one by one, with the tips of her fingers, biting them with the front of her teeth. Her teeth were surprisingly level and white and he could see the whiteness of the new grains on her tongue as she bit them.

'They're milky,' she said.

'Still want a few more days, I think,' he said.

As they walked back up the field she plucked an ear of wheat as high as the girl herself, rustled in her fingers. When she bent down to blow on the husks a small gust of wind suddenly turned and blew the chaff up into her face. She laughed rather loudly, showing her teeth again, and he said:

'Here, you want to do it like this. You want to bring your thumbs over so that you can blow down there and make a chimney.'

'How?' she said.

A moment later he was holding her hands. He stood slightly behind her and held her hands and showed her how to cup them so that the chaff could blow out through the chimney made by her fingers.

'Now blow,' he said.

'I can't blow for laughing.'

Her mouth spluttered and a new gust of laughter blew into her hands and a dancing cloud of chaff leapt up in a spurt from her fingers. She laughed again and he felt her body shaking. A few husks of wheat blew into her mouth and a few more stuck to the moist edges of her lips as she laughed.

She pulled out her handkerchief to wipe her lips, still laughing, and suddenly he found himself trying to help her and then in a clumsy way trying to kiss her face and mouth at the same time.

'Elsie,' he said. 'Here, Elsie—'

She laughed again and said, 'We don't want to fool here. Somebody will see us if we start fooling here. Mrs Mortimer will see us. Not here.'

'You were always so quiet,' he said.

'It isn't always the loud ones who say most, is it?' she said. She began to shake herself. 'Now I've got chaff down my neck. Look at me.'

She laughed again and shook herself, twisting her body in a way that suddenly reminded him of the twist of dark air running among the ripening corn. He tried to kiss her again and she said:

'Not here I keep telling you. Some time if you like but not here. Not in broad daylight. I don't like people watching me.'

'All right—'

'Some other time. It's so public here,' she said. 'There'll be another time.'

By the end of August the corn was cut and carted. The stubbles were empty except for the girl and Mrs Mortimer, gleaning on fine afternoons, and a few brown hens scratching among the straw. 'I could never quite give up the hens,' Mrs Mortimer said. 'It would be an awful wrench to give them up. I didn't mind the cherries and I didn't even mind the calves so much. But the hens are company. I can talk to the hens.'

About the house, in the yard, bright yellow stacks stood ready for threshing, and there was a fresh clean smell of straw on the air. During summer the face of the girl had reddened with sun and air and as autumn came on it seemed to broaden and flatten, the thick skin ripe and healthy in texture.

'Soon be winter coming on, Elsie,' Mrs Mortimer said. 'You think you'll stay up here with us for the winter?'

'Well, I expect I shall if nothing happens,' Elsie said.

'Happens? If what happens?'

'Well, you never know what may happen,' Elsie said, 'do you?'

'I want you to stay if you can,' Mrs Mortimer said. 'They get a lot of snow up here some winters, but perhaps we'll be lucky. Stay if you can. I got now so as I think of you as one of our own.'

In a growing fondness for the girl Mrs Mortimer occasionally remembered and reflected on the incident of the baby. It was very strange and inexplicable to her, the incident of the baby. It filled her with mystery and wonder. It was a mystery beyond comprehension that a girl could conceive and bear a child and then, having delivered it, give it away. She felt she would never be able to grasp the reasons for that. 'You'd think it would be like tearing your own heart out to do a thing like that,' she thought.

Towards the end of November the first snow fell, covering the hillsides down to within a hundred feet of the valley. The house stood almost on the dividing line of snow, like a boat at the edge of a tide, between fields that were still fresh green with winter corn and others smooth with the first thin white fall.

'I got something to tell you,' the girl said to Mrs Mortimer. 'I don't think I'll be staying here much longer.'

'Not staying?'

'No.'

'Why not?'

'I don't think I will, that's all.'

'Is it the snow? You don't like the snow, do you? That's what it is, the snow.'

'It's not the snow so much.'

'Is it us then?' Mrs Mortimer said. 'Don't you like us no more?'

'I like you. It isn't that,' the girl said.

'What is it then, Elsie? Don't say you'll go. What is it?'

'It's the baby,' Elsie said.

'The baby?' Mrs Mortimer felt a pain of tears in her eyes. 'I somehow thought one day you'd want it back. I'm glad.'

'Not that baby,' the girl said. 'Not that one. I'm going to have another.'

Mrs Mortimer felt a strange sense of disturbance. She was shaken once again by disbelief and pain. She could not speak and the girl said:

'In the Spring. April I think it'll be.'

'How did you come to do that?' Mrs Mortimer said. 'Up here? With us—?'

'I know somebody,' the girl said, 'I got to know somebody. That's all.'

'I don't understand,' Mrs Mortimer said. She spoke quietly, almost to herself. She thought, with the old pain, of her years of sterility. She remembered how, in distraction, she had so much despised herself, how she had turned, out of pride, into isolation, away from Joe. 'I don't understand,' she said.

At night she turned restlessly in her bed. Splinters of moonlight between the edges of the curtains cut across her eyes and kept them stiffly open.

'Can't you sleep again?' Joe said.

'It's the girl,' she said. 'Elsie. I can't get her out of my mind.'

'What's wrong with Elsie?'

'She's having another baby,' she said. 'In the Spring.'

'Oh! no!' he said. 'Oh! no. No. You don't mean that? No.'

'It seems she got to know somebody. Somehow,' she said. She felt across her eyes the hard stab of moonlight. She turned and put her hand out and touched Joe on the shoulder. 'Joe,' she said. 'That doesn't seem right, does it? It doesn't seem fair.'

Joe did not answer.

'It doesn't seem fair. It's not right. It seems cruel,' she said.

The following night she could not sleep again. She heard a westerly wind from across the valley beating light squalls of rain on the windows of the bedroom. The air was mild in a sudden change and she lay with her arms outside the coverlet, listening to the rain washing away the snow.

Suddenly Joe took hold of her hands and began crying into them.

'I didn't know what I was doing. She kept asking me. It was her who kept asking me.'

She could not speak and he turned his face to the pillow.

'I didn't think you wanted me. You used to say so. I got so as I thought you didn't want me any more. You used to say—'

'I want you,' she said. 'Don't be afraid of that.'

'Did she say anything?' he said. 'Did she say it was me?'

'No. She didn't say.'

'Did you think it was me?'

'I'd begun to think,' she said. 'I thought I could tell by the way you couldn't look at her.'

She heard him draw his breath in dry snatches, unable to find words. Suddenly she was sorry for him, with no anger or reproach or bitterness, and she stretched out her long bare arms.

'Come here to me,' she said. 'Come close to me. I'm sorry. It was me. It was my fault.'

'Never,' he said. 'Never. I won't have that—'

'Listen to me,' she said. 'Listen to what I say.'

As she spoke she was aware of a feeling of being uplifted, of a depressive weight being taken from her.

'Listen, Joe, if I ask her perhaps she'll give it to us. You remember? She gave the other away.'

'No,' he said. 'You couldn't do that—'

'I could,' she said. She began smiling to herself in the darkness. 'Tomorrow I'll ask her. We could do it properly – so that it was ours.'

'If you forgive me,' Joe said. 'Only if you do that—'

'I forgive you,' she said.

She went through the rest of the winter as if she were carrying the baby herself. 'You mustn't do that, Elsie. Don't lift that,' she would say: 'Take a lie down for an hour. Rest yourself – it'll do you the world of good to rest.' She looked forward to Spring with a strange acute sensation of being poised on a wire, frightened that she would fall before she got there.

When the baby was born she wrapped it in a warm blanket and succoured it like the early chickens she had once wrapped in flannel, in a basket, under the stove.

'And I can have him?' she said. 'You haven't changed your mind? You won't change your mind will you?'

'No,' the girl said. 'You can have him. I don't want the bother. You can look after him.'

'We'll love him,' she said. 'We'll look after him.'

On a day in late April she took the baby and carried him down through the yard, in the sunshine, to where the fields began. Hedgerows were breaking everywhere into bright new leaf. Primroses lay in thick pale drifts under the shelter of them and under clumps of ash and hornbeam. In every turn of wind there was a whitening of anemones, with cowslips trembling gold about the pasture.

She lifted the baby up, in the sunshine, against the blue spring sky, and laughed and shook him gently, showing him the world of leaf and flower and corn.

'Look at all the flowers!' she said. 'Look at the corn! The corn looks good, doesn't it? It's going to be good this year, isn't it? Look at it all! – isn't the corn beautiful?'

High above her, on the hill, there was a sound of endless lark song and in the fields the young curved lines of corn were wonderfully fresh and trembling in the sun.

**Symbols**

A *symbol* is something which stands for or represents something else.

eg

   may represent a cross-roads

   may represent love

Red may represent danger or anger
A stormy night may represent a violent argument

Writers and poets often use symbols to reinforce certain ideas. These symbols could be almost anything and they could represent almost anything too.

# Assignments

○ ☞ **1**   **a** A number of details in the story are used in a *symbolic* way. Read the information in the box, and then refer back to the story to see whether you can complete the list below. There are no absolutely right or wrong answers – you may disagree with the interpretations given as examples.

- Saving half the money represents a future for their child
- The newborn chickens represent . . . .
- The eggs represent . . . .
- . . . . represents Mrs Mortimer's failure to have children
- The change to corn farming represents . . . .
- The winter represents . . . .
- The summer represents . . . .
- . . . . represents the girl's ripeness and fertility
- The wheat grains in the girl's mouth represent her appeal to Joe's senses
- The April sunshine represents . . . .
- The spring flowers represent . . . .
- The good corn represents . . . .

**b** What other symbols can you find in the story?
**c** What do you think the symbols add to the story? For example, could the story have been written without any reference to nature, do you think?

**2**   **a** Write the job advertisement which Elsie answers.
**b** Write the doctor's report on Mrs Mortimer.
**c** Write the conversation Joe might have had with Elsie after Mrs Mortimer has been told who the father of the baby is.

**3**   Write two or three letters from Elsie to her mother.

**4**   Write some entries from *either* Mrs Mortimer's *or* Joe's diary from the time they first move to the new farm until Elsie gives them the baby to adopt.

**5**   Try writing a poem, description or story which uses symbolism. You can do this in any way you like, but the following ideas may help you to get started:

- Someone feeling happy on a bright day or sad on a miserable day
- A photograph symbolises a memory of the past
- An item of clothing symbolises a certain event in the wearer's life
- An ex-convict is always reminded of his past when he sees keys and locks
- Colours represent moods or feelings.

This poem is about the First World War but it is written by a modern poet, Roger McGough. Begin by reading the poem aloud or listening to it being read.

**A Square Dance**
In Flanders fields in northern France
They're all doing a brand new dance
It makes you happy and out of breath
And it's called the Dance of Death

Everybody stands in line                                          5
Everybody's feeling fine
We're all going to a hop
1–2–3 and over the top

It's the dance designed to thrill
It's the mustard gas quadrille[1]                                 10
A dance for men – girls have no say in it
For your partner is a bayonet

See how the dancers sway and run
To the rhythm of the gun
Swing your partner dos-y-doed                                     15
All around the shells explode

Honour your partner form a square
Smell the burning in the air
Over the barbed wire kicking high
Men like shirts hung out to dry                                   20

If you fall that's no disgrace
Someone else will take your place
'Old soldiers never die . . .'
        . . . only young ones

In Flanders fields where mortars blaze
They're all doing the latest craze                               25
Khaki dancers out of breath
Doing the glorious Dance of Death
*1 square dance*    Doing the glorious (CLAP, CLAP) Dance of Death.

# Assignments

○ ☞ **1** A square dance is a country dance in which four couples face inwards from four sides (thus forming a square). One example of a square dance is the quadrille.

Referring to the box when you need to, try to answer the following questions about the poem. (In most cases there are no right or wrong answers – use the questions as a framework for your group discussion.)

**a** The central idea of the poem is a comparison between a square dance and a battlefield. Each of the following phrases may refer to a square dance. What actions on the battlefield do they refer to in the poem?

- stands in line (*line 5*)
- sway and run (*line 13*)
- swing your partner (*line 15*)
- form a square (*line 17*)
- kicking high (*line 19*)
- CLAP CLAP (*line 28*)

**b** Which of the following words or phrases are puns?

- out of breath (*line 3*)
- sway and run (*line 13*)
- 'Old soldiers never die' (*line 23*)
- Honour your partner (*line 17*)
- going to a hop (*line 7*)
- thrill (*line 9*)
- quadrille (*line 10*)
- craze (*line 25*)
- fall (*line 21*)

In each case explain the double meaning.

**c** Which of the following rhymes are particularly startling, in your opinion? Why?

- line/fine (*lines 5–6*)
- dos-y-doed/explode (*lines 15–16*)

- blaze/craze (*lines 24–25*)
- say in it/bayonet (*lines 11–12*)
- breath/death (*lines 3–4*)

**d** As far as the *rhythm* is concerned, which do you think is the most important line in the poem? Why?

**e** Place the following five lines in order of how *sarcastic* you think they are: line 20; line 23; line 13; line 6; line 22.

**f** Place the following five lines in order of how *scornful* you think they are: line 28; line 23; line 6; line 20; line 10.

**g** Which of the following phrases would you say best describes the poet's *tone*? (See page 127.)

- witty irony
- scornful sarcasm
- subtle innuendo
- mock jollity
- biting contempt

**h** In order to achieve the total effect of the poem, the poet uses at least all the following devices: rhythm; sarcasm; puns; rhyme; simile; contrast.

Place them in what you think is their order of importance to the poem's success.

Can you identify any other devices the poet uses?

**2** Write about any aspects of the poem you find interesting. As well as referring closely to the language and form of the poem, you may like to discuss what you think the poet feels about war and what questions the poem makes you ask yourself.

**3** Try writing something satirical yourself. It's not easy, but the following ideas may help you to get started:

- Use the form of a skipping rhyme, nursery rhyme or children's song to treat a serious subject. (War? Injustice? Poverty?)
- Choose a subject you feel strongly about. Write in a humorous way about the people who oppose your view.
- Write a jokey comedy sketch which has a serious point to make about human morals or the stupidity of human behaviour.

**THE LOST SISTER**
**Dorothy M. Johnson**

Before Major Harris got there with half a dozen cavalrymen, civilian scouts were out searching for the missing woman. They were expert trackers. Their lives had depended, at various times, on their ability to read the meaning of a turned stone, a broken twig, a bruised leaf. They found that Bessie had gone south. They tracked her for ten miles. And then they lost the trail, for Bessie was as skilled as they were. Her life had sometimes depended on leaving no stone or twig or leaf marked by her passage. She travelled fast at first. Then, with time to be careful, she evaded the followers she knew would come.

Aunt Mary kept saying pitifully, 'Oh, why did she go? I thought she would be contented with me!'

The others said that it was, perhaps, all for the best.

Aunt Margaret proclaimed, 'She has gone back to her own.' That was what they honestly believed and so did Major Harris.

My mother told me why she had gone. 'You know that picture she had of the Indian chief, her son? He's escaped from the jail he was in. The fort got word of it, and they think Bessie may be going to where he's hiding. That's why they're trying so hard to find her. They think,' my mother explained, 'that she knew of his escape before they did. They think the interpreter told her when he was here. There was no other way she could have found out.'

They scoured the mountains to the south for Eagle Head and Bessie. They never found her, and they did not get him until a year later, far to the north. They could not capture him that time. He died fighting.

After I grew up, I operated the family store, disliking storekeeping a little more every day. When I was free to sell it, I did, and went to raising cattle. And one day, riding in a canyon after strayed steers, I found – I think – Aunt Bessie. A cowboy who worked for me was along, or I would never have let anybody know.

We found weathered bones near a little spring. They had a mystery on them, those nameless human bones suddenly come upon. I could feel old death brushing my back.

'Some prospector,' suggested my riding partner.

I thought so too until I found, protected by a log, sodden scraps of fabric that might have been a dark, respectable dress. And wrapped in them was a sodden something that might have once been a picture.

The man with me was young, but he had heard the story of the captive child. He had been telling me about it, in fact.

I tried to push the sodden scrap of fabric back under the log, but he was too quick for me. 'That ain't no shirt, that's a dress!' he announced. 'This here was no prospector – it was a woman!' He paused and then announced with awe, 'I bet you it was your Indian aunt!'

I scowled and said, 'Nonsense. It could be anybody.'

He got all worked up about it. 'If it was *my* aunt,' he declared, 'I'd bury her in the family plot.'

'No,' I said, and shook my head.

We left the bones there in the canyon, where they had been for forty-odd years if they were Aunt Bessie's. And I think they were. But I

237

would not make her a captive again. She's in the family album. She doesn't need to be in the family plot.

If my guess about why she left us is wrong, nobody can prove it. She never intended to join her son in hiding. She went in the opposite direction to lure pursuit away.

What happened to her in the canyon doesn't concern me, or anyone. My Aunt Bessie accomplished what she set out to do. It was not her life that mattered, but his. She bought him another year.

# Assignments

○ ☞ **5** Were your predictions on page 54 correct?

    **a** Why did the narrator not have the aunt buried in the family plot? Do you agree with his decision?
    **b** What evidence was there in the first part of the story (pages 48–52) that Bessie might act in this way?
    **c** Do you like the way the story ends?
    **d** Do you think it is a well-written story?

    **6** Write a paragraph about Aunt Bessie as if you were each of the following:

    **a** The boy's mother
    **b** The interpreter
    **c** Major Harris
    **d** Aunt Margaret
    **e** Aunt Mary
    **f** Aunt Bessie herself

    **7** Imagine you are *either* Aunt Margaret *or* Aunt Bessie. Rewrite the story from that point of view, ending at the point when Bessie leaves the aunts' house.

238

**ALL BUT EMPTY**
Part 5

All the while I held the receiver I watched the curtain, and presently it began to shake and billow, as if somebody was fumbling for the way out. 'Hurry, hurry,' I called down the telephone, and then as the voice spoke I saw the old man wavering in the gap of the curtain. 'Hurry. The murderer's here,' I called, stumbling over the name of the cinema and so intent on the message I had to convey that I could not take in for a moment the puzzled and puzzling reply: 'We've got the murderer. It's the body that's disappeared.'

Well, did anyone predict this ending?

# Assignments

☞ **1** Look back at the story (pages 16, 17, 92, 98, 141). Were there any clues as to how it might end? How did Graham Greene manage to mislead his readers?

✔ 📖 **2** Try writing your own story with a 'twist' at the end. For instance:

- The one person the reader thought was the killer is not
- The one who seems guilty is innocent
- The thing the reader thought could never happen does happen
- Nothing is quite the way it seemed to be

✔ 📖 **3** To make it really complicated, you could write a story with a 'double twist'. To do this, you must lead your readers to expect that there will be a twist and then, at the end, have the predictable ending after all!

# U·N·I·T 59 *Weighing up the evidence*

When an important issue is being considered, there are usually many factors and points of view to take into account. Take, for instance, the issue of nuclear power.

Traditionally, electricity has been made from coal. However, in recent years many countries have used nuclear power to generate some of their electricity. Nuclear power is created by splitting atoms of uranium – a process which releases heat. This heat produces steam, which drives the turbines to generate electricity. In the process radioactivity is discharged, but this is contained within the reactor.

After use, the spent nuclear fuel is taken to a reprocessing plant, where it is separated into uranium and plutonium (which can be recycled for further use) and radioactive waste material.

Some people are very much against nuclear power for a number of reasons; others feel equally strongly that it is a good thing. You can read some of the evidence for both views on these pages.

1    **We could do without nuclear power. Britain has a glut of energy. It's an island with over 300 years' reserves of coal, sitting in a sea of oil and gas, with the longest coastline in Europe – good for wind, tidal and wave sources of energy. Nuclear power only supplies about 4% of all our energy needs in a form – electricity – which is either impractical or too expensive for most of our energy needs – industrial and domestic heating.**

2    *We need nuclear generated electricity to preserve a balanced energy policy and avoid over-dependence on one fuel for all our electricity. A single source of supply can be affected by shortage, interruption because of technical difficulties or disruptive industrial action. Coal, gas and oil reserves will eventually run out. Petrol and diesel oil are needed for road transport, and coal can be used as an oil substitute in the manufacture of plastics and pharmaceuticals. Uranium, on the other hand, is found in many places in the world and has no other significant commercial use except in nuclear power stations. Nuclear energy is a clean and cheap method of generating electricity. Nuclear power stations are cheaper to run overall than equivalent coal-fired stations, and pollution is negligible. Nuclear energy supplies about 20% of the electricity in the UK.*

3    Other forms of energy could be developed which are better than nuclear power. For instance, even in cloudy northern countries like Britain there is more than enough solar energy for our needs – the total falling on this country every year is more than one hundred times greater than all the energy used. We also have an ideal climate for wind power, which could generate at least 20% of our electricity. Wave energy has been developed in Britain in recent years and there is also the possibility of generating electricity from tides, like the one at the Severn estuary. These methods have been tested out but research and development have been delayed because of a shortage of cash and political commitment. In 1985 £220 million was given to the development of nuclear power, but only £14 million to develop these renewable sources of energy.

4    **The sun directs a vast amount of energy towards Britain each year, but it is a very diluted form of energy and is very unevenly distributed. One day it may be possible to harness the sun's energy on a large scale, but as far as can be seen ahead, it will only be practical in Britain to heat water for use in homes by means of solar panels. Even this looks as though costs may be too high to make it economic. The waves of the sea could provide energy, but they are very variable and difficult to use. It would probably take a line of devices as much as 60 miles long to produce the same amount of electricity as a large power station. Tides could also be used, but the cost of building huge structures to trap the water would be very high. To provide enough wind power to generate electricity for a city like Liverpool would require about 200 giant windmills each with blades 200 ft long.**

5    *Two-thirds of the energy in the coal burnt in coal power stations is thrown away as waste heat. We could reclaim more than half of this to heat buildings. Britain is almost alone in Europe in not having developed this concept. We could also avoid wasting about a third of the energy we use by*

*insulating buildings and by using efficient equipment. Money spent on conservation is far more efficient than that spent on electricity generation, and creates far more jobs throughout the economy.*

6    Radiation is dangerous. You can't feel it, see it, smell it or taste it, but it can cause cancer, genetic damage and premature ageing by weakening the body's resistance to many common diseases. The effects can take years or generations to become visible, so it is often very difficult to prove that radiation exposure years before caused the damage. There is no safe level of exposure: any exposure adds to the risk. Even very small doses can cause serious damage.

7    **We live in a radioactive world and would do so whether there was nuclear power or not. Man is exposed to radiation from the sun and outer space, from rocks and soil and therefore from building materials. Radiation is even present in the human body itself. The air we breathe also contains radioactive gases such as radon. In addition to natural radiation, man is exposed to sources of radiation he has created. These include X-rays, therapeutic use of radiation and diagnosis by radiology. Manufacture of items such as luminous watches and smoke detectors as well as industrial radiography also involves people in work with radiation. The amount of radiation resulting from the UK nuclear industry is only 0.1% of the public's average exposure dosage.**

8    *People say there are risks in producing electricity from nuclear energy. There are, but there are risks in producing electricity from any source of energy. Coal miners and men on the North Sea oil rigs run risks. In fact no one can live without running any risks at all. Every time we cross a busy road, or travel by car or aeroplane, we run a risk. The risks from nuclear energy are very small compared with the benefits it can bring us.*

9    The nuclear fuels industry is licensed to operate its sites by the Nuclear Installations Inspectorate of the Health and Safety Executive. The sites are subject to inspection by the NII and the licence contains requirements and conditions designed to safeguard workers and the general public. The standards of radiation protection are based on internationally accepted recommendations. Nuclear plants are designed, constructed and operated with safety in mind. Safety precautions are duplicated or even triplicated and are complemented by extensive monitoring of the environment, the workplace and employees themselves. Air, milk, fish, shellfish, seaweed, grass, soil and other materials are all analysed to check radiation levels. In addition, Government departments carry out their own independent surveys.

10   **All industrial processes produce waste in a variety of physical and chemical forms, each of which needs consideration. So it is with the nuclear industry. A great deal of nuclear waste is stored at nuclear sites like power stations and the fuel reprocessing plant at Sellafield. When some of its radioactivity has died away, it can be disposed of outside. Low-active liquid waste may be discharged into the sea, while low-active solid waste is buried**

242

in trenches, like the one at Drigg. Discharge of these wastes is carried out under authorisations set by the Government to ensure that radiation doses to the public are kept within recommended limits.

11   *Radioactive waste is dangerous for enormous periods of time: 250 000 years in the case of high-level wastes and 300 years in the case of low-level wastes. Vast amounts of radioactive effluent have now been discharged into the sea from Sellafield. House dust in the Sellafield area now shows up to 6000 times higher plutonium levels than elsewhere. Nuclear waste dumps like the one at Drigg pose a number of potential hazards to the public. The radioactivity may leak from the site and find its way into rivers and reservoirs. Half the dumps in the USA have been closed down because contamination has spread outside the site. Even if the radioactivity is safely contained under normal conditions, the site may be disturbed by an earthquake (these do occasionally occur in Britain) or by someone accidentally or deliberately interfering with the waste site. A dump containing long-lived radioactivity will have to be isolated for thousands of years.*

12   Nuclear reactors currently rely upon finite sources of uranium, a metal not found in economic quantities in Britain. In order to prolong the lifespan of nuclear power, therefore, the Fast Breeder Reactor has been developed, using plutonium as a fuel. Plutonium can also be used to make nuclear weapons, and is one of the most dangerous substances known to mankind. Reactors using uranium operate at extremely high temperatures and generate heat long after production has stopped. This means that they must be kept cool at all times. A loss of coolant accident could lead to the release of large quantities of radiation into the atmosphere.

13   **On 26 April 1986 an accident occurred to the Number 4 reactor at the nuclear power station in Chernobyl, 60 miles north of Kiev in the Soviet Union. Increased radioactivity levels were subsequently detected in a number of countries including the UK, but by the time the radioactivity reached the UK it was to a large extent diluted. The type of reactor used at Chernobyl has a number of serious defects, and would not be acceptable in the UK. The principal feature in common between the Chernobyl reactors and UK reactors is the use of a graphite moderator. But in the Soviet design the graphite operates at a much higher maximum temperature, 700°C, compared with 350–550°C for the UK reactors. This, together with the close proximity of the graphite to water used as a coolant, poses much greater safety problems.**

14   *It was admitted by the authorities in Britain that we shall probably suffer between 50 and 150 fatal cancers as a result of the Chernobyl accident which happened over 1000 miles away. Had the accident happened in France or in Britain itself, the consequences would have been far far worse. In Russia, they face the likelihood of several thousand cancers over the next 30 years, and the long-term contamination of hundreds of square miles of farmland and water supplies.*

**15** 'I would like to emphasise that the safety standards in this country, the whole licensing process and the procedure by which the safety of nuclear power stations is regulated is different from other countries' – and in our country I am convinced that it is very good indeed. The care which is taken is so thorough and so complete that I believe it is at least as good as anything in the world. I am sure that the reactors which are operating at the moment present no risk – no undue risk – to people at all.'

**16** **US nuclear experts now believe that the Soviet nuclear plant at Chernobyl, previously dismissed as having a dangerously unsafe design, has similar safety standards to Western reactors and many features common to US designs. Experts say that although Chernobyl may have not passed Nuclear Regulatory Commission standards, the plan is similar in many respects to US plants.**

# Assignments

All the extracts above are taken from books and leaflets published either by manufacturers who produce nuclear power or by organisations who campaign for its abolition. For this reason, there are many contradictions in the evidence presented here. Not all the extracts are exclusively about nuclear power; some touch on other related issues which must also be considered in the debate.

○ ☞ **1**

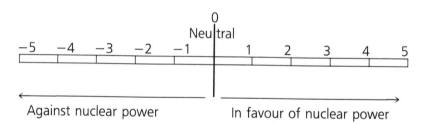

Consider each of the pieces of evidence, **1–16**. Give each a number from −5 to +5 according to the view you think it takes of nuclear power (eg +5 would be a very positive view, −2 a moderately negative view, 0 would be neutral).

**2** **a** Make a list of the main factors to be considered when trying to establish whether nuclear power is a good or a bad thing.
**b** For each of these factors write down *in note form* (ie very briefly) the arguments for and against.
**c** Fifth-form pupils at your school are to hold a debate on nuclear power. Use your notes for **a** and **b** to help you write a report (see page 19) which all fifth formers will read before the debate. Use the headings which you prepared in **a** to subdivide your report, and keep it as simple as possible.

**3** Hold a formal debate on the motion: 'We totally condemn nuclear power.' (See page 134 to find out how this kind of debate is organised.)

**4** **a** Decide whether you are in favour of or against nuclear power. (You cannot be neutral for this assignment.)
**b** List what you feel are the four best reasons to support your opinion.
**c** List four arguments someone disagreeing with your view might raise.
**d** These eight points can form the basis of an eight-paragraph essay. Make brief notes for each of them, showing how the main point can be developed with evidence, examples etc.
**c** Write an article for your school magazine with this title:

*Nuclear power is one of the key issues of our time. Are you for it or against it?*

Your main purpose in writing the article is to persuade readers that your view is the only sensible one. (The box shows you one way you could organise your ideas.)

---

**Argument essays**

An argument essay is one in which you put forward a particular point of view and explain in full the reasons for your view. The aim of the essay is to *persuade* your reader(s) that your view is the right one.

- Plan your essay carefully first.
- Begin by capturing the reader's interest with something surprising or interesting.
- Write four paragraphs putting forward the arguments you disagree with and explain why you disagree.
- Write four more paragraphs on the points you support and why you support them.
- Save your strongest arguments until last.
- In the last paragraph leave the reader with something to think about.
- Organise your paragraphs in a logical way, bearing in mind how one paragraph can be linked to the next.

---

**5** Follow the same method to write a persuasive article on another issue you feel strongly about. Remember to research your chosen subject carefully first.

# U·N·I·T 60 Asking yourself the questions

In the course of this book you can read and study texts of all sorts in many different ways. Generally speaking, you are guided fairly closely. In this unit, however, you will have to do more of the work yourself!

Begin by reading this story by Ray Bradbury. It is set in the not too distant future.

**THE MURDERER**

Music moved with him in the white halls. He passed an office door: 'The Merry Widow Waltz.' Another door: 'Afternoon of a Faun.' A third: 'Kiss Me Again.' He turned into a cross corridor: 'The Sword Dance' buried him in cymbals, drums, pots, pans, knives, forks, thunder, and tin lightning. All washed away as he hurried through an anteroom where a secretary sat nicely stunned by Beethoven's Fifth. He moved himself before her eyes like a hand; she didn't see him.

His wrist radio buzzed.

'Yes?'

'This is Lee, Dad. Don't forget about my allowance.'

'Yes, son, yes. I'm busy.'

'Just didn't want you to forget, Dad,' said the wrist radio. Tchaikovsky's 'Romeo and Juliet' swarmed about the voice and flushed into the long halls.

The psychiatrist moved in the beehive of offices, in the cross-pollination of themes, Stravinsky mating with Bach, Haydn unsuccessfully repulsing Rachmaninoff, Schubert slain by Duke Ellington. He nodded to the humming secretaries and the whistling doctors fresh to their morning work. At his office he checked a few papers with his stenographer,[1] who sang under her breath, then phoned the police captain upstairs. A few minutes later a red light blinked, a voice said from the ceiling:

'Prisoner delivered to Interview Chamber Nine.'

He unlocked the chamber door, stepped in, heard the door lock behind him.

'Go away,' said the prisoner, smiling.

The psychiatrist was shocked by that smile. A very sunny, pleasant warm thing, a thing that shed bright light upon the room. Dawn among the dark hills. High noon at midnight, that smile. The blue eyes sparkled serenely above that display of self-assured dentistry.

'I'm here to help you,' said the psychiatrist, frowning. Something was wrong with the room. He had hesitated the moment he entered. He glanced around. The prisoner laughed. 'If you're wondering why it's so quiet in here, I just kicked the radio to death.'

Violent, thought the doctor.

The prisoner read this thought, smiled, put out a gentle hand. 'No, only

*1 Typist*

246

to machines that yak-yak-yak.'

Bits of the wall radio's tubes and wires lay on the gray carpeting. Ignoring these, feeling that smile upon him like a heat lamp, the psychiatrist sat across from his patient in the unusual silence which was like the gathering of a storm.

'You're Mr Albert Brock, who calls himself The Murderer?'

Brock nodded pleasantly. 'Before we start . . .' He moved quietly and quickly to detach the wrist radio from the doctor's arm. He tucked it in his teeth like a walnut, gritted and heard it crack, handed it back to the appalled psychiatrist as if he had done them both a favor. 'That's better.'

The psychiatrist stared at the ruined machine. 'You're running up quite a damage bill.'

'I don't care,' smiled the patient. 'As the old song goes: "Don't Care What Happens to Me!"' He hummed it.

The psychiatrist said: 'Shall we start?'

'Fine. The first victim, or one of the first, was my telephone. Murder most foul. I shoved it in the kitchen Insinkerator! Stopped the disposal unit in mid-swallow. Poor thing strangled to death. After that I shot the television set!'

The psychiatrist said, 'Mmm.'

'Fired six shots right through the cathode. Made a beautiful tinkling crash, like a dropped chandelier.'

'Nice imagery.'

'Thanks, I always dreamt of being a writer.'

'Suppose you tell me when you first began to hate the telephone.'

'It frightened me as a child. Uncle of mine called it the Ghost Machine. Voices without bodies. Scared the living hell out of me. Later in life I was never comfortable. Seemed to me a phone was an impersonal instrument. If it *felt* like it, it let your personality go through its wires. If it didn't *want* to, it just drained your personality away until what slipped through at the other end was some cold fish of a voice all steel, copper, plastic, no warmth, no reality. It's easy to say the wrong thing on telephones; the telephone changes your meaning on you. First thing you know, you've made an enemy. Then, of course, the telephone's such a *convenient* thing; it just sits there and *demands* you call someone who doesn't want to be called. Friends were always calling, calling, calling me. Hell, I hadn't any time of my own. When it wasn't the telephone it was the television, the radio, the phonograph. When it wasn't the television or radio or the phonograph it was motion pictures at the corner theater, motion pictures projected, with commercials on low-lying cumulus clouds. It doesn't rain rain any more, it rains soap-suds. When it wasn't High-Fly Cloud advertisements, it was music by Mozzek in every restaurant; music and commercials on the busses I rode to work. When it wasn't music, it was inter-office communications, and my horror chamber of a radio wrist watch on which my friends and my wife phoned every five minutes. What is there about such "conveniences" that makes them so *temptingly* convenient? The average man thinks, Here I am, time on my hands, and there on my wrist is a wrist telephone, so why not just buzz old Joe up, eh? "Hello, hello!" I love my friends, my wife, humanity, very much, but when one minute my wife calls to say, "Where are you *now*, dear?" and a friend calls and says, "Got the best off-color joke to tell you. Seems there was a guy—" And a stranger calls and cries out, "This is the Find-Fax Poll. What gum are you chewing at this very *instant!*" Well!'

'How did you feel during the week?'

'The fuse lit. On the edge of the cliff. That same afternoon I did what I did at the office.'

'Which was?'

'I poured a paper cup of water into the intercommunications system.'

The psychiatrist wrote on his pad.

'And the system shorted?'

'Beautifully! The Fourth of July on wheels! My God, stenographers ran around looking *lost!* What an uproar!'

'Felt better temporarily, eh?'

'Fine! Then I got the idea at noon of stomping my wrist radio on the sidewalk. A shrill voice was just yelling out of it at me. "This is people's Poll Number Nine. What did you eat for lunch?" when I kicked the Jesus out of the wrist radio!'

'Felt even *better*, eh?'

'It *grew* on me!' Brock rubbed his hands together. 'Why didn't I start a solitary revolution, deliver man from certain conveniences'? "Convenient for Who?" I cried. Convenient for friends: "Hey, Al, thought I'd call you from the locker room out here at Green Hills. Just made a sockdolager hole in one! A hole in one, Al! A *beautiful* day. Having a shot of whisky now. Thought you'd want to know. Al!" Convenient for my office, so when I'm in the field with my radio car there's no moment when I'm not in touch. In *touch! There's* a slimy phrase. Touch, hell. *Gripped!* Pawed, rather. Mauled and massaged and pounded by FM voices. You can't leave your car without checking in: "Have stopped to visit gas-station men's room." "Okay, Brock, step on it!" "Brock, what *took* you so long?" "Sorry, sir." "Watch it next time, Brock." "*Yes, sir!*" So, do you know what I did, Doctor? I bought a quart of French chocolate ice cream and spooned it into the car radio transmitter.'

'Was there any *special* reason for selecting French chocolate ice cream to spoon into the broadcasting unit?'

Brock thought about it and smiled. 'It's my favorite flavor.'

'Oh,' said the doctor.

'I figured, hell, what's good enough for me is good enough for the radio transmitter.'

'What made you think of spooning *ice cream* into the radio?'

'It was a hot day.'

The doctor paused.

'And what happened next?'

'Silence happened next. God, it was *beautiful*. That car radio cackling all day, Brock go here, Brock go there, Brock check in, Brock check out, okay Brock, hour lunch, Brock, lunch over, Brock, Brock, Brock. Well, that silence was like putting ice cream in my ears.'

'You seem to like ice cream a lot.'

'I just rode around feeling of the silence. It's a big bolt of the nicest softest flannel ever made. Silence. A whole hour of it. I just sat in my car; smiling, feeling of that flannel with my ears. I felt *drunk* with Freedom!'

'Go on.'

'Then I got the idea of the portable diathermy machine.[2] I rented one, took it on the bus going home that night. There sat all the tired commuters with their wrist radios, talking to their wives, saying, "Now I'm at Forty-third, now I'm at Forty-fourth, here I am at Forty-ninth, now turning at Sixty-first," One husband cursing, "Well, get *out* of that bar, damn it, and get home and get dinner started, I'm at Seventieth!" And the transit-system radio playing "Tales from the Vienna Woods," a canary singing words about a first-rate wheat cereal. Then – I switched on my diathermy! Static! Interference! All wives cut off from husbands grousing about a hard day at the office. All husbands cut off from wives who had just seen their children break a window! The "Vienna Woods" chopped down, the canary mangled! *Silence!* A terrible, unexpected silence. The bus inhabitants faced with having to converse with each other. Panic! Sheer, animal panic!'

'The police seized you?'

'The bus *had* to stop. After all, the music *was* being scrambled, husbands and wives *were* out of touch with reality. Pandemonium, riot, and chaos. Squirrels chattering in cages! A trouble unit arrived, triangulated on me instantly, had me reprimanded, fined, and home, minus my diathermy machine, in jig time.'

'Mr Brock, may I suggest that so far your whole pattern here is not very – practical? If you didn't like transit radios or office radios or car business radios, why didn't you join a fraternity of radio haters, start petititons, get legal and constitutional rulings? After all, this *is* a democracy.'

'And I,' said Brock, 'am that thing called a minority. I *did* join fraternities, picket, pass petitions, take it to court. Year after year I protested. Everyone laughed. Everyone else *loved* bus radios and commercials. *I* was out of step.'

'Then you should have taken it like a good soldier, don't you think? The majority rules.'

'But they went too far. If a little music and "keeping in touch" was charming, they figured a lot would be ten times as charming. I went *wild!* I got home to find my wife hysterical. *Why?* Because she had been completely out of touch with me for half a day. Remember, I did a dance on my wrist radio? Well, that night I laid plans to murder my house.'

'Are you *sure* that's how you want me to write it down?'

'That's semantically accurate.[3] Kill it dead. It's one of those talking, singing, humming, weather-reporting, poetry-reading, novel-reciting, jingle-jangling, rockaby-crooning-when-you-go-to-bed houses. A house that screams opera to you in the shower and teaches you Spanish in your sleep. One of those blathering caves where all kinds of electronic Oracles make you feel a trifle larger than a thimble, with stoves that say, "I'm apricot pie, and I'm *done*," or "I'm prime roast beef, so *baste* me!" and other nursery gibberish like that. With beds that rock you to sleep and *shake* you awake. A house that *barely* tolerates humans, I tell you. A front door that barks: "You've mud on your feet, sir!" And an electronic vacuum hound that snuffles around after you from room to room, inhaling every fingernail or ash you drop. Jesus God, *I* say, Jesus God!'

'Quietly,' suggested the psychiatrist.

2 *Machine which heats body tissues – for medical purposes*
3 *That is exactly what I mean*

249

'Remember that Gilbert and Sullivan song – "I've Got It on My List, It Never Will Be Missed"? All night I listed grievances. Next morning early I bought a pistol. I *purposely* muddied my feet, I stood at our front door. The front door shrilled, "Dirty feet, muddy feet! Wipe your feet! Please be *neat!*" I shot the damn thing in its keyhole. I ran to the kitchen, where the stove was just whining, "Turn me *over!*" In the middle of a mechanical omelet I did the stove to death. Oh, how it sizzled and screamed, "I'm *shorted!*" Then the telephone rang like a spoiled brat. I shoved it down the Insinkerator. I must state here and now I have *nothing* whatever against the Insinkerator: it was an innocent bystander. I feel sorry for it now, a practical device indeed, which never said a word, purred like a sleepy lion most of the time, and digested our leftovers. I'll have it restored. Then I went in and shot the televisor, that insidious beast, that Medusa,[4] which freezes a billion people to stone every night, staring fixedly, that Siren[5] which called and sang and promised so much and gave, after all, so little, but myself always going back, going back, hoping and waiting until – bang! Like a headless turkey, gobbling, my wife whooped out the front door. The police came. Here I *am!*'

He sat back happily and lit a cigarette.

'And did you realize, in committing these crimes, that the wrist radio, the broadcasting transmitter, the phone, the bus radio, the office intercoms, all were rented or were someone else's property?'

'I would do it all over again, so help me God.'

The psychiatrist sat there in the sunshine of that beatific smile.

'You don't want any further help from the Office of Mental Health? You're ready to take the consequences?'

'This is only the beginning,' said Mr Brock. 'I'm the vanguard of the small public which is tired of noise and being taken advantage of and pushed around and yelled at, every moment music, every moment in touch with some voice somewhere, do this, do that, quick, quick, now here, now there. You'll see. The revolt begins. My name will go down in history!'

'Mmm.' The psychiatrist seemed to be thinking.

'It'll take time, of course. It was all so enchanting at first. The very *idea* of these things, the practical uses, was wonderful. They were almost toys to be played with, but the people got too involved, went too far, and got wrapped up in a pattern of social behavior and couldn't get out, couldn't admit they were *in*, even. So they rationalized their nerves as something else. "Our modern age," they said. "Conditions," they said. "High-strung," they said. But mark my words, the seed has been sown. I got world-wide coverage on TV radio, films; *there's* an irony for you. That was five days ago. A billion people know about me. Check your financial columns. Any day now. Maybe today. Watch for a sudden spurt, a rise in sales for French chocolate ice cream!'

'I see,' said the psychiatrist.

'Can I go back to my nice private cell now, where I can be alone and quiet for six months?'

'Yes,' said the psychiatrist quietly.

'Don't worry about me,' said Mr Brock, rising. 'I'm just going to sit around for a long time stuffing that nice soft bolt of quiet material in both

*4 Female monster whose terrible appearance turned men to stone*
*5 Sea-nymph whose singing lured sailors to their deaths on the rocks*

ears.'

'Mmm,' said the psychiatrist, going to the door.

'Cheers,' said Mr Brock.

'Yes,' said the psychiatrist.

He pressed a code signal on a hidden button, the door opened, he stepped out, the door shut and locked. Alone, he moved in the offices and corridors. The first twenty yards of his walk were accompanied by 'Tambourine Chinois.' Then it was 'Tzigane,' Bach's Passacaglia and Fugue in something Minor, 'Tiger Rag,' 'Love Is Like a Cigarette.' He took his broken wrist radio from his pocket like a dead praying mantis. He turned in at his office. A bell sounded; a voice came out of the ceiling, 'Doctor?'

'Just finished with Brock,' said the psychiatrist.

'Diagnosis?'

'Seems completely disorientated, but convivial.[6] Refuses to accept the simplest realities of his environment and work *with* them.'

'Prognosis?'[7]

'Indefinite. Left him enjoying a piece of invisible material.'

Three phones rang. A duplicate wrist radio in his desk drawer buzzed like a wounded grasshopper. The intercom flashed a pink light and click-clicked. Three phones rang. The drawer buzzed. Music blew in through the open door. The psychiatrist, humming quietly, fitted the new wrist radio to his wrist, flipped the intercom, talked a moment, picked up one telephone, talked, picked up another telephone, talked, picked up the third telephone, talked, touched the wrist-radio button, talked calmly and quietly, his face cool and serene, in the middle of the music and the lights flashing, the two phones ringing again, and his hands moving, and his wrist radio buzzing, and the intercoms talking, and voices speaking from the ceiling. And he went on quietly this way through the remainder of a cool, air-conditioned, and long afternoon; telephone, wrist radio, intercom, telephone, wrist radio, intercom, telephone, wrist radio, intercom, telephone, wrist radio, intercom, telephone, wrist radio, intercom, telephone, wrist radio . . .

*6 Jolly*
*7 Medical forecast*

251

# Assignments

○ ✔ ☞ **1**　**a** Each member of your group should write a list of about five general questions which s/he wants to ask about this story. The questions should concern anything which seems puzzling, interesting, important or significant in any way.

**b** Discuss everyone's questions and then, in your group, draw up a list of the five questions which you think are the most crucial to an understanding of the story.

**c** Exchange lists of questions with another group. Try to answer their questions. (After this it is a good idea to have a general feedback session.)

**d** In your group (or even as a whole class) decide on the *one* key question which seems to get at the heart of the story. (You need not answer it!)

---

✔ ◇ **2**　The discussion you have carried out should help you to write an essay on *The Murderer*. If you wish, you could use these questions as a title:

*What do you think is Bradbury's intention in writing 'The Murderer'? How well do you think he achieves this?*

Remember to plan your essay before writing anything.

---

✔ ◇ **3**　Write the report the psychiatrist makes (see page 19) after his interview with Brock. Use these headings to sub-divide your report:

- The patient himself
- His problems
- My interview with him
- My conclusions based on this interview
- Advice for the future

---

✔ ◇ **4**　Write a poem or short story inspired by *The Murderer*.

# Answers to exercises

**UNIT 1**
**Skimming a book** (pages 3–4)

**1** 272
**2** 60
**3** 1–8 pages
**4** **a** Yes, **b** No, **c** Yes, **d** No, **e** No
**5** **a** No, **b** No, **c** Yes, **d** No, **e** Yes
**6** **a** Yes, **b** Yes, **c** Yes, **d** Yes, **e** Yes
**7** **a** Nuclear power, **b** a football match, **c** crime, **d** interviewing a teacher, **e** tourism in Europe, **f** using a video camera
**8** **a** poems, **b** factual passages **c** newspaper report, **d** advertisements and factual information, **e** factual information and a diagram
**9** **a** No, **b** Yes, **c** Yes, **d** Yes, **e** Yes, **f** Yes, **g** Yes, **h** Yes, **i** Yes
**10** They sum up important guidelines and points to remember

**UNIT 2**
**Scanning a text** (pages 5–7)

**a** 30, **b** 20, **c** 500, **d** 30–40, **e** Yes, **f** apple, **g** single, **h** same, **i** Yes, **j** cottage, **k** butter, haricot, **l** plain, 10, **m** pineapple, **n** Yes, **o** 10, **p** 1 pint jelly, **q** celery, courgettes, marrow, cucumber, lettuce, mushrooms, rhubarb, spring greens, vinegar, **r** canned apricots, currants, nuts, **s** tuna in oil

**UNIT 4**
**Solving the clues** (pages 12–15)

*The right face* (story about actor) **c, d, p, i, b, f, n, l, k**
*Surprise* (story about Fatty Brown) **o, a, j, e, h, g, m**

**UNIT 17**
**Revising a poem** (pages 65–67)

The final version of the poem is the one at the top.

**UNIT 28**
**Absorbing the details** (pages 103–107)

**4** **a** Waiyaki, **b** Kinuthia, **c** Kamau
**5** **a** False, **b** True (or at least partly true), **c** False, **d** Partly true, **e** True, **f** Partly true
To find out more about how these characters grow up and what becomes of them, read *The River Between* by Ngugi wa Thiong'o.

## UNIT 29
**Fighting talk** (page 112)

*Down*  1 Frank Bruno

*Across*  2 Champion of, 3 rigidity, 4 paraphernalia, 5 neutral, 6 shook, 7 beginning, 8 corridor, 9 unanimous, 10 affection, 11 opponent

## UNIT 32
**Writing for an audience** (page 123–131)

| 1 | h | 2 | c | 3 | i |
|---|---|---|---|---|---|
| 4 | g | 5 | b | 6 | d |
| 7 | a | 8 | j | 9 | l |
| 10 | f | 11 | k | 12 | e |

## UNIT 33
**Judging the tone** (page 127–131)

2  **a** xiii, **b** iv, **c** iii, **d** viii, **e** xii, **f** xi, **g** i, **h** x, **i** xiv, **j** vi, **k** vii, **l** ii, **m** ix, **n** v

## UNIT 34
**What's said where** (pages 132–134)

| 1 | c | 2 | j | 3 | e |
|---|---|---|---|---|---|
| 4 | b | 5 | h | 6 | d |
| 7 | f | 8 | g | 9 | a |
| 10 | i | | | | |

Correct order: **b, f, c, i, h, e, j, g, d, a**

## UNIT 35
**Same subject, different lives** (pages 135–141)

Lear's response to Cordelia is to say that she is no longer his daughter and may inherit none of his kingdom. Ironically, she is the daughter who loves him most.

If you can, try to see *King Lear* on stage – or perhaps you can borrow a videotape of it.

## UNIT 36
**Clear instructions** (pages 142–145)

The book actually uses these words:

| 1 | familiarise | 2 | mobile | 3 | knobs |
|---|---|---|---|---|---|
| 4 | switches | 5 | work | 6 | jerking |
| 7 | accurately | 8 | sharper | 9 | employed |
| 10 | critical | 11 | equipment | 12 | on-the-move |
| 13 | restful | 14 | expensive | 15 | blessing |

Answers to labelling the camera:

**1** H, **2** I, **3** J, **4** A, **5** K, **6** G, **7** F, **8** C, **9** E, **10** B, **11** L, **12** D

## UNIT 40
### Choosing the right words (pages 162–163)

The word Frost actually chose were:

| | | |
|---|---|---|
| **1** snarled | **2** rattled | **3** snarled |
| **4** rattled | **5** saved | **6** knew |
| **7** meant | **8** leaped | **9** leap |
| **10** laugh | **11** spilling | **12** boy |
| **13** man | **14** child | **15** puffed |
| **16** nothing | **17** ended | **18** the |
| **19** one | **20** dead | |

## UNIT 41
### More space than words (pages 164–165)

I lied to you. There is no original version of this poem because I never did complete it. (Thank you for doing it for me.)

## UNIT 48
### The odd words out (188–190)

| 'cheerily' | should be | 'gruffly' |
|---|---|---|
| 'steal' | " " | 'buy' . |
| 'comical' | " " | 'intolerable' |
| 'policeman' | " " | 'sentry' |
| 'child' | " " | 'patient' |
| 'slimy' | " " | 'gleaming' |
| 'crying' | " " | 'smiling' |
| 'raindrops' | " " | 'snowflakes' |
| 'bright' | " " | 'dismal' |
| 'raging' | " " | 'sad-eyed' |

## UNIT 56
### Efficient reading (pages 219–220)

**1**  **a** 4, **b** 1, **c** 5, **d** 6, **e** 3, **f** 2
**2**  **a** 31, **b** 2, **c** 22, **d** Sgt. Pepper, **e** 3, **f** 8, **g** Elvis Presley and Cliff Richard, **h** Elvis Presley **i** Beatles, **j** 11, **k** 30

# AT-A-GLANCE GUIDE TO PUPIL TASKS

Tasks (rows):

1. Analysing language
2. Argumentative/discursive writing
3. Artwork
4. Assessing logic
5. Autobiography/diary writing
6. Character study
7. Classifying
8. Comparing/contrasting
9. Debating
10. Devising diagram
11. Devising questions/exercises
12. Dramawork
13. Editing/revising
14. Filling in gaps
15. Following instructions
16. General discussion work
17. Giving instructions
18. Giving talk
19. Interpreting visual information
20. Labelling diagram
21. Making chart/plan
22. Making notes
23. Predicting
24. Problem solving
25. Reading aloud
26. Report writing
27. Rewriting in new form
28. Scanning
29. Sequencing
30. Skimming
31. Summarising
32. Tape recording
33. Timed assignments
34. Vocabulary work
35. Writing about literature
36. Writing dialogue/script
37. Writing for specific audience
38. Writing letter
39. Writing newspaper/magazine items
40. Writing poem
41. Writing stories etc

Columns: UNIT 1–60

256

## Index of authors and poets

## Index of language topics

# Acknowledgements

The author would like to thank the following for all their help with this book: Alan Black, Jean Warden, Terry Ward, Geraldine and Peter Daw, Virginia Waterhouse, Lynsay Swan, Anna Gregory, Gail Riminton, Joyce Hatwell.

The author and publishers are grateful to the following for permission to use material:

Sara Lee Ltd (Unit 3); Laurence Pollinger Ltd for *All but empty* by Graham Greene (Unit 5); The *Observer* (Unit 6); Harvey Unna and Stephen Durbridge Ltd for *Maniacs* by Peter Whalley (Unit 10); Faber and Faber Ltd for 'Trout' from *Death of a Naturalist* by Seamus Heaney (Unit 11); Andre Deutsch Ltd for extracts from *The Lost Sister* by Dorothy M Johnson (Unit 14); Chatto and Windus and the author's estate for 'Anthem for Dommed Youth' from *The Collected Poems of Wilfred Owen* edited by C Day Lewis (Unit 17); Simon Rae for 'Night Driving' (Unit 19); Maurice Temple Smith Ltd for extracts from *The Victorian Underworld* by Kellow Chesney (Unit 20); The Advertising Standards Authority for extracts from the *British Code of Advertising Practice* (Unit 22); Ilfracombe Publicity Association for tourist information and Ken Ward and John H N Mason for extracts from *Guide to the South-west peninsula coastal path* (Unit 24); The Office of Fair Trading for *Motorbikes* (Unit 26); Heinemann Educational Books for an extract from *The River Between* by Ngugi wa Thiong'o; Mail Newspapers plc and the *Guardian* (John Rodda) (Unit 29); Laurence Pollinger Ltd and the estate of Mrs Freida Lawrence Ravagli for an extract from *Sons and Lovers* by D H Lawrence (Unit 30); Collins Publishers Ltd for an extract from *Free Dinners* by Farukh Dhondy (Unit 30); Methuen Ltd for an extract from *1066 and all that* by W C Sellar and R J Yeatman (Unit 33); Penny Chorlton and the *Guardian* (Unit 34); Hamish Hamilton Ltd for extracts from *How to make your own video programmes* by Hannen Foss (Unit 36); Jonathan Clowes Ltd for 'Flight' from *The Habit of Loving* by Doris Lessing (Unit 38); Save the Children Fund (Unit 39); Jonathan Cape Ltd for 'Out, out' from *The Poetry of Robert Frost* (Unit 40); Routledge and Kegan Paul Ltd for extracts from *Adolescent Boys of East London* by Peter Willmott (Unit 43); *Women's Own* Magazine (Unit 44); Jonathan Cape Ltd for 'Naming of Parts' from *A Map of Verona* by Henry Reed (Unit 46); Secker and Warburg Ltd for *Children are civilians too* by Heinrich Böll (Unit 48); A M Heath Ltd for an extract from *So much unfairness of things* by C D B Bryan (Unit 50); Laurence Pollinger Ltd and the estate of Mrs Freida Lawrence Ravagli for an extract from *The Rainbow* by D H Lawrence (Unit 51); Penguin Books Ltd for an extract from *The First Year of Teaching* ed Smyth, Hannam and Stephenson (Unit 51); Harvey Unna and Stephen Durbridge Ltd for *Always in Love with Amy* by Ken Whitmore (Unit 53); Laurence Pollinger Ltd for 'The Good Corn' from *Seven by Five* by H E Bates (Unit 57); A D Peters and Co Ltd for 'A Square Dance' from *The Mersey Sound* by Roger McGough (Unit 58); British

Nuclear Fuels plc and Friends of the Earth (Unit 59); William Collins Ltd for *The Murderer* by Ray Bradbury.

We would also like to thank the following for permission to reproduce photographs and illustrations:

Walter Stiner: front cover (from *Faces* 27)

Sue Merrick: pages 8, 21, 57, 140, 144

Mik Heslin: pages 1, 2, 79, 168

All-Sport Ltd (Units 29, 45); BBC Hulton Picture Library (Units 5, 14, 56); Central Electricity Generating Board (Units 59); Ilfracombe Publicity Association (Unit 24); Imperial War Museum (Unit 17); Mary Evans Picture Library (Unit 20); Save the Children Fund (Unit 39); Graham Topping (Units 41, 57).

Every effort has been made to contact copyright holders. We apologise for any inadvertent omissions and will, of course, be happy to make corrections at the earliest opportunity.